MCSE:
Windows 2000 Directory
Services Design

Exam Notes

MCSE:
Windows® 2000 Directory Services Design

Exam Notes™

Robert King
Gary Govanus

San Francisco • Paris • Düsseldorf • Soest • London

SYBEX®

Associate Publisher: Neil Edde
Contracts and Licensing Manager: Kristine O'Callaghan
Acquisitions and Developmental Editor: Jeff Kellum
Editor: Dale Good
Production Editor: Elizabeth Campbell
Technical Editor: Mark Kovach
Book Designer: Bill Gibson
Graphic Illustrator: Tony Jonick
Electronic Publishing Specialist: Maureen Forys, Happenstance Type-O-Rama
Proofreaders: Laurie O'Connell, Nancy Riddiough
Indexer: Ted Laux
Cover Designer: Archer Design
Cover Illustrator/Photographer: Natural Selection

Library of Congress Card Number: 00-107344
ISBN: 0-7821-2765-7

To my wife and best friend, Suze.
—Robert King

To Bobbi, my very best friend
in the whole world.
—Gary Govanus

Acknowledgments

It's funny how life throws you curveballs from time to time. When I accepted this project, I was living just north of Tampa, was self-employed, and planned to use the traditional slow period at the beginning of the year to write. By the time we started working, I was moving to Grand Rapids, had a new job, and ended up using all of my free-time trying to keep up! Special thanks go to my little girls, Katie and Carrie, with whom I missed a lot of bedtime stories and Disney videos! My wife, Susan, who (because of the business I'm in) has experienced single parenting for the last few months (I'll take some time off now—I promise!)

I'd also like to thank the guys at Ingram Micro who donated a couple of killer Everest computers to my home lab so I could test my theories before I committed them to print! Ingram Micro doesn't sell to the public, but if you're a reseller I give them two thumbs up for service! (You can visit them at `www.ingrammicro.com`.)

—Bob King

I think Bob will agree that whenever we take on these projects, they sure sound good. It should be really easy to knock these books out. It usually takes about two weeks before the enormity of the task hits and we start looking at the page count and thinking we may never finish. And then, someone is asking us for our dedications and acknowledgements. My how time does fly.

Because Bob and I live so far apart (I live in Minnesota and at last check, he lived in Michigan), I can't tell you what he is like during the book writing process. I do know that I am not the most fun person in the world to live with. I am never the most fun person in the world to live with, but while writing a book, I can be an absolute bear. So, I really have to thank all those people closest to me.

Thanks to my wife Bobbi; the best daughters a guy can have, Dawn and Denise; and my three grandchildren, Brandice, CJ, and Courtney; and finally to my dear and loving parents, Dolly and Jack Govanus. Thanks all for sticking by me.

—*Gary Govanus*

We'd both like to thank everyone at Sybex who helped us put this book together: Special thanks to Associate Publisher Neil Edde and Developmental Editor Jeff Kellum. Thanks to Technical Editor Mark Kovach, Production Editor Elizabeth Campbell, Editor Dale Good, Electronic Publishing Specialist Maureen Forys, Graphic Artist Tony Jonick, and to the proofreaders, Laurie O'Connell and Nancy Riddiough. Without your hard work and dedication, this project could never have happened.

Thanks to my wife Bobbi; the best daughters a guy can have, Dawn and Denise; and my three grandchildren, Brandice, CJ, and Courtney; and finally to my dear and loving parents, Dolly and Jack Govanus. Thanks all for sticking by me.

—*Gary Govanus*

We'd both like to thank everyone at Sybex who helped us put this book together: Special thanks to Associate Publisher Neil Edde and Developmental Editor Jeff Kellum. Thanks to Technical Editor Mark Kovach, Production Editor Elizabeth Campbell, Editor Dale Good, Electronic Publishing Specialist Maureen Forys, Graphic Artist Tony Jonick, and to the proofreaders, Laurie O'Connell and Nancy Riddiough. Without your hard work and dedication, this project could never have happened.

Contents

Introduction

Microsoft's new Microsoft Certified Systems Engineer (MCSE) track for Windows 2000 is the premier certification for computer industry professionals. Covering the core technologies around which Microsoft's future will be built, the new MCSE certification is a powerful credential for career advancement.

This book has been developed, in cooperation with Microsoft Corporation, to give you the critical skills and knowledge you need to prepare for one of the new MCSE certification programs; Directory Services Infrastructure Design. You will find the information you need to acquire a solid understanding of Windows 2000 Directory Services Design, to prepare for Exam 70-219: Designing a Directory Services Infrastructure, and to progress toward MCSE certification.

Is This Book for You?

The MCSE Exam Notes books were designed to be succinct, portable exam review guides that can be used either in conjunction with a more complete study program (book, CBT courseware, classroom/lab environment) or as an exam review for those who don't feel the need for more extensive test preparation. It isn't our goal to give the answers away, but rather to identify those topics on which you can expect to be tested and to provide sufficient coverage of these topics.

Perhaps you're already familiar with the features and functionality of Windows 2000. The thought of paying lots of money for a specialized MCSE exam preparation course probably doesn't sound too appealing. What can they teach you that you don't already know, right? Be careful, though. Many experienced network administrators have walked confidently into test centers only to walk sheepishly out of them after failing an MCSE exam. As they discovered, there's the Microsoft of the real world and the Microsoft of the MCSE exams. It's our goal with these Exam Notes books to show you where the two converge and where they diverge. After you've finished reading through this book, you should have a clear idea of how your understanding of the technologies involved matches up with the expectations of the MCSE test makers in Redmond.

Or perhaps you're relatively new to the world of Microsoft networking, drawn to it by the promise of challenging work and higher salaries. You've just waded through an 800-page MCSE Windows 2000 study guide or taken a class at a local training center. Lots of information to keep track of, isn't it? Well, by organizing the Exam Notes books according to the Microsoft exam objectives, and by breaking up the information into concise manageable pieces, we've created what we think is the handiest exam review guide available. Throw it in your briefcase and carry it to work with you. As you read through the book, you'll be able to identify quickly those areas you know best and those that require more in-depth review.

NOTE   The goal of the Exam Notes series is to help MCSE candidates familiarize themselves with the subjects on which they can expect to be tested in the MCSE exams. For complete, in-depth coverage of the technologies and topics involved, we recommend the MCSE Windows 2000 Study Guide series from Sybex.

How Is This Book Organized?

As mentioned above, this book is organized according to the official exam objectives list prepared by Microsoft for Exam 70-219. The chapters coincide to the broad objectives groupings, such as Analyzing Business Requirements, Analyzing Technical Requirements, and Designing a Directory Service Architechture. These groupings are also reflected in the organization of the MCSE exams themselves.

Within each chapter, the individual exam objectives are addressed in turn. Each objective's coverage is further divided into the following sections of information:

Critical Information

This section presents the greatest level of detail on information for the objective. This is the place to start if you're unfamiliar with or uncertain about the objective's technical issues.

Exam Essentials

In this section, we've put together a concise list of the most crucial topics that you'll need to comprehend fully prior to taking the MCSE exam. These summaries can help you identify subject areas that might require more study on your part.

Key Terms and Concepts

Here you'll find a mini-glossary of the most important terms and concepts related to the specific objective. This list will help you understand what the technical words mean within the context of the related subject matter.

Sample Questions

For each objective, we've included a selection of questions similar to those you'll encounter on the actual MCSE exam. Answers and explanations are provided so you can gain some insight into the test-taking process.

How Do You Become an MCSE?

Attaining MCSE certification has always been a challenge. In the past, people could acquire detailed exam information—even most of the exam questions—from online "brain dumps" and third-party "cram" books or software products. For the new MCSE exams, however, this simply will not be the case.

To avoid the "paper-MCSE syndrome" (a devaluation of the MCSE certification because unqualified individuals manage to pass the exams), Microsoft has taken strong steps to protect the security and integrity of the new MCSE track. Prospective MSCEs will need to complete a course of study that provides not only detailed knowledge of a wide range of topics, but true skills derived from working with Windows 2000 and related software products.

In the new MCSE program, Microsoft is heavily emphasizing hands-on skills. Microsoft has stated that "nearly half of the core required exams' content demands that the candidate have troubleshooting skills acquired through hands-on experience and working knowledge."

Fortunately, if you are willing to dedicate time and effort with Windows 2000, you can prepare for the exams by using the proper tools. If you work through this book and the other books in this series, you should successfully meet the exam requirements.

TIP This book is part of a series of MCSE Study Guides and Exam Notes published by Sybex that covers the five core requirements as well as the electives you need to complete your MCSE track.

Exam Requirements

Successful candidates must pass a minimum set of exams that measure technical proficiency and expertise.

- Candidates for MCSE certification must pass seven exams, including four core operating system exams, one design exam, and two electives.

- Candidates who have already passed three Windows NT 4 exams (70-067, 70-068, and 70-073) may opt to take an "accelerated" exam plus one core design exam and two electives.

NOTE If you do not pass the accelerated exam after one attempt, you must pass the five core requirements and two electives.

The following tables show the exams that a new certification candidate must pass. *All* of these exams are required:

Exam #	Title	Requirement Met
70-216	Implementing and Administering a Microsoft Windows 2000 Network Infrastructure	Core (Operating System)
70-210	Installing, Configuring, and Administering Microsoft Windows 2000 Professional	Core (Operating System)
70-215	Installing, Configuring, and Administering Microsoft Windows 2000 Server	Core (Operating System)
70-217	Implementing and Administering a Microsoft Windows 2000 Directory Services Infrastructure	Core (Operating System)

One of these exams is required:

Exam #	Title	Requirement Met
70-219	Designing a Microsoft Windows 2000 Directory Services Infrastructure	Core (Design)
70-220	Designing Security for a Microsoft Windows 2000 Network	Core (Design)
70-221	Designing a Microsoft Windows 2000 Network Infrastructure	Core (Design)

Two of these exams are required:

Exam #	Title	Requirement Met
70-219	Designing a Microsoft Windows 2000 Directory Services Infrastructure	Elective
70-220	Designing Security for a Microsoft Windows 2000 Network	Elective
70-221	Designing a Microsoft Windows 2000 Network Infrastructure	Elective
Any current MCSE elective	Exams cover topics such as Exchange Server, SQL Server, Systems Management Server, Internet Explorer Administrators Kit, and Proxy Server (new exams are added regularly)	Elective

NOTE For a more detailed description of the Microsoft certification programs, including a list of current MCSE electives, check Microsoft's Training and Certification Web site at www.microsoft.com/trainingandservices.

Exam Registration

You may take the exams at any of more than 1,000 Authorized Prometric Testing Centers (APTCs) and VUE Testing Centers around the world. For the location of a testing center near you, call Sylvan Prometric at (800) 755-EXAM (755-3926), or call VUE at (888) 837-8616. Outside the United States and Canada, contact your local Sylvan Prometric or VUE registration center.

You should determine the number of the exam you want to take, and then register with the Sylvan Prometric or VUE registration center nearest to you. At this point, you'll be asked for advance payment for the exam. The exams are $100 each. Exams must be taken within one year of payment. You can schedule exams up to six weeks in advance or as late as one working day prior to the date of the exam. You can cancel or reschedule your exam if you contact the center at least two working days prior to the exam. Same-day registration is available in some locations, subject to space availability. Where same-day registration is available, you must register a minimum of two hours before test time.

TIP   You may also register for your exams online at www.sylvanprometric.com or www.vue.com.

When you schedule the exam, you'll be provided with instructions regarding appointment and cancellation procedures, ID requirements, and information about the testing center location. In addition, you'll receive a registration and payment confirmation letter from Sylvan Prometric or VUE.

Microsoft requires certification candidates to accept the terms of a nondisclosure agreement before taking certification exams.

What the Designing a Microsoft Windows 2000 Directory Services Infrastructure Exam Measures

The Designing a Microsoft Windows 2000 Directory Services Infrastructure exam covers concepts and skills required for the design of an Active Directory structure in an organization or business environment. It emphasizes the following areas of Active Directory design:

- Analysis of the business environment
- Analysis of the physical environment

- Planning for the use of Active Directory and Windows 2000 features

- Creating an optimized Active Directory environment

This exam differs from the core MCSE examinations in that there are no objectives that represent physical tasks. The test objectives guide you in analyzing given situations and suggesting solutions that meet the business needs of that environment. System analysis is not a skill that can be quantified into a series of facts or procedures to be memorized. Because of Microsoft's emphasis on providing business solutions, much of this book (and most of the exam objectives) focus on enabling you to create an Active Directory structure that is stable, optimized, and designed in such a way that it fulfills true business needs.

Tips for Taking Your Exam

Here are some general tips for taking your exam successfully:

- Arrive early at the exam center so you can relax and review your study materials, particularly tables and lists of exam-related information.

- Read the questions carefully. Don't be tempted to jump to an early conclusion. Make sure you know *exactly* what the question is asking.

- When answering multiple-choice questions you're not sure about, use a process of elimination to get rid of the obviously incorrect questions first. This will improve your odds if you need to make an educated guess.

- This test has many exhibits (pictures). It can be difficult, if not impossible, to view both the questions and the exhibit simulation on the 14- and 15-inch screens usually found at the testing centers. Call around to each center and see if they have 17-inch monitors available. If they don't, perhaps you can arrange to bring in your own. Failing this, some have found it useful to quickly draw the diagram on the scratch paper provided by the testing center and use the monitor to view just the question.

- You are allowed to use the Windows calculator during your test. However, it may be better to memorize a table of the subnet addresses and to write it down on the scratch paper supplied by the testing center before you start the test.

Once you've completed an exam, you'll be given immediate, online notification of your pass or fail status. You'll also receive a printed Examination Score Report indicating your pass or fail status and your exam results by section. (The test administrator will give you the printed score report.) Test scores are automatically forwarded to Microsoft within five working days after you take the test. You don't need to send your score to Microsoft. If you pass the exam, you'll receive confirmation from Microsoft, typically within two to four weeks.

Contact Information

To find out more about Microsoft Education and Certification materials and programs, to register with Sylvan Prometric, or to get other useful information, check the following resources. Outside the United States or Canada, contact your local Microsoft office or Sylvan Prometric testing center.

Microsoft Certified Professional Program—(800) 636-7544

Call the MCPP number for information about the Microsoft Certified Professional program and exams, and to order the latest Microsoft Roadmap to Education and Certification.

Sylvan Prometric testing centers—(800) 755-EXAM

Contact Sylvan to register to take a Microsoft Certified Professional exam at any of more than 800 Sylvan Prometric testing centers around the world.

Microsoft Certification Development Team—
www.microsoft.com/trainingandservices

Contact the Microsoft Certification Development Team through their Web site to volunteer for participation in one or more exam development phases or to report a problem with an exam. Address written correspondence to the Certification Development Team, Microsoft Education and Certification, One Microsoft Way, Redmond, WA 98052.

Microsoft TechNet Technical Information Network— (800) 344-2121

This is an excellent resource for support professionals and system administrators. Outside the United States and Canada, call your local Microsoft subsidiary for information.

How to Contact the Publisher

Sybex welcomes reader feedback on all of its titles. Visit the Sybex Web site at www.sybex.com for book updates and additional certification information. You'll also find online forms to submit comments or suggestions regarding this or any other Sybex book.

Chapter

1

Analyzing Business Requirements

For the MCSE Design exams, Microsoft has added content to test your ability to suggest, install, configure, and maintain its products in a real business environment. The end result for us, the MCSEs and potential MCSEs of the world, is that we need to have a broader sense of the business world. Therein lies the problem—many people have a background in technology, and many people have a background in business, but few people have experience in both arenas. That's where the Windows® 2000 Directory Services Design comes in—this examination will test your ability to analyze a business environment and suggest a solution that will fill a business need.

This first group of exam objectives, "Analyze the Existing and Planned Business Models," are designed to test your knowledge of basic business environments. How a business works has a great influence on how technology should best be implemented. We'll start by describing and defining basic business models that can act as guidelines when designing an Active Directory (AD) structure. While no business will match a model exactly, most will match a model close enough to make some generic decisions.

After analyzing the business models we'll move to a discussion of company processes. Knowing how information is used, how the business deals with change, and how decisions are made can help to fine-tune an AD environment to match the needs of the company. We'll also look at the existing Information Technology (IT) structure. The ways in which a company currently implements and manages technology, how it makes decisions, and even how it acquires funding can also influence your decisions about which technologies you would recommend and how you would implement them.

Analyze the existing and planned business models.

- **Analyze the company model and the geographical scope. Models include regional, national, international, subsidiary, and branch offices.**

- **Analyze company processes. Processes include information flow, communication flow, service and product life cycles, and decision-making.**

If you take a few courses in business management, you soon discover that no matter how diverse the economy, and no matter how varied the products and services that are available, most successful businesses are organized along one of a few management philosophies. These philosophies, or *business models*, define the internal structures used to manage the complex interrelationships among the functions necessary to successfully conduct business. To put it more simply, a business model defines how work gets done. From a design perspective, knowing how work gets done allows you to design an Active Directory structure that matches (and maybe even enhances) the company's management structure.

The bottom line for this section is that you must be able to look at a company, ask a few questions, and from that, be able to determine what technical solutions you would recommend for that environment. Microsoft expects you to understand the basics of business—the various types of management styles that exist, the difference technological needs based upon a company's physical diversity, and how business processes affect technology. In this first section you are really reviewing "Business 101"—getting a background in the business of business.

Critical Information

If you approach these exam objectives as if you were really performing an Active Directory design, one of the first things you would do is try to get a feel for the size and complexity of the project. This is known as the *scope* of the project. The process involves gathering information about the physical and business aspects of the environment. We will discuss these processes in the sections that follow.

Analyze the Company Model and Geographical Scope

When you are determining the scope of a design project, there are certain aspects of the environment that you can use to rate the network. For exam purposes, Microsoft has defined a set of standards that you can use as a yardstick to determine the scope of a design project. There are two sets of standards, or models, mentioned in the examination objectives:

Geographic Scope The *geographic scope* of a company is determined by the number of physical locations that make up the network and the connectivity between them. There are three levels of geographic models—regional, national, and international. The differences between them will be examined a little later in this section.

Business Model The *business model* refers to the business relationship between sites and services. In other words, you'll look at each location and determine its relationship to the company. You might, for instance, have a research site that is technically part of your network but is in reality a completely separate entity, using none of the corporate resources and not requiring complete access to the company infrastructure. On the other hand, you might have a location that is the central distribution point for all order processing for your company. Employees at this site might need to read data or use other resources at every location within the company. Each of these two examples would require a different level of access and would be handled differently in your final AD system design.

NOTE For testing purposes Microsoft defines two business models—the subsidiary and branch offices.

In the next sections, we discuss each of these two standards: the geographic scope and the business model.

Understanding the Geographic Scope

One of the most expensive components of any network consists of the connections between physical locations (hereafter known as *sites*). With this in mind, one of the first design goals for any network should be to reduce, or at least control, the network traffic that crosses any expensive wide area links. The bigger the network, or the larger the number of links in the network, the more important this first goal becomes! Microsoft defines three sizes of networks based upon the amount of wide area connectivity inherent in the geographic layout of facilities—regional (small), national (medium), and international (large). To this add one more class of network—the simple-network model, which often consists of just a single site. Microsoft doesn't include this as a design model because a simple-network environment shouldn't take a whole lot of planning. For testing purposes, though, you'll need to know when to plan and when to go with the defaults.

SIMPLE-NETWORK MODEL

Remember, you're not going to see this name on the exam, but you might see a case study or a question that revolves around a network that really doesn't take much planning. The definition of a simple network is an environment in which all resources are connected over fast, reliable lines that have ample bandwidth available. In most cases, the simple network will be made up of a single site, and the company will have no need to create network relationships with outside vendors, customers, or other foreign systems. A simple network will not require any extensive planning—it will be a single domain, it will contain no special connectivity issues, and the existing network traffic will not push the limits of whatever topology (Ethernet, Token Ring, etc.) is currently in place. The simple network will be the most common environment in the market—very few of us will be able to work on the design of large networks.

We won't go into great deal about the simple network, but you should be aware that systems so small that they do not fit into one of Microsoft's defined environments are probably simple networks. It's important to remember the following distinctions about a simple network:

- No wide area links, unless those links are high speed, reliable, and have plenty of available bandwidth

- No special relationships with outside systems
- Single NT domain

REGIONAL MODEL

A *regional model* is one in which all sites are contained within a well-defined geographic area. Although this definition is vague, it works well in conjunction with the other two models defined by Microsoft. To make it a bit more specific, we would add that, in most cases, a regional network will be made up of connections that travel through a single vendor's lines. If, for instance, all of a company's lines are purchased through one of the regional Bells, then it follows that the network itself is regional in scope. The network in Figure 1.1 is a perfect example of a regional environment.

FIGURE 1.1: A regional network

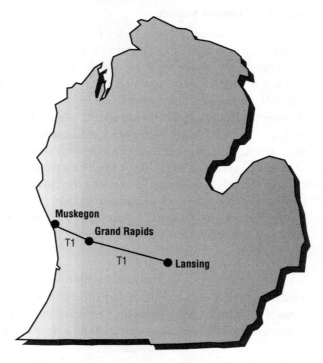

In this example the network consists of two wide area links: one from Grand Rapids to Muskegon and another from Grand Rapids to Lansing. In this case, the region can be defined as western Michigan, and the same vendor probably provides both wide area lines.

Notice that no time zone is crossed, nor is any state boundary. You will not have to be concerned with the time differences on any scheduled processes, and you will not have to know more than one set of legal issues. Unfortunately, there is no definitive description of a regional network. The network depicted in Figure 1.2 is considerably larger in area (but no more complex) than the first example, and it too qualifies as a regional environment.

FIGURE 1.2: A larger regional network

As you can see from Figure 1.2, geographic confinement is not the only criterion for ranking an environment as a regional network. You will also have to take into account the relative complexity of the environment. Take, for example, the network depicted in Figure 1.3. Outwardly, it appears almost identical to the network presented in Figure 1.2, but it has one additional site.

FIGURE 1.3: A more complex network

This network is much more complex than the preceding example. In this network you will have to consider an unreliable dial-up connection and a potential bottleneck on the 64K line. You also need to note that all traffic from both the Atlanta and the Washington sites must travel across a single T1 line to reach Grand Rapids. There is also a straight-line path for data to travel from one end of the network to another. If either Grand Rapids or Boston becomes unavailable, the continuity of communication will be broken. Based upon the additional complexity of the environment, this network would not be classified as regional. It would more likely fit into the next category— the national network model. The important distinctions to remember about a regional model are these:

- Simple infrastructure design
- Well defined geographic boundaries
- No complex setup issues

NATIONAL MODEL

A *national model* environment is one that, as the name implies, covers all or parts of an entire country. The network infrastructure is complex, it crosses time zones, rules and regulations might differ from site to site, complex services are part of the mix, and/or in general, it services a larger number of users. If any one of these conditions is met, it *might* be a national network. Sound confusing? Welcome to the world of Microsoft testing. Let's start our discussion by breaking down each of these points to get a clearer understanding of what each represents.

Complex Infrastructure   If the network in question is made up entirely of fast, reliable links that have plenty of available bandwidth, you don't *really* have to take them into account for your design. You could assume that the Wide Area Network (WAN) links would not have an appreciable effect on network performance. Luckily for consultants, few networks match these specifications. A typical national network will be made up of the following components:

- Different speed dedicated lines (T1, 256K, 64K, etc.)
- Dial-up connections
- Different network topologies, such as Asynchronous Transfer Mode (ATM), Frame Relay, etc.
- Different connectivity vendors

- Different hardware configurations (switches, routers, etc.)
- Different levels of available bandwidth

When a network becomes a heterogeneous mix that fulfills some of the bulleted items above, it is probably a national network. Each of these considerations will add complexity to the design and length to the design process.

Time Zones   Multiple time zones in and of themselves would not mandate a national network design (although crossing time zones is almost a given in any national network in the United States). Crossing them can, however, add complexity to such issues as scheduled over-the-Net backups, time-sensitive database entries, and any other process that relies on a timed function. If your environment includes time-sensitive processes in more than one time zone, you might have a national network.

Laws and Regulations   What is acceptable in one community might not be acceptable in *every* community. If your network crosses cultural boundaries, it should probably be considered national in scope.

A great example of this type of issue is offering gambling services across the Internet. Consider Reno, Nevada—a place where gambling is just another business. Consider also Provo, Utah—a place where gambling is frowned upon. If you had a business that included services for gamblers, you would have to be aware of the legal ramifications of offering services in both states. As the network administrator for a business with offices in both locations, you would have to be aware of the laws in both communities and design your network services accordingly.

Complex Services   Most of today's networks offer a complex set of services to end users. Networks still provide the basics, such as file and print services, but are now also expected to support advanced messaging systems (such as Exchange Server), Internet Web servers (such as Internet Information Server), and even voice-over-IP phone service. The more complex the services, the more complex the design will have to be to support those services.

Larger Number of Users   This is the most subjective of the considerations. Because Windows 2000 and Active Directory can support a million objects in a single domain, "large" is hard to define in straight numbers. It would more likely be defined as a large number of users with diverse business needs. A group of accountants might need to download large amounts of investment information from the Internet, another group might need large amounts of bandwidth to support a streaming video application, and yet another group might need to access only the e-mail servers. If you stop to think about these three examples, you will find that they each demand different physical capabilities of the network. Add them together in the same business, and you'll have to control your network traffic patterns carefully.

The bottom line is that a network will be national in scope if it is more complex than a regional network but does not cross any international boundaries.

INTERNATIONAL MODEL

The name of the *international model* sums up the definition—international networks cross national borders. In many respects, the makeup of most international networks will be similar to most national networks. Their size alone mandates a certain amount of complexity. Like national networks, international networks will usually have the following characteristics:

- They may have a complex infrastructure.

- They may cross time zones.

- They move through areas with different laws and regulations.

- They may offer complex services to their end users.

- There may be language differences between sites.

From a design standpoint, there are two major differences between a national network and an international network:

1. Laws and regulations of two (or more) different countries will have to be taken into account.

2. There will usually be multiple providers for connectivity services, and those services will probably vary in quality and reliability.

Laws and Regulations   Understanding the laws and regulations involved in a multicountry environment can be a full-time job. You will have to stay up-to-date on the export laws of each country (the U.S., for instance, is very careful about the technology that it allows to be exported), the acceptable content for each area (many parts of the Pacific Rim, for instance, do not allow full access to the Internet), and even standard worker compensation customs (Germany, for instance, has a standard 37.5-hour work week for all employees). Knowledge of these items allows you to plan for implementation of technology, person-hours available, and tariffs that might affect your environment.

Multiple Providers   A typical international network, like the one shown in Figure 1.4, will span the territories of multiple providers of communication services. A working knowledge of the reliability of services and the cost of those services is critical when you are planning the budget for your design project.

FIGURE 1.4: An international network

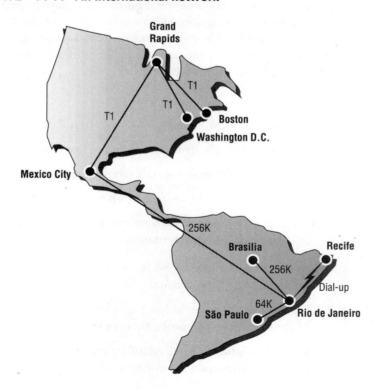

The costs involved in international connectivity can be astronomical! It is important that you fully understand how those costs are applied when designing your network. One network engineering company, for instance, saved a client 40 percent per month by changing which side of a WAN link initialized the line. The client had an office in Los Angeles and another in the Pacific Rim. When the engineers looked over the client's wide area connectivity, they noticed that the Pacific Rim site called the U.S. site every evening to download production information. After looking over the rates for the two telecommunications companies involved, they discovered that it was 40 percent less expensive to have the U.S. site call the Pacific Rim site than the other way around. This one change saved (and is still saving) the client over $12,000.00 per year!

With the release of Windows 2000 and Active Directory, and with the changes to the MCSE program, Microsoft has changed the scope of your responsibilities. You are no longer allowed to focus solely on the technology. As network administrators, you are being asked to understand the business side of the equation. You are going to have to learn how companies do business, why they do business as they do, and how Microsoft software can improve the business environment. Detailed analysis of the environment and the ability to integrate technology and business to provide a solution are the keys to success in the new MCSE program!

Understanding the Business Model

You've seen how the physical infrastructure of a company can affect the scope of the upgrade or migration process, but this is only half of the equation. To fully understand a project, you must become knowledgeable about the relationships between the components that make up that infrastructure. This requires an analysis of more than just network bandwidth. It requires you to analyze at least these three issues:

- The political relationships between sites, departments, and individual managers

- The uses to which the connections will be put (just e-mail versus real-time database access, for instance)

- The similarities and differences between the sites, both in physical makeup and in management philosophy

As you can see, this is where real-world business experience and knowledge come in handy!

The exam objectives mention two different business models to consider at this point in the design project: subsidiary offices and branch offices. As a measure of comparison, we're going to add one more type of facility: corporate offices. Once you have finished analyzing the geographic scope of the environment—in other words, after you have gathered the information necessary to fully understand the physical infrastructure of the network—you must take a good look at the end points of that structure. The end points represent the physical locations where work is done—be it administrative, production, research, or what have you. The geographic models help you map the network infrastructure; the business models help you map the business infrastructure. Remember that the goal of the Design exams is to produce MCSEs that can suggest whole-business solutions, so the ability to analyze the underlying business processes of a company is critical to successfully passing these tests.

In the following sections, we will discuss each of the business models: the corporate office, branch office, and subsidiary office.

CORPORATE OFFICES

Remember, the designation "corporate office" is our own creation. We'll use the definition that follows for comparison purposes to determine which type of location any given site represents. A *corporate office* represents a full-blown business site—a location in which the company has invested heavily in facilities, information services staff, and hardware, or a location that is heavily staffed. Some or all of the following statements will describe a corporate office environment:

- It has a diverse environment made up of varying client types, hardware, software, and supporting staff.

- It has multiple servers or specialized servers.

- It acts as a hub for the network infrastructure.

- It provides company-wide access to data or services.

- It has large (relative to the overall size of the company) numbers of employees.

- It houses the management staff of the company.

- It represents a key location in the company's political structure.

- It has the "feel" of a permanent facility.

- It is fully controlled by the company (as opposed to a partner relationship).

NOTE We know that a few of the characteristics of a corporate office environment are rather subjective—what can we say? Many of the decisions you'll be making during an ADS design project will indeed be subjective. For testing purposes, though, you should get enough of a feel for each location from the text to be able to categorize it.

The bottom line for corporate office sites is that they feel like permanent facilities. They will act as a central point for something within the company—management, production, delivery, and so on. If the company as a whole could not continue without a particular location, that location can be considered a corporate office.

NOTE "Why," you might ask, "did they bother adding this definition of a business model to this discussion?" For the simple reason that, for testing purposes, anything that does not fit into the corporate office class of location will be defined as one of two other classes of sites: branch or subsidiary. By knowing what *not* to include, you can eliminate some of the variables in the case studies you see on the exam.

BRANCH OFFICES

A *branch office* can be defined as a wholly controlled facility that does not meet the criteria to be classified as a corporate office.

Although this definition is not very descriptive in and of itself, when you compare a branch office location to the list of attributes for a corporate site, it becomes fairly straightforward to make the distinction. The following statements do *not* describe branch offices:

- They have a diverse client base.
- They have multiple or specialized servers. (Often, branch offices do not contain any servers.)
- They usually act as a hub for the network infrastructure.
- They provide access to company-wide data or services.
- They usually house the company's management staff.
- They act as a key location for the company.

The following statements *do* describe branch offices:

- They are fairly permanent facilities.
- They are fully controlled by the company.

Although these distinctions allow you to classify locations fairly easily, there are also a few desirable design factors that you would like to find in the branch offices for your company. Most of the time, companies that have branch offices will set them up in a fairly standard fashion. These similarities allow you to set up standard management strategies, or policies, that can be applied to all branch office sites. As an example, let's look at the facilities in the Last National Bank of Michigan (LNB). The network for LNB is shown in Figure 1.5.

The LNB office in Detroit houses the corporate IS department, the legal staff, the CEO, the CIO, and the CFO. It processes all transactions with the Federal Reserve Bank, provides a central database of client and account information, and houses the corporate marketing department. All other offices have dedicated lines that link to Detroit, so it also acts as the hub of the network infrastructure. As you have probably already guessed, the Detroit facility qualifies as a corporate office. The question remains: "Are any of the other sites also corporate offices?"

FIGURE 1.5: The network for the Last National Bank of Michigan

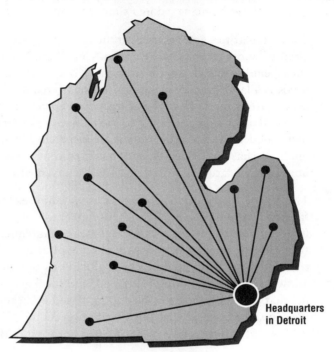

The outlying sites represent actual community banks. Each site is connected to the Detroit office by either a 56K or 256K dedicated line
(depending upon the volume of business generated at the facility). All
sites have between four and eight computers used by the bank tellers,
between two and four computers used by loan officers, one or two
computers used by the bank's management staff, and two to four
printers. Each facility also contains a Backup Domain Controller
(BDC) that belongs to the single domain defined for the current NT 4
implementation (this prevents a complete loss of functionality in the
event of the WAN link going down).

The other sites have fairly similar environments. None is critical to
the continued functioning of the company as a whole. In other words,
all other sites can be classified as branch offices. The branch offices all

have fairly consistent environments, provide no company-wide services, and can be managed in a similar manner.

These similarities among sites within a company are not unusual. Granted, most companies are not as "clean" as LNB, but many have consistent layouts. Take, for example, KMK, Inc. in Minnesota. KMK is a large grocery company headquartered in Hutchinson. Its headquarters meets all of the criteria for a corporate office designation—all other sites are managed there, inventory databases are kept there, all deliveries to retail outlets are dispatched from there, and so on. It also has three other types of facilities: central distribution warehouses, KMK grocery stores, and KMK convenience stores.

The central distribution centers act as warehouses for the retail facilities within a region. They house inventory database servers (that connect to the corporate databases in Hutchinson), complete shop floor management software to control order fulfillment and truck routing (connected to a cool global positioning system that allows real-time rerouting of trucks), and local accounting personnel that control billing for the region. Based upon this description, we can safely assume that the distribution centers are *not* branch offices and can therefore be considered corporate offices.

The KMK grocery stores also have inventory control software that is connected to their point-of-sale bar-code scanning system. Local inventory is stored on a local database that uploads changes to the local distribution center each evening. The IS environment consists of 5 to 10 networked cash registers and 2 to 3 computers used by store management. Because the computer environments are fairly simple and no single store is critical to the company as a whole, we can classify the grocery stores as branch offices.

The KMK convenience stores can best be described as smaller versions of the grocery stores with a few additional considerations. The convenience stores also sell gasoline and so have a complete inventory control system built into the gas pumps. Typical stores have two to three cash registers that are tied into a bar-code scanning package used for inventory control. Each store has one server (though the computers are usually old and out-of-date) that stores local sales information and connects to the local distribution center each night to update the central database. Because the computer environments are fairly simple and no single store is critical to the company as a whole, we can classify the convenience stores as branch offices.

Are you seeing a pattern yet? The easiest way to determine if a site is a branch office is to first determine if it is *not* a corporate office!

You are probably asking yourself why this is important. Take another look at Figure 1.5. At first glance, this network looks fairly complex. There are 10 to 20 sites connected over a regional network infrastructure. Based solely upon the physical network, you might classify this as a complex project. The reality is that the Last National Bank of Michigan would be a fairly easy system to work with—only one site contains any complex technology. Without looking at the business model, you would overbid the project and probably lose the job, or if you were on the LNB staff, you might decide that the upgrade would cost too much in dollars and time and cancel or delay your upgrade plans.

From a design perspective, you should look at all of the sites, determine how many corporate offices are involved and treat them as a separate design component, and then group branch offices into management clusters that can be seen as a single design element. (You will have to design only one consistent plan for each type of branch office instead of each separate office.)

SUBSIDIARY OFFICES

Subsidiary office locations are sites that are part of the overall business but are not controlled by the company. Partner companies, franchise sites, and separate business divisions are the best examples of true subsidiary offices, but any office that is beyond the control of corporate management can qualify. As you can image, gathering information from such entities can be difficult.

Unfortunately, the business relationships with subsidiary offices are often more complex than those with corporate-owned facilities. Complex business relationship usually imply complex IS relationships. You might, for instance, need to access sales information from an independently owned franchise, but its IS department might want complete control over the transfer of information. Take, for example, the Mom's Apple Pie (MAP) company shown in Figure 1.6.

FIGURE 1.6: Mom's Apple Pie company

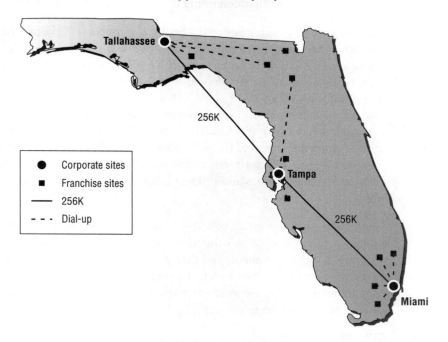

Mom's Apple Pie sells pies, cakes, and cookies. It started with one small location in Tampa, Florida, and soon expanded to three sites (marked as corporate sites in Figure 1.6). A few years ago, the company decided to franchise its name, and it has been going strong ever since. Each franchise is independently owned and managed but reports sales figures and orders supplies through the parent company.

When a person or company buys a franchise license from MAP, they attend a month-long training session during which they are brought up to speed on the computer software and hardware used to connect to MAP's corporate system for placing orders and reporting sales figures.

Designing an ADS environment (or any other operating system, for that matter) that includes autonomous entries is quite a bit more complicated than putting together a system controlled by a single IS department. In our Mom's Apple Pie example, you will have to write new training materials for the management course, talk to each franchise owner to gather information about his or her interaction with MAP's system, and plan for additional security to control the access that the franchisees have when they connect.

Analyze Company Processes

In terms of a design project, we are still in the beginning stages. As we stated earlier, the first task is to get a feel for the complexity of the environment. For this exam subobjective, you will be tested on your ability to analyze standard business processes.

Microsoft defines five main business processes that will have major influences on AD design:

- Information flow
- Communication flow
- Services
- Product and services life cycles
- Decision-making

Achieving an in-depth understanding of each of these issues is critical to a good AD design. The analysis process itself is mostly a matter of interviewing key personnel and surveying groups of employees. On a large project, this process can take quite a bit of time and effort, but it pays off in an AD design that functions flawlessly!

Analyzing Information Flow

Information flow refers to the actual access of data. A typical company has numerous sources and types of information that is critical to the functioning of the business. For our purposes, let's define *information* as anything that crosses the network. Using this definition expands the analysis process but gives you a more detailed look at network traffic patterns—and *that* is what this section is really about. Most companies will have one or more of the following:

- Customer database

- Sales information

- Marketing material

- Inventory database

- Accounting data

Along with this "hard" data, most companies also have what we call "soft information." *Soft information* is data that is not easily quantified or qualified. This would include the following:

- E-mail

- Web site content

- Call logs

- Contact information

- Miscellaneous documents (including everything from legal contracts to templates for marketing material)

Another type of information that is often handled by the network is software. Software installations and upgrades are easier to perform across the network, and standards are easier to enforce. Many companies are moving back to the old school of moving applications from the desktop and storing them on the server (thus making upgrades, patches and fixes, and version control easier to manage). Another form of information that is becoming quite popular is the use of terminal services, which are available on most servers. Because terminal services are built into Windows 2000 Server software, it is safe to assume that more and more companies will be looking at this option.

The ultimate design goal of analyzing the information flow of an environment is to optimize the placement of that data and minimize its effect on the network. To accomplish this, you'll have to gather a list of all of the information sources within a company, the location of those resources, and who accesses them. From there, you can begin to think about moving data in ways that will reduce its load on the rest of your network. From our experience, the best way to accomplish this is to build a set of matrices (as shown in Table 1.1) that cross-reference information sources with users. This helps later, because it aids in defining the group objects you'll want to create within AD. Unfortunately, the process of gathering this information can be long and tedious.

TABLE 1.1:   Information Flow Matrix

User	Bob	Susan	Katherine	Caroline
Customer list	X		X	
Inventory database		X		X
Sales database	X		X	X
Accounting Information		X		X
Document templates	X		X	
Office 2000	X	X	X	X

For a large company with hundreds of users, this process is not feasible. For these types of environments, analyze the data access of a few key people in each department and then be prepared to deal with any issues during implementation. It can also be helpful to survey all employees a few times during this process—once at the beginning as you build your list of information sources and again when you are trying to see who uses which source. We've run across numerous examples where a large number of people are using a data source (such as a shared contact list or custom-made database) that management didn't even know existed.

> **TIP** Exam Hint: What you learn from your analysis of information flow can be used to provide a business solution. If the analysis shows redundant data entry, for instance, your solution might include a consolidation of data. (Microsoft loves this type of answer, especially if it involves the sale of a copy of SQL Server or Exchange Server!) Taking multiple Access databases, for instance, and moving them to a central SQL Server database can reduce traffic and provide central management.

It's always important to keep your goal in mind during each step of the design process, so to reiterate—the goal of analyzing information flow is to control network traffic. You'll use this information when planning your server placement, when planning the placement of various services when designing your site boundaries for AD replication, and even during design (or redesign) of the network infrastructure. These various services include Primary Domain Controller (PDC) Emulator, Domain Name System (DNS) services, Dynamic Host Configuration Protocol (DHCP) services, and so on. Once you're done with the AD design, this information can be used to help choose and configure routers and other network components, purchase new servers, and even implement new software. In other words, in a real-life scenario, having a good grasp of information flow is critical to good administration, not just good design.

> **TIP** Exam Hint: If a Microsoft exam question starts discussing data sources and their locations on the network, you can bet you'll be asked to analyze and optimize the information flow. All of the design issues listed in the preceding paragraph might be involved in the final answer.

It's been said that the phrase "Money is power" has changed to "Information is power." In any consulting work, whether it is an AD design or just an optimization of an existing network, one of the first questions we ask is "Can you give us a list of all of the data sources on your network?" You'd be surprised at the number of times we get an answer from upper management and the IS staff (sometimes even they don't match), and then after investigation, we supply them with an entire list of information they didn't even know existed on their network. Or worse, we'll be talking with someone from marketing and they'll describe an information source that they would like to have created, and we'll inform them that accounting already has that data available. The latter problem is really one of communication flow (which is our next topic), but its roots start in information management. You can manage information only if you know what you have and where it is located—in other words, you have to analyze the information flow.

Analyzing Communication Flow

Once you have analyzed the information flow for a company, the next step is to analyze how that information is used. Here, once again, business knowledge rather than technical knowledge is key. First we should define the difference between information flow and communication flow. As we discussed in the last section, information flow refers to the actual access of data. *Communication flow*, on the other hand, refers more to the sharing of information and the free flow of ideas within a company. As such, it is both a physical aspect (who talks to whom) and a philosophical aspect (how much freedom of information exists) of AD design.

During your analysis of the information flow, you gathered a list of all of the data sources within the company. To analyze the communication flow, you must now start asking about how that data is used as information. The word *data* refers to a bunch of facts; *information*, on the other hand, refers to useful (and usable) facts. To visualize the difference, think about all of the databases and documents on the Internet. If there were no way of linking those resources, it would be data—good facts, but no real context. Now add a search engine and the HTML protocol. Suddenly, all of those documents and databases become useful—and the moment they become useful, they become information.

Start the analysis of communication flow by asking questions about who uses what data for what purposes. Create another matrix that lists all of the data sources, who maintains them, and who uses them, as shown in Table 1.2.

TABLE 1.2: Communication Flow Matrix

Data Source	Maintained By	Users
Inventory database	Purchasing	Purchasing, Production, Sales, Accounting
Customer database	Sales	Sales, Marketing
Sales figures	Sales	Sales, Accounting
Document templates	Marketing	Marketing, Sales
Price list	Accounting	Sales, Accounting
Vendor list	Purchasing	Purchasing, Production
Marketing material	Marketing	Marketing, Sales
Product designs	Research and Development	R&D, Production, Purchasing, Accounting
Software	IS	All departments

Once you have a list of what we call the hard facts—who uses what—you must continue your investigation into communication flow by analyzing the soft facts. You need to ask about other types of information: Who uses the Web and what kind of content do they access? Who uses e-mail and how much mail is sent and received? Who uses the printers, what do they print, and how often? Is there a fax server, and if so, who uses it and how much? In other words, now you have to look at anything that might generate network traffic. For each of these soft network uses, you need to gather three pieces of information:

- Who generates it?

- How frequently is it generated?

- How much traffic does it create?

Once again, the goal of analyzing communication flow is controlling network traffic—what is generated and where it goes on the network. You'll be using this information extensively later in your design process.

Analyzing Services on the Network

By this time in your quest for MCSE certification, you should be quite familiar with the various network services that Windows 2000 can provide. You should understand the installation, configuration, and maintenance of DHCP, DNS, Windows Internet Naming Service (WINS), and all of the other network services available. Don't forget some of the hidden services, such as user authentication, AD replication, and proxy services. There are also numerous add-on services available—e-mail, system management, software distribution, and remote management. Each of these components provides a valuable service to your network. Each also comes with a price—in dollars, time, and/or network traffic. Those costs are what network design is all about.

This phase of the design process begins with an analysis of each service your network provides. The process can be divided into three steps:

1. Isolate

2. Re-create

3. Extrapolate

First, isolate a test network so that your analysis isn't affected by other traffic on the wire. Second, re-create the traffic generated by the service. Use one of the tools provided by Microsoft (Performance Monitor, Network Monitor, Replication Monitor, and so on) to measure the amount of traffic the service generates. From this information, you can then extrapolate the effects of the service for as many users as necessary.

As an example, let's look at the traffic generated during the initialization of a DHCP client. The DHCP process generates four packets during initialization—Discovery, Offer, Selection, and Acknowledgment. Knowing this, you can then determine the amount of traffic that would be generated by 100 clients initializing—4 packets each times 100 clients equals 400 packets. You could get even more detailed if necessary, measuring the number of bytes involved and dividing your available bandwidth by that number. This should give you the number of computers that can initialize simultaneously. Of course, this isn't the whole picture yet. DHCP traffic is not the only traffic generated during client initialization. You will have to measure *all* traffic generated and extrapolate from that figure to see the true effects of client initialization.

Once again, the goal in analyzing the traffic generated by services on your network is to control that traffic. Knowing how many bytes or packets are generated by a given process might seem a bit extreme, but in the long run, you can use that information to control network traffic, decreasing the chance that network congestion will adversely affect network performance.

Product and Service Life Cycles

Unfortunately, there are two ways to define the phrase "product and service life cycles": with an internal perspective and with an external perspective. When using the internal definition, it is the length of time the company's products or services are valid—in other words, the amount of time its products and services remain viable in the marketplace. Using the external definition, "product and service life cycle" can be defined as the length of time the environment is valid—in other words, the amount of time the environment will remain static (no hardware or software upgrade required). Both definitions are valid considerations during an AD design.

A short life span for products or services creates a very dynamic network. Each time a product goes to market, a slew of resources is assigned to that product. In the quick world of retail, when the product no longer sells, all of those resources have to be reassigned to other projects. This means that objects within the AD structure regularly will be moving from container to container—not the kind of AD structure you would want to design for a company with no internal IS staff (unless you are a consultant who sells hourly support). If, however, the client has an adequate and experienced IS department, then a dynamic structure might be the best business solution.

More germane to our discussion is the external definition of product life cycles. We recently read that the average life span of software is down to about 18 months. That means that 18 months (on average) after you install a piece of software, an upgrade will be available, which in turn means that, if Microsoft follows the industry average, a significant change to Windows 2000 can be expected around July 2001. Scary, isn't it? Luckily, two factors influence this estimate:

- Operating systems usually have longer life spans than applications.

- Microsoft was years late in releasing Windows 2000, so maybe it'll be late with its next one as well.

Applications, on the other hand, offer no such exceptions. You can expect that the word processor you are currently using in-house will need to be upgraded within a year or so. This also applies to any other software you have installed. Luckily, Windows 2000 includes software publication as a core component of Group Policy, so upgrades should get easier and less time consuming.

Hardware is another story. There are vast numbers of processors being released, faster network components being brought to market, faster printers, better hard drives, more fault-tolerant servers—in other words, constant improvements are being made to the equipment we use on our networks. Keeping hardware up-to-date is a losing battle. But we must keep up to remain competitive. Here, product life cycles are measured in days rather than months. A new computer is often outdated before you even open the box. As servers have become faster, more fault tolerant, and more reliable, IS experts are returning to the days of consolidated resources. Multiple servers regularly are being migrated to one replacement server. Hardware upgrades should have a minimal influence on a well-designed network, but there will be times where the consolidation of services to a central computer will affect the availability of data and services.

Analyzing the Decision-Making Process

At some point in the design process, you will need someone to make a decision about some aspect of your proposal. This is true for both staff IS personnel and outside consultants. There is a sales theory that says basically that you can't make a sale without talking to the decision maker. This same theory holds true in network design—you'll never get a design approved unless you are talking to the decision maker or makers. This is the case with purchases of hardware and software as well.

Exam Essentials

This first section presents a challenge to both an author and to a potential test taker. Most of this material will not be tested in a direct manner. In most cases you'll be presented with a case study question that describes a company. Based upon the case study, you'll be asked to suggest business solutions. Choosing the correct solution will depend on your ability to analyze the given environment, and determine which of the business models it represents. The answers to the questions will often depend on your making the proper analysis.

Understand the differences between the three geographic scopes. You must be able to read a case study and determine which of the three geographical models it fits into—regional, national, or international.

NOTE   Since the simple-network model was our own creation, you will not see it listed as a choice.

Be aware that if an environment matches the criteria for our "simple-network" everything can be left at the default configuration. While the simple-network definition is our own creation, it can be used to determine if the environment can be left "as is"—i.e., single domain, and no advanced configuration options.

Understand the differences between types of locations.   Once again, after reading a case study, you'll need to be able to analyze the information presented and classify each location into either a subsidiary or branch office model (or our classification—a corporate office.)

Know the difference between information flow and communication flow.   Information flow is a description of where data moves within the infrastructure. Communication flow is how employees use information.

Key Terms and Concepts

Geographical Scope   A description of the number of physical locations that make up the network and the connectivity between them.

Business Model   A description of the relationships among sites and services.

Simple-Network Model   Our term (not Microsoft's) that refers to a single-domain environment in which no complex issues exist.

Regional Model   An environment in which all sites are contained within a well-defined geographic area.

National Model   An environment in which all sites are located within the borders of a single country.

International Model   An environment in which the company has locations in multiple countries.

Corporate Office   Our term (not Microsoft's) that refers to a location in which the company has invested heavily in facilities, information services staff, and hardware, or a location that is heavily staffed.

Branch Office   A wholly controlled facility that does not meet the criteria to be classified as a corporate office. (See the "Critical Information" section for details.)

Subsidiary Office   A location that is part of the overall business but is not controlled by the company.

Information Flow   A description of the movement of information across the network infrastructure.

Soft Information   Information that is not easily quantified as to size or use. (See "Critical Information" for details.)

Data   A series of facts.

Information   Data that has been organized into a useable format.

Product and Service Life Cycles   There are two types:

- The length of time that a company's products or services are valid.
- The length of time that the implemented technology will remain viable.

Sample Questions

1. You are beginning an AD planning project for a company in St. Paul, Minnesota. The company has offices throughout Wisconsin, Minnesota, Illinois, and western Michigan. Each office connects to the headquarters facility with a dedicated line appropriate to its needs. (The company has a contract with a local provider of dedicated lines, which means that bandwidth is never an issue.) Use of the network is limited to printing, file access, and e-mail.

Which of the geographic models best describes this environment?

A. Simple

B. Regional

C. National

D. International

Answer: B. In most respects, this company could be a simple model, except that it includes wide area links. For this reason, it is best described as a regional model.

2. You are beginning an AD planning project for a company in St. Paul, Minnesota. The company has offices throughout Wisconsin, Minnesota, Illinois, and western Michigan. Each office connects to the headquarters facility with a dedicated line appropriate to its needs. They occasionally have bandwidth issues on some of these lines in remote areas—often these lines are unavailable for hours at a time. To combat this, each remote site has a dial-up connection available to use during these periods.

Which geographic models best describes this environment?

A. Simple

B. Regional

C. National

D. International

Answer: C.   The addition of variable quality WAN links and dial-up connections moves this example from a regional to a national model.

3. You are beginning an AD planning project for a company in St. Paul, Minnesota. The company has offices throughout Wisconsin, Minnesota, Illinois, western Michigan, and parts of Canada. Each office connects to the headquarters facility with a dedicated line appropriate to its needs. They occasionally have bandwidth issues on some of these lines in remote areas—often these lines are unavailable for hours at a time. To combat this, each remote site has a dial-up connection available to use during these periods. The Canadian offices are managed by a separate branch of the IT department, and all software is installed using the French versions.

Which geographic models best describes this environment?

A. Simple

B. Regional

C. National

D. International

Answer: D.   Because this network crosses international boundaries, one would assume that this would qualify as an international model. Although the answer is correct, the reason is wrong. Given the limited boundaries of the network, this could be considered a regional or national network. What sets it apart (and moves it to the international model) is the fact that different languages are in use across the network and different laws and regulations might apply at various locations.

4. A business model is _____

A. The marketing plan for a product line

B. A document used to apply for a business license

C. A definition of the management philosophy of a company

D. The wiring schematic of a network

Answer: C.   Business models define the relationships between groups within a company.

Analyze the existing and planned organizational structures. Considerations include management model; company organization; vendor, partner, and customer relationships; and acquisition plans.

After looking at the overall structure of the company and its environment, the next step in a design process it to analyze specific aspects of the way that the company approaches common business processes. In this section, we'll discuss those processes that are included in the Microsoft MCSE exam.

Critical Information

In keeping with Microsoft's emphasis on providing business solutions, you will need to understand some of the basic management philosophies used in real-life companies. Knowing the relationships between internal and external groups can help to design an AD structure that makes life easier for both end users and administrators.

NOTE Remember that one of your major design goals is to design an environment in which technology matches business rather than one in which business must change to match technology. If you ever utter the words "You *can't* do it that way because the system won't allow it," you need to reevaluate your design.

Analyzing the Management Model and Company Organization

Microsoft defines four major business models:

- Departmental
- Project based

- Product/service based

- Cost centers

Each of these models represents a different way of looking at the same thing—the structure of a business. In reality, most businesses do pretty much the same stuff—accounts payable, accounts receivable, marketing, sales, and so on. What differs from company to company is the way these functions interrelate. The relationships among functions are what business models are all about.

NOTE   Microsoft's use of the terms *management model* and *company organization* can be a bit confusing. They both mean the same thing on the exam—how internal relationships are managed within a company. For testing purposes, the two terms are interchangeable. In order to reduce confusion, we've decided to refer to them as *business models,* which is a more accurate description.

When you're trying to determine the business model used by a company, a great place to start is with the company's organizational chart. Look at how branches of the chart are named and look at the chain of command. For each model, we'll provide a sample organizational chart to try to drive home the differences. Another great way to determine the business model is to listen to how management refers to processes, personnel, or projects. We'll also include a few examples of how management refers to internal processes with each model.

TIP   In the case study exam questions, Microsoft will often include quotes from staff. Read these quotes carefully—not only do they give you clues about the company's business needs and goals, they also hint at the management philosophy of the environment. Knowing how the business is managed can help you determine which solution would be the best answer for the case study company.

Understanding the Departmental Model

The *departmental model* is the traditional method of managing a business. The basics of the departmental model are quite simple—look at the tasks that make up the business processes of a company, group them according to function, and manage each group. For any company from a small tavern to a large international corporation to be successful, certain tasks must be completed. These tasks can be grouped into departments. Some of the traditional departments include, but are not limited to, the following:

Accounting   Manages the money—both incoming and outgoing. This department is usually also responsible for ensuring that the former outpaces the latter!

Marketing   Ensures that the public (or some portion thereof) knows about the company and its goods or services.

Sales   Convinces someone to actually buy a product or service.

Research and Development   Defines the goods or services offered by the company.

Production   Makes the goods or performs the service.

Information Services   Manages the hardware and software the computer environment comprises.

Most of us are quite comfortable with the functions performed by these traditional departments. This is what makes it an attractive business model—familiarity with function is built in. If you hire Katie to be a salesperson, you don't have to teach her what the accounting department does—she already knows (at least superficially).

Some businesses have departments that are specific to their function. If you were designing an AD structure for a city, for instance, your departments would probably include the standard ones *and* a few that are specific to city management, such as the following:

- Water works
- Sanitation
- Fire control

- Health and welfare

- Law enforcement

- Animal control

- Road construction and repair

Once again, though, the power of this business model is that the overall function (if not the specific tasks) of each department is well known. If there's a big pothole in the street in front of your house, you instinctively know which city office to call.

NOTE Understanding the departments a city government would have is a good example of the extra knowledge required to design an international network. The list of departments will often differ by culture.

The organizational chart for a company managed using the departmental model, as shown in Figure 1.7, will be familiar to anyone who has worked for a large corporation.

FIGURE 1.7: A departmental organizational chart

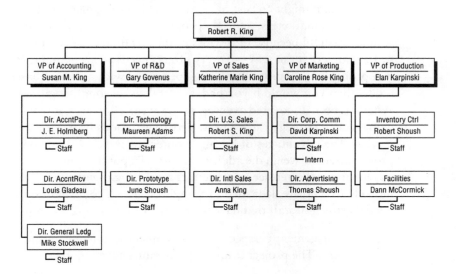

Discovering the management model in use for a company usually involves talking to upper management. Listen for clues in the way that they reference business procedures. Ask for the organizational chart and then ask a few questions about the interrelationships among areas of functionality. If the chain of command is straightforward and it is easy to explain who reports to whom, the odds are the company is using a departmental management model.

TIP   Exam Hint: Many of the case study questions include quotes from different people within the sample company, but very few of the questions will include an organizational chart. You'll have to read the material carefully, looking for clues to these internal relationships.

Understanding the Project-Based Model

For quite some time, the *project-based model* was considered the "new age" of management. In it, the company is broken into small groups, or teams (to use the vernacular). Each team contains all of the resources necessary to support a company project. At first glance, this might seem like the same as the departmental model, but in the case of a project-based model, teams are "cross-discipline." In other words, a team might consist of research and development staff, accountants, marketers, and salespeople. For many years, this was seen as wasteful because of the loss of the advantages of centralized staff. (Think of it this way—if every project needs an accountant, you will probably need more accounting personnel with a project-based model than you would if you had a centralized accounting group.) What has been discovered over the last few years, however, is that this management strategy is the fastest way to get goods or services to market. The advantages of having "content experts" working on a project often outweigh the additional costs. To put that another way, a company will often see faster results by putting together a team of individuals who are dedicated to a single project as compared to having departmental staff that have to split their time among all projects.

From a management perspective, this is the most dynamic business environment. The project teams are constantly forming, reforming, and breaking up as projects are created, finished, or dropped. The chain of command is often disjointed—people report to project heads who often report to other project heads or upper management. These kinds of companies are often in industries in which the ability to make quick decisions is critical (many companies in the computer industry use the project-based business model).

To a consultant or inside staff administrator trying to create an AD structure, the project-based model can often be a nightmare to design for. The same dynamics that make this model good for cutting-edge businesses can make it difficult to design a stable directory structure. Your AD structure must be designed to take into account the constant reassignment of personnel and other resources.

Organizational charts for companies using a project-based management model usually follow one of two forms: matrix or free-flow. The matrix chart is basically just a spreadsheet that crosses references to projects and personnel, as shown in Table 1.3. Most such charts will also include a column (as shown) to indicate each person's skill set. This view is handy when individuals might be assigned to multiple projects.

TABLE 1.3: A Project-Based Organizational Matrix

Name/ Project	Expertise	Beef Dog Food	Tuna Cat Food	Dog Treats	Cat Treats	Pet Toys
Susan K.	Accounting	X				
Bob K.	Project Lead					X
Katie K.	Packaging	X				
Carrie K.	Design					X
Kodiak	Product Tester	X		X		X
Fluffy	Product Tester		X		X	X

TABLE 1.3: A Project-Based Organizational Matrix *(continued)*

Name/ Project	Expertise	Beef Dog Food	Tuna Cat Food	Dog Treats	Cat Treats	Pet Toys
Tom S.	Project Lead	X				
Robert S.	Project Lead		X			
June S.	Accounting		X			
Anna K.	Production	X	X	X	X	X
Elan K.	Purchasing	X		X		

As you can see, this type of organizational matrix is great for seeing who is working on what project, but it's not too good at portraying who reports to whom. The free-flow organizational chart, as shown in Figure 1.8, is better at this.

FIGURE 1.8: A project-based, free-flow organizational chart

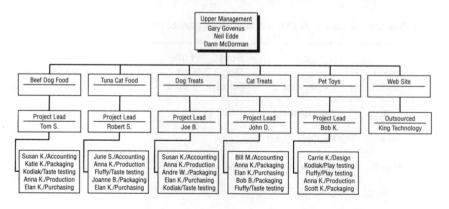

During your interviews with management, you will hear a few key words that will indicate a project-based model. If you hear things like

the following, then it's probably a project-based model (we've made the key words bold):

- "Joe is working on the new widget **team**." (As opposed to Joe is "in production.")

- "Jane is **doing accounting for** the support **group**." (As opposed to Jane is "in accounting.")

- "Accounting **data is spread out** over multiple projects." (One of the worst aspects of the project-based model is that, because resources are dedicated to each group, information is often disjointed and distributed across multiple locations.)

TIP   Exam Hint: Watch for statements that contain key words in the case study questions—they'll clue you in to the management philosophy of the company.

Understanding the Product/Service-Based Model

The *product/service-based model* is quite similar to the project-based model. Once again, resources are dedicated to specific functions, but in this model, those groups are specifically organized to support whatever products or services the company sells. Companies that start out using the project-based model often mature into the product/service-based model. The organizational chart will look exactly like that of a company using the project-based approach except that the groupings will be by product or service rather than internal projects.

In Figure 1.9, we see a part of the organizational chart for a product-based environment. The only real difference between this and a project-based company is that the product lines might include product-based projects.

The biggest clue you'll get when interviewing management is that all references are made specific to a product or service. You might hear, for instance, something like the following (we've made the key words bold):

- "Joe's working on the **dog food** team." (A product-based environment)

- "Our **network integration** division...." (A service-based environment)

FIGURE 1.9: A product-based organizational chart

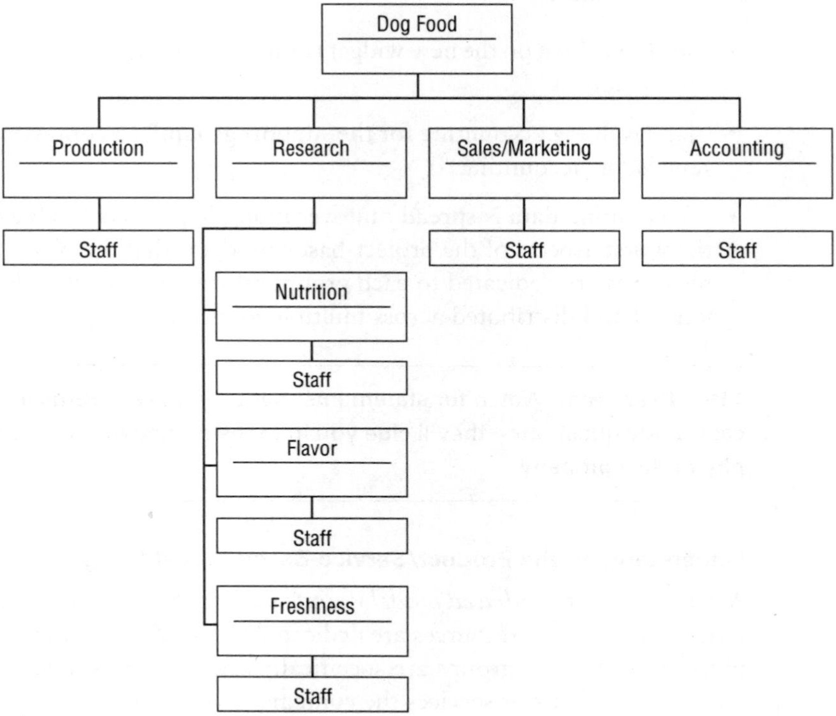

Understanding the Cost-Center Model

The *cost-center model* is usually a hybrid of all of the other models. In this model, the functions of business are once again divided into groups—based on projects, products/services, or traditional departments—just as they are in the other models we have discussed. The big difference is in how those groups interact. Each group is seen as a separate business entity within the company. Groups charge each other for the services they provide. The IS department, for instance, might charge the sales department for server disk space usage or e-mail functionality.

From an Active Directory design perspective, this business model mandates some specific functionality—the most important is the ability to track and control the use of resources. The organizational chart can follow the format of any of the other models (departmental, project, or product/service). The clues to a cost center model will come during your analysis of information flow, funding, priorities, and growth strategies. (We'll discuss these topics later in this chapter.)

Analyzing Business Relationships

So far, we've concentrated on the internal business structure of a company. Because no business survives in a vacuum, we'll now expand our discussion to include the various forms of relationships that exist with outside entities—vendors, partners, customers, and acquisitions. In many legacy operating systems, you really don't have to worry about outside relationships because their focus is limited to internal resources. In Windows NT 4, for instance, whether or not a company has close ties with its vendors would have little (if any) effect on the domain structure. But in Windows 2000 (and Active Directory), these outside entities can have large effects on AD design.

In the sections that follow, we will talk about each of these relationships, paying particular attention to what you must know to pass the exam.

Analyzing Vendor Relationships

A few years ago, the term *vendor* referred only to an outside company that provided services or goods to a company. Today, markets have shifted, and this shift has resulted in relationships with vendors that are much closer than those that existed only five years ago. In our consulting firm we do business with a particular vendor; let's call it XYZ. The vendor has worked hard to build a relationship with our company because of the volume of hardware and software that we order. Right now, we can access XYZ's Web site (with an authenticated logon) and access its part numbers and inventory. The vendor's system is so advanced that we can access its inventory database through its Web page and find pricing and availability of its products. We've built such a strong relationship with this vendor that we get faxes, e-mails, and phone calls about daily specials and new technologies. The point here is that the vendor has almost become another department of our company.

During your design considerations, you will have to consider ways to increase the effectiveness of the vendor relationship. Remember that the vendor is trying to sell to you (or your client), not the other way around. This puts you in the position of power. Any administrative work that can be placed at the other end will be good for your company. With this in mind, consider giving your vendors access to some of the information on your network. If, for instance, your company builds widgets and you purchase some of the widget parts from company ABC, why not give company ABC access to some of your shop floor data? It could be responsible for checking your production schedule to ensure that you have enough stock on hand. Active Directory is the perfect tool for granting access to some resources while protecting others.

From an examination perspective, Microsoft is pushing the cooperative aspects of AD. If your vendors are also using Windows 2000, it is easy to add their AD trees to your forest. If not, it is easy to set up a certificate server to allow secure access to resources across the Internet. Don't forget to consider other Microsoft products for your complete business solution. You might, for instance, want to use Exchange Server to create a series of public folders that can be used as a communication channel with vendors. Or you might think about using the filtering capabilities of Proxy Server to control access from certain IP subnets.

TIP Exam Hint: The bottom line for analyzing vendor relationships is access to information. The more your vendors know about your needs, the better the vendors will be able to serve you. Use the capabilities of Windows 2000 and Active Directory to grant that access!

Analyzing Partner Relationships

One of the keys to success in today's competitive markets is to partner with other companies. A *partner* can be defined as another business entity that exists as a separate company but works with your company to achieve a mutual goal. The biggest problem (until the release of Windows 2000) was controlling the flow of information between the two companies. Windows 2000 and Active Directory make it easy to tie two systems together and limit or prevent access to confidential information while still allowing access to the information or resources that are necessary for the partnership to work. Once again, your analysis of the partner relationships should concentrate on shared resources. Consider all of the ways that Windows 2000 allows outside entities to access internal resources and use those capabilities to facilitate the partnership.

Analyzing Customer Relationships

Among the most important relationships that a business can build are those with its customer base. There are many ways to foster these relationships, and our job in IS is to offer technological solutions that help sustain these relationships (one of the most important statistics in business is the number of customers who would do business with a company again or recommend the company to friends). When analyzing the customer relationships of a company, there are two questions you need to answer:

- What is the nature of the relationship with the customer base?
- What technologies can be used to increase these relationships?

There are as many types of relationships with customers as there are types of business. You need to analyze the amount of customer contact—both before and after the sale—the nature of those contacts (technical support, installation support, reordering supplies, and so on), and the frequency of contact. Dietary consultants, for instance, are constantly contacted by their client base. Those contacts would probably be either to ask a series of questions (such as "How many calories are in a candy bar?" or "Which vegetables have the vitamins I need?") or to purchase additional items, such as books or packaged meals.

The nature of the contact will directly affect the technologies you might suggest to the client. A company in which the contact is mostly conversation, such as a psychic hot line, would probably love a telephony product that ties into a contact database (something that would read the incoming caller ID and automatically bring up any information about the customer's former calls). A company that offers technical support, on the other hand, would probably benefit from a full-blown help-desk package. In either case, match the technology to the type of customer contact.

NOTE You will also want to consider the technical sophistication of the customer base. It makes no sense to offer Internet support, for instance, if the demographics show that most of the customers do not own a computer.

Analyzing Acquisition Plans

If your company has plans to acquire other companies or to merge with them, you will want to ask some very specific questions. Your overall design strategy can be affected by the results of this type of growth. Ask about the process of integration between the two companies. Will the two companies be merged into one or will both companies continue to function as separate business units? Does the newly acquired company have a registered domain name? If so, will it continue to use it? (Remember that the Active Directory root domain name defines the scope of the name space—if the two companies need separate identities, you might be forced to create two AD trees and tie them together in a forest.) What new physical locations will be added to the WAN? (Don't forget to include them in the material you gathered during your analysis of the network infrastructure.) Is the new company using Windows 2000? If not, can you suggest a comprehensive migration to it or will you have to deal with a heterogeneous environment? Which IS staff will be responsible for the merging of the two networks?

The bottom line for analyzing business acquisitions or mergers is to remember that you are, in effect, dealing with two separate companies. There will be political, cultural, and philosophical differences between the two businesses. You job will be to wade through all of that and come up with the best technical and business solution available.

Exam Essentials

This section covered the basic formulas used to manage businesses.

Be able to describe the differences between the four business management models. The four models are departmental, project based, product/service based, and cost centers. (See the "Critical Information" section for details.)

Understand how Windows 2000 and Active Directory can be used to build better vendor and partner relationships. Building a forest of AD trees can facilitate the sharing of resources.

Key Terms and Concepts

Business Model   A description of the relationships among sites and services.

Departmental Business Model   A management philosophy in which tasks and processes are grouped according to function.

Project-Based Business Model   A management philosophy in which a company is broken into small groups, or teams. Each team contains all of the resources necessary to support a company project.

Product/Service-Based Business Model   A management philosophy in which company resources are dedicated to a particular product or service.

Cost Center Business Model   A management philosophy in which tasks and processes are divided in some manner (usually using one of the other three models) but each group charges for the services that it provides to the others.

Vendor   An outside company that provides services or goods to another company.

Partner   A business entity that exists as a separate company but works with a company to achieve a mutual goal.

Sample Questions

1. Golf Stuff, Inc., established in 1924, manufactures golf-related accessories. During your interviews with staff members, you discover that each business function is managed by a vice president, is overseen by a director, and is responsible for specific business needs. Which of the following business models would best describe Golf Stuff, Inc.?

A. Departmental

B. Project based

C. Product/service based

D. Cost center

Answer: A.   Most long-established firms will be managed along traditional departmental guidelines. The clue here is the strict chain of command (VPs and directors) and the function-specific areas of responsibility.

2. New Age Art is a medium-sized firm that specializes in inspirational office décor. During your interviews with the staff, you discovered that there are groups of "content experts" who specialize in, and are responsible for, specific types of art: motivational, therapeutic, and even aromatic influencers. These groups find artists, negotiate purchase prices, and bring the articles to market. Which of the following business models would best describe New Age Art?

A. Departmental

B. Project based

C. Product/service based

D. Cost center

Answer: C.   Because each group appears to be totally responsible for a different product line, it is safe to assume that the management philosophy is product based.

3. OverAll, Inc. is a holding company for a group of firms involved in the manufacture and distribution of computer peripherals. Each of the firms is autonomous and responsible for its own financial well being. During your investigation of the company, you discovered a database that tracks invoices among the various firms; for instance, the marketing firm bills the sales firm for any collateral produced. Which of the following business models would best describe OverAll, Inc.?

A. Departmental

B. Project based

C. Product/service based

D. Cost center

Answer: D.   Because each of the child firms is an autonomous business, assuming its own fiscal responsibilities, the cost center model would be the best fit.

4. Which of the following business models is usually the most dynamic?

A. Departmental

B. Project based

C. Product/service based

D. Cost center

Answer: B.   In a project-based environment, resources are constantly being moved from one project to another. This results in frequent changes to the Active Directory database.

5. The CEO of a company says, "Accounting has all of the figures you have asked for." Which business model do you suspect is used within the company?

A. Departmental

B. Project

C. Product/service

D. Cost center

Answer: A.   The CEO implies that there is a group of people whose job is handling the accounting needs for the company.

Analyze factors that influence company strategies.

- **Identify company priorities.**
- **Identify the projected growth and growth strategy.**
- **Identify relevant laws and regulations.**
- **Identify the company's tolerance for risk.**
- **Identify the total cost of operations.**

At some point in the design process, you will need someone to make a decision about some aspect of your proposal. This is true for both staff IS personnel and outside consultants. There is a theory in sales that basically says that you can't make a sale without talking to the decision-maker. This same theory holds true in network design— you'll never get a design approved unless you are talking to the decision maker or makers. This is the case with purchases of hardware and software as well.

There are numerous factors that can influence the decision-making process within a company. Some are political, some are legal, and some are financial. Before you begin, you should analyze these factors to see what effect they will have on your final AD design. You wouldn't, for instance, suggest 50 new servers to a company that has a tight budget for the project or plan for 128-bit encryption for a company that has offices overseas. (Of course this example might change as our laws change.)

Critical Analysis

Company Priorities

We in the IS industry tend to think that we are the center of the world (after all, everyone comes to us for answers), but the reality is that the migration or upgrade to Windows 2000 might be only one small project in the scheme of things. In any given company, at any given time, there are probably numerous projects in the works. We recently worked on the directory design team for a company that was dealing with the following issues simultaneously:

- Planning an upgrade to Windows 2000

- Finishing its ISO9000 compliance testing

- Moving from a legacy e-mail package to Microsoft Exchange Server

- Setting up Internet access at every desk

- Designing an e-commerce Web site

- Checking for Y2K issues at every client computer

Our design project was definitely *not* at the top of the list. We had numerous problems gathering the information we needed to complete a good AD design—either personnel were not available, or that part of the network was undergoing changes so the information would not be valid in a couple of weeks, or some other issue would come up and the design team would be split up to put out IS fires. We had committed the cardinal sin of consultants: we believed that our project was the most important project going on, when in reality, internal politics made the e-mail upgrade the hot ticket.

Find out what is going on within the company and how important each project is in the scheme of things. Knowing that your design is considered a low-priority project can help you to plan deadlines and person-hours, and plan for changes of direction in the process. (There's nothing worse than getting halfway through a project only to have it canceled due to a lack of interest.)

Projected Growth and Growth Strategy

We were recently involved in the design of a network for a company that was moving from one facility to another. We got to design the network from the wiring on up—not only was it fun, it was satisfying as well because the company accepted just about every suggestion we made. We set up the network, configured the workstations, and moved the 200 users to the new location. Only then did we find out that another business in the new building was planning to buy out the company and the move to the new facility was made to ease the transition. Now our network that was designed to easily support 200 users would have to support over 1,000 users. Luckily, we had planned for a little growth, so all we had to do was move a few servers to reposition the services they provided. This *could*, however, have been a major problem had our design not been flexible. Always discuss the future of the company. Ask about mergers, acquisitions. Even ask whether the company might be sold. Each of these factors can, and will, influence your AD structure.

Even the normal growth that occurs in a healthy company must not be taken for granted. Look at the past few years' revenue: Has the company's revenue grown each year? If so, does there appear to be a pattern? How many new employees has the company hired in the last few years, and again, is there a pattern? In a retail business, for instance, what happens when a new store is added to the company? What is the average number of new employees, what hardware and software is involved, what WAN links are added to the infrastructure? Is there a seasonal increase in business activity that should be taken into account? Persistent Images did some work for a couple of ski resorts at Tahoe. We were making changes during its slow season (summer) but had to plan for the additional overhead that would be added to the network once the ski season opened.

Companies often have a set of goals for growing their business—as for example, 10-percent increase in sales, one new location each quarter, an additional five employees each month, and so on. Ask about growth goals and the strategies that exist to handle the additional network overhead. During your analysis of the management model and the business procedures, consider how these things would change given a 10-percent growth in staff.

Laws and Regulations

Throughout the world, there are laws and regulations that govern how business can be conducted. Some of these laws and regulations are so obscure that they are virtually unknown. We were working with a small company in Germany recently that drove this fact home. The company had a typical central management policy for all IS resources, including databases. We set them up so that all user information was managed from that central site. Only later did we find out about the German law that prohibits employee personal information from being managed from another state. In other words, we had set them up so that users were managed from the company's main location in Europe—located in Amsterdam—and that was illegal in Germany. The only way to get around the law was to have every employee sign a waiver allowing the administrative staff to manage personal information. The moral of this story is that you must conform to the local laws and regulations when creating a business solution.

Conformity with local laws and regulations can be fairly easy if you always work in the same basic location—if for no other reason than repetition, you will soon know the regulations for your area. If you travel, however, this changes. We almost always bring in local consultants to look over physical aspects like cabling or electrical work. For the business side, we will either rely on the staff at the company or, once again, bring in a local consultant to look over our proposed design. Although this adds to the original bid, it saves time and money in the long run.

Risk Tolerance

In business, as in life, there are different tolerances for risk. We're the kind of guys who will jump out of airplanes or dive deep to meet a shark face-to-face, but we have friends who get nervous driving over the speed limit (not that we would ever do that!). There are some businesses that are willing to take big risks in the hope of big gains, just as there are businesses for which risk is a four-letter word. How much risk a company is willing to take will certainly influence your design process. A low-risk company will be best served by a slow methodical approach to the migration to Windows 2000 and Active Directory. You'll have to set up *every* contingency in a test lab before moving into a production environment. A high-risk company will be more willing to move Windows 2000 into its production environment and work out the bugs (oops—deal with the opportunities that present themselves) as they appear. We've found that the best approach is usually somewhere in the middle—put together a test lab, and practice, and then pick an area or department to act as the proving ground for your procedures.

From a design perspective, knowing the risk tolerance of a company helps in creating the project schedule (the lower the tolerance, the longer the project will take) and in budgeting (the lower the tolerance, the higher the cost). It can also help you to determine the level of fault tolerance that should be implemented. Windows 2000 Advanced Server, for instance, includes clustering capabilities that reduce downtime due to equipment failures. Or you might want to configure redundant WAN links between sites to ensure reliable communication.

Cost of Operations

In Bob's office, there is an old poster that hung in his father's transmission shop. It reads, "We can give you two out of three: Good, Fast, or Cheap!" Bob's dad used to call it his first law of business physics. Whenever we have a client that wants all three, we have to remind ourselves that not everyone has a background in "physics." The rule holds true for every aspect of business—including AD design. During your analysis of the business environment, you will have to find out which two the client is expecting. Not surprisingly, most clients want all three.

Budgeting for a design project is tricky business: Ask for too much and the project gets canceled (or some other consultant gets the job); ask for too little and your funding runs out before the project is finished. Microsoft's dream is that every AD design will provide a complete business solution for the client. The reality is that funding often determines how much of the dream you can provide. One of the skills that Microsoft expects you to demonstrate in the Design exams is the ability to prioritize tasks. Given a budget and a prioritized list of goals, you can then determine which goals can be met now, which should be deferred until later, and which are just not realistic given the current business situation. Funding will play a large role in making these decisions.

There are many costs involved in running a business. *Hard costs*—such as payroll, rent, and insurance—are easy to budget because they usually do not change over time. Given a list of hard costs, it is easy to budget for a month, a quarter, or even a year. There are other costs that are not so easy to budget, sometimes referred to as soft costs. *Soft costs* include time lost due to server downtime, person-hours lost due to sick leave, and any other costs that are variable over time. Soft costs are much more difficult to budget. When justifying the expense of an upgrade or migration to Windows 2000, you must include the savings in both hard and soft costs.

Earlier in this chapter, we stated that Microsoft is expecting MCSE candidates to show business skills as well as technical skills. Creating and justifying a budget for a design project is one of those skills. Many of us technologists have never really taken the time to learn the process involved in budgeting. (Many of us have actually avoided this aspect of information services.) We don't know how many times we have heard someone say, "Can't do it, not in the budget." There are times when this is an accurate description, but more often than not, this is a statement made by someone who doesn't know how to justify costs to upper management.

Budget creation should start with an overall analysis of the company's finances. What are the total costs of running the business? What percentage of that amount is the IS budget? Have IS costs been increasing over the last few years? How about overall costs—does it cost more to keep the business running today than it did last year or the year before? Break down the overall cost of operations by department—which departments cost the most? In each department, break down the costs of business processes. Analyze the procedures involved in "doing business." What does it cost to produce one widget (or whatever product or service the company produces)? What does it cost to generate one invoice? What expenses are involved in maintaining the inventory database? Ask about the help desk—what is the average time to close each trouble call?

The goal of compiling this list of business expenses is to determine if a move to Windows 2000 can be economically justified. Spend some time thinking about each of the processes in the business model—exactly how is an invoice generated, and can the process be streamlined through the use of technology? Why does the company have such a large inventory? Would a better production control system provide better order-on-demand options? How often were the servers down last quarter, and what can be done to reduce the effect (or better yet, reduce downtime)? Look at every business cost to determine if a feature of AD can reduce them.

NOTE This philosophy of providing business solutions rather than technology is a paradigm shift in how Microsoft wants to present its products. Each of the Design tests will emphasize the skills necessary to analyze the business needs of an environment.

Exam Essentials

In this section we looked at various business considerations that must be taken into account during an AD design project.

Remember that even though you are taking a Microsoft exam, Windows 2000 (and Active Directory) might not be the highest priority to a company in the case studies. Always examine the issues to determine the order in which actions should be taken (based upon business needs.)

Keep in mind that laws and regulations might differ from area to area. Look through the description of the case study to determine if the AD design will be affected by different sets of rules.

Change means risk! Examine the case studies to see if there is a hint about the company's risk tolerance. You might have to take a more conservative approach with a client whose tolerance for risk is low.

Analyze the effects of costs on the company. A company with cash flow problems might need to wait for a better time to implement new technology. (Or, better yet, new technology might save them enough money to justify the implementation.)

Key Terms and Concepts

Risk Acceptance Level The amount of risk a company is willing to take during an upgrade or migration to Windows 2000.

Sample Questions

1. Company ABC is concerned that employee productivity will suffer during the migration to Windows 2000 and is considering staying with its current operating system to avoid this. Which of the following would best describe its attitude?

   A. High risk tolerance

   B. Low risk tolerance

   C. Nervous client syndrome

   D. Buyers regret

   Answer: B.   Company ABC has a low risk tolerance level. You should produce a safe and secure design implementation plan to alleviate its concerns.

2. The date is November 12, 1999. Your company is currently A) preparing a year-end stockholders report, B) testing all IT systems for Y2K compliance, C) configuring a firewall to control access across a new Internet connection, and D) designing an AD structure for a planned migration to Windows 2000. Prioritize these projects from most critical to least.

   A. A, B, C, D

   B. B, C, D, A

   C. C, B, A, D

   D. D, C, B, A

   Answer: C.   The most critical project is to protect your current environment. That means controlling a new Internet connection has to be done immediately. This should be followed by the Y2K testing (even though in retrospect Y2K didn't seem like much of an issue, its small effect was mostly due to businesses being prepared), then keep the stockholders happy by getting the report done. In this case, the move to Windows 2000 is the lowest priority project in the list.

Analyze the structure of IT management. Considerations include type of administration, such as centralized or decentralized; funding model; outsourcing; decision-making process; and change-management process.

At this point in the design process, you are still gathering information to help you make wise decisions during later discussions. Some would argue that the IT department is just another business group and therefore should have been discussed in earlier objectives. There are two good reasons for isolating the IT department for analysis. First and foremost, given the nature of this text, Microsoft separates the information technology department in the exam objectives. There are a series of exam objectives focused on analyzing the technical environment of a company (you will see more about this in the next chapter.) Second, the IT department is not just a consumer of IT services, it also provides them. Because the IT department will support the final implementation of Windows 2000 and AD, it is important to have a firm grounding in the current and expected IT department.

Critical Information

Before you can begin the process of suggesting and implementing new technologies (or even business procedures), you must have an understanding of the department that will implement those suggestions— the IT department. How the IT department is managed is critical to many of the issues we will be discussing in later chapters. Once again, this chapter's main focus is gathering information that will be used later in the design process.

Just as businesses have models for management (as discussed earlier), so too do departments. Because a departmental management philosophy is more granular (or to put that another way, more dependent upon the function of the department), there are no real cookie-cutter models that will fit every department. Each department has its own management considerations. This first section describes the considerations that are relevant when discussing an IT department.

Central or Decentralized Management

There are two basic philosophies of IT management: central control and decentralized control. In a shop using a central control management model, all IT resources are managed by a small group of people in a single location. In a decentralized model, resources are managed locally. There are advantages and disadvantages to both management techniques.

NOTE The management technique used by the IT department often mimics the overall philosophy of the company. In companies where the headquarters staff is in complete control of all facets of the business, the IT staff is more likely to use a central management model. Conversely, in companies where sites or departments are more autonomous, the IT staff is more likely to used decentralized management techniques.

Central Management

Centralized management mirrors the "glass room" philosophy of the mainframe era. All IT decisions and management come from a central location (hence the name of the model) by a small administrative staff. These IT professionals need to have a high level of expertise because they support all IT resources—from workstations to servers and everything in between. In larger environments, the workload is often distributed by expertise. Each component of the overall environment—WAN, server, workstation, and applications—will have one or more individuals who specialize in it.

There are often fewer organizational units (OUs) in the AD tree because management does not need to be delegated to local staff. The directory administrators have complete control over the entire AD structure. Although this means that the administrator must have more experience and training, and therefore a higher salary, these costs are usually offset by a reduction in personnel and the number of people who need to be brought up to speed on Active Directory.

Because there is no local IT staff at each location, components of the environment must be as reliable as possible. Imagine a company with offices around the globe, as shown in Figure 1.10. This company is headquartered in New York City and has offices in Minneapolis, Tampa, London, Paris, and Frankfurt.

FIGURE 1.10: An international environment

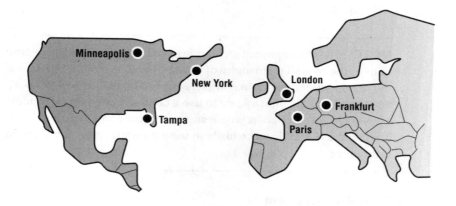

Assuming a central IT management philosophy, if a server goes down in Paris, someone from New York City must fly to France to effect repairs. Not only is this costly, it implies an unacceptable amount of downtime. This is probably the number-one problem with a centrally controlled IT environment in a large company: fixes generally take longer and cost more at remote facilities. Part of the drawback can be eased by means of your AD design—the more IT resources located near the IT staff, the less cost (and time) involved in repair and maintenance. In most cases, the overall design of the network will be to place critical resources near the IT staff (rather than near the users who access them).

Automation is the key to avoiding the costs involved in long-range management. Most centrally controlled IT departments use tools to automate the distribution of applications, regular backups, and even the occasional server reboot. Remote management tools and scripted actions are used to accomplish the majority of IT functions. From an AD design perspective, this means that features such as *Group Policy Object (GPO) software publishing* will be used extensively.

The separation of the IT staff from the end users can also result in a slower support process. Often, any type of change, fix, or maintenance must be submitted to IT (often in triplicate) in the form of a request. The request will then be placed in a queue, awaiting completion. This sounds like a terrible system (from the users' perspective), but it is often extremely effective. Because many of the requests will originate in locations with no IT staff, most changes are made using remote management tools of one sort or another.

Given the distance between the IT staff and the users they support, most decisions are made after thorough analysis. A mistake *could* mean someone would have to travel to the remote site (not to mention the downtime or loss of productivity until the problem is fixed). In many ways, a centrally controlled IT department will be easier to migrate to Windows 2000—they are used to taking the time to design processes and procedures and are familiar with the concepts of many of the central management features.

Based upon the time it takes for actions to take place, centrally controlled IT departments are often considered more conservative than their decentralized colleagues. In reality, though, because of the need for cutting-edge management tools, central IT departments are often more up-to-date. They use the latest tools, master the processes of automation, and are always looking for new technologies to make maintenance of the network faster and more efficient.

From an AD design perspective, the Active Directory structure of a centrally controlled IT environment is often simpler to design and maintain. Because a centrally controlled IT environment does not involve delegation of management roles, the tree often has fewer domains and organizational units. This simplicity is also reflected in the security strategy—fewer domains, fewer organizational units, fewer administrative staff, and better trained (or more experienced) IT staff all add up to a simpler AD implementation.

> **NOTE** For more information about security strategies, please see *MCSE: Windows 2000 Network Security Design Study Guide*, by Gary Govanus and Robert King (Sybex, 2000).

Decentralized Management

In stark contrast to a centralized management model, an environment that uses *decentralized management* has administrative staff at most sites. These local administrators often have complete control over the resources at their location. This management model creates a completely different type of environment for the AD design team. Look at the network of Katie's Dive Shops, shown in Figure 1.11. Here we have another company with multiple remote locations. It has stores in San Diego, San Francisco, Seattle, Chicago, Miami, Tampa, and New Orleans. The corporate headquarters are in Minneapolis.

FIGURE 1.11: Katie's Dive Shops

Each shop is a retail outlet, an equipment maintenance shop, and a training facility approved by the Professional Association of Diving Instructors (PADI). Most shops also offer dive excursions, often working with local travel agencies to arrange package deals. Each shop is connected to a corporate network and has access to shared information from across the nation. (One of the trademarks of a Katie facility is that information about weather and water conditions for every location is posted in each store at the beginning of each day.) Students can take their classroom lessons at one shop, do their pool exercises at another, and finish with their open water dives at another. This flexibility has made Katie's Dive Shops a big success. Katie has taken great pains to ensure that someone with IT experience works at each shop (usually as the equipment maintenance and repair person). Her corporate IT staff trains these individuals on both the network and the specific retail store software packages that are used.

If a server goes down in one of the facilities, there is an IT professional available to fix the problem immediately. This is one of the hallmarks of a decentralized IT department—local maintenance of the IT resources. Rather than waiting for a headquarters staff member to fix any problems—either remotely or, worse yet (in terms of downtime and expense), by coming to the site—problems are dealt with by a local staff member. The drawback to this is that the local person might not have the in-depth knowledge or experience necessary to deal with more complex issues. This is probably the biggest drawback to a decentralized management model. Based on the smaller environment for which they are responsible, local staff members often do not have extensive experience or training to deal with more complex issues.

The overall AD structure is usually more complex in a decentralized environment. More divisions of responsibility exist, and to facilitate this, more organizational units are required. Of course, this also results in a more complex security strategy. *Delegation of responsibility must be done responsibly!* Care must be taken to avoid giving local administrators too much power in the AD structure. Although this is not necessarily a difficult task, it *does* take careful planning.

One of the biggest advantages of a decentralized environment is local support. When users express a need, the local IT representative can fulfill it quickly. There is usually no lengthy procedure of "Submit your request in triplicate (and we'll get around to it when we can)." Our experience has been that this responsiveness results in a much better relationship with end users. From a business perspective, the ability to respond to end-user needs on-site and in minimal time can be a great asset.

In general, the IT staff in a decentralized environment often has less training and is less experienced overall than those in a centrally managed department. On the flip side though, the local IT representative is often more knowledgeable about the components of his facility. Given the opportunity to work on-site, the IT person has a chance to learn each aspect of the local environment inside and out.

Environments that are decentralized are often viewed as less conservative than those that are classified as centralized. There is no greater motivation to improvise and get the job done than having an end user staring at you!

Funding Model

Funding is usually a touchy subject for IT departments. On the one hand, everyone knows the value of the services he or she provides, but on the other hand, many of those services are intangible and therefore hard to quantify. This is no more apparent than when trying to justify the expense of moving to a new operating system such as Windows 2000. Unfortunately, there is a catch-22 in funding: If everything is working well, no one wants to spend the money (if it works, don't fix it). On the other hand, if there are problems, no one will trust the judgment of the staff (fix what we have before we move to something new). The most important thing to remember about funding an IT department is that upper management (especially accountants) are looking for a *return on investment (ROI)*. Basically, the ROI describes the ways in which a change will reduce costs (or improve profits) and the amount of time it will take for these lower costs (or better profits) to outweigh the cost of the change. For example, let's say your company makes widgets. Under your current system, each widget costs $1.00 to produce. If you suggested a technology that costs $100.00 to implement but would reduce the cost of producing widgets to $0.50, the ROI would be 200 widgets (200 × $0.50 = $100.00). To be more accurate, your ROI would be the amount of time it takes to produce 200 widgets.

The problem with the concept of ROI as it pertains to the costs of information technologies is that many IT benefits are intangible. If, for instance, you implement an on-line, customer-support system that improves customer satisfaction (thereby increasing repeat business), how would you quantify the benefit in dollars? One way to justify the expense is to assume that the better support system will probably reduce the amount of time it takes to close each incident. You could then quantify the dollar savings by calculating the amount of time spent on each call before and after the on-line support system was implemented and multiplying the time saved by the number of employees involved. Always justify your solutions with dollars (either saved or received).

Various groups have done surveys that estimate the costs of upgrading to Windows 2000. Rather than list a series of dollar amounts that would be out-of-date by the time you read them, let us suggest that those surveys will always be available on the World Wide Web. Perform an Internet search with the keywords "Windows 2000," "cost," and "justify" and you should find numerous Web sites with information. When planning your budget, start with these figures and then adjust them to fit your environment. Your area, for instance, might have much lower salaries than those used in the surveys (thus lowering expected costs), or you might find that your hardware costs are lower than their estimates.

There are three costs to include in your budget: software, hardware, and time. The software and hardware costs are easy enough to calculate; just use the information gathered in the physical analysis. You should have a complete list of the hardware and software currently in your environment. In your earlier studies for the MCSE, you were presented with minimum and recommended hardware configurations. Compare what you have in place (your current inventory) with the recommendations in order to build a list of the purchases necessary.

More difficult to estimate is the amount of time that will be involved in the process. Many a good consulting contract has ended up being a losing proposition because of low estimates. Although there are no magic figures, your estimate should include the following criteria:

Design Time   Remember that the time spent planning will decrease the time spent implementing (hence the value of this manual!).

Travel Time and Costs   In a larger environment, you might end up visiting remote locations to perform upgrades or training.

Hardware Purchases and Configuration   Hardware vendors always promise fast delivery, but add extra time to account for delays. Also add time to configure and test the hardware once it arrives.

Software Purchases, Installation, and Configuration   Perform a few installations and upgrades that simulate the processes you'll be doing in the field. Always add extra time here—nothing goes as smoothly in the field as it does in the lab!

Training Time   Both your IT staff and your end users will probably require some sort of training on the new operating system (and any new applications) that you install.

Support Time   This is one area that many IT professionals forget to budget. No implementation ever goes exactly as planned! Set aside some time dedicated to user support after the upgrade.

The bottom line with funding is to do your homework. Calculate the total cost of the upgrade as closely as possible. We always try to bounce our budgets off a few colleagues before we present them to management. They often find items that we have missed (or offer a suggestion to lower costs).

Once you've calculated your budget, be prepared to justify those costs. If you are a consultant, you will be asked some very tough questions: Why do you need that expensive server? Why does each workstation need 128MB of RAM? Why do we need to upgrade the line between Chicago and Detroit? You should be prepared with a logical explanation for the expense of every item on your budget. You should also be prepared for the ultimate question: Why should we upgrade to Windows 2000? Don't rely on the computer-geek answer, "Because it's the latest thing!" During your preparation for the MCSE exams, you have seen all of the features of Windows 2000 (not the least of which is AD). Look at the business environment and be prepared to list those features and the business solutions that they provide *in this specific environment*.

TIP   Exam Hint: The preceding paragraph describes a few of the case study questions you might see on the exam. Microsoft will present you with the solution and then a series of answers that justify that solution. You will have to pick the correct justification (not just the correct technology).

Outsourced Services

Over the last few years, more and more companies have started to outsource IT tasks. *Outsourcing* is hiring an outside firm to perform an IT task. Some outsourced functions are short term, such as hiring a consultant to lead the design process for your new AD structure. Other tasks that might be outsourced are ongoing, such as maintenance of a DNS server. In either case, processes that are outsourced will take careful consideration during your AD implementation. You will have to analyze each outsourced function and ask yourself these questions:

- Should it continue to be outsourced? Find out why the task was outsourced in the first place. If the situation has changed, determine if it would be better to bring the responsibility back in-house. If, for instance, the task was outsourced due to lack of experience, determine whether the skill has since been gained through experience or training. If the reason was costs, analyze the costs based upon Windows 2000. (As hard as it might be to believe, Windows 2000 makes many tasks much easier and cheaper than they were in Windows NT or some other legacy operating systems.)

- Should it be taken over by internal staff? There are many tasks that were once secondary skills and are now critical to a Windows 2000–based network. It is often preferable to have critical tasks performed by your IT staff rather than an outside consultant. Look at each outsourced function to determine if it is mission critical. For each task that is critical to the IT environment, you will have to determine the benefits (and costs) of performing it in-house.

- Is it no longer needed? Many network services that were required in legacy networks are no longer required in a Windows 2000 environment. WINS, for instance, is not really required in a network in which all computers are running Windows 2000. (Beware. Although Windows 2000–based computers might not need a particular service, be aware that you might have to continue to offer it to provide backward compatibility with older software.)

The biggest—and in our experience, most common—outsourcing decision will concern DNS. Because DNS has never been critical to Windows networking, and because DNS expertise is fairly rare, many companies have chosen to outsource the DNS service. Most Internet Service Providers (ISPs) offer DNS as a piece of their standard service package. We'll discuss the role of DNS in an AD environment in Chapter 3, "Designing a Directory Service Architecture." For now, though, you should already be aware of the critical nature of DNS in a Windows 2000 network. Windows 2000 Professional–based computers use DNS to "find" domain controllers. Without DNS, the logon service does not function. This leads to various design issues, such as whether clients should have to access an outside (rather than local) DNS server each time they log on to the network.

Another commonly outsourced service is the help desk. Many companies engage an outside firm to handle PC maintenance, software support, and server maintenance. If that is the case in your company, you will have to determine if your current vendor has the skills necessary to support a Windows 2000 network. If not, you will have to either find another source of support or move those services back into the realm of your IT department. If you decide to take over the help desk function, you will have to ensure that your help desk personnel have been given the opportunity to work with (or be trained on) Windows 2000.

Decision-Making Process

Earlier we discussed the decision-making process as it pertained to the entire company. Now that we are discussing an individual department, we must add a few new twists. The biggest change is that, in many companies, a decision made at the department level is not really a decision—it's a suggestion that will be kicked upstairs for further consideration. As consultants, we have actually been hired to provide technical and business justifications for a decision already made by the IT department. In other words, the technologists had already chosen a course of action but were unable to justify it in a manner that would be acceptable to upper management.

When presenting a suggestion for the use of technology, many of us IT professionals make the mistake of relying on the technical knowledge of our audience. We spend most of our careers presenting ideas to the departmental staff that is the easiest audience to sell on technology. Often, we are not even required to describe the benefits—our "techie" peers already know what it does, how it's implemented, and what the costs are. Although this may be sufficient within our department, we need to remember that at some point, an accountant is going to look over our suggestion. That accountant is going to want bottom-line justification for the costs involved.

The same rules that apply within the context of the company as a whole also apply within the context of a department. Your presentation of new technology should be made with an eye toward reducing costs or increasing profits. Intangible benefits should be extra—do not rely upon them to completely justify the idea. Break down costs into small chunks—it's easier to get multiple small expenses past the accountants than it is to get one big one past them.

Within the IT department, there are usually certain individuals who are considered responsible for a particular area of expertise. You might find, for instance, that one person is responsible for server maintenance, another for messaging systems, and yet another for wide area networking. When presenting an idea for a new use of an existing technology or the implementation of something completely new, it is usually best to bounce the idea off of the person responsible for that area of the IT environment. That person, having both experience and a unique perspective, might point out flaws in your idea that would lessen its value. On the other hand, because that person is the "expert," the department and company management probably values their opinion. Presenting your idea to them first, and garnering their support, can help you avoid the political battles that sometimes ensue over changes to the business procedures or processes.

The bottom line with decision-making within the IT department is that no decision should be made without due consideration. Your job is to determine who does the considering, who presents the options to management, and in the end, who make the choice. When it comes right down to it, you are selling technology to management. There's an old sales adage that says that the closer you are to the decision-maker, the closer you are to a sale. The same holds true when selling IT—knowing who makes (or helps to make) the final decisions will tell you who you need to focus on.

Current Change-Management Process

The *change-management process* defines how the IT department handles changes to the environment. If the company decides to upgrade from Microsoft Office 97 to Microsoft Office 2000, for instance, the change-management process would define how that upgrade is accomplished. To put things in focus, the upgrade or migration to Windows 2000 can be considered a change, and so the procedures used to accomplish this should be defined as part of the change-management strategy. Not all changes will be as major as the preceding two examples—a change can be as simple as upgrading the Network Interface Card (NIC) driver on client computers or installing printer drivers for a new printer. No matter how small the change, every company will have a change-management policy to perform the task.

Unfortunately, the change-management process used within a company is not always well defined. Upgrading drivers, for instance, is often the responsibility of non-IT personnel or local "gurus" recruited for the task. Even that, however, is a policy of sorts. Your job as part of the AD design team will be to document how changes are handled and then suggest alternatives that are more efficient or less costly. This is usually one of the most difficult of the early phases of the design process. In many companies, the change-management strategy is both undocumented and haphazard. For some reason, we, as an industry, seem to place more importance on the occasional task (like server installation or operating system upgrade) than we do the day-to-day administration that keeps our businesses running. One of the reasons for the success of Windows NT was that it popularized the automation of processes. Although Microsoft didn't invent Dynamic Host Configuration Protocol (DHCP)—okay, maybe the protocol, though that's arguable, but not the process—NT made it a common component of business networks. NT also introduced the concept of printer server management of print drivers. (Before NT, you had to manually install print drivers on every workstation.) These first steps in the direction of a centrally controlled change-management process were the precursors of many of the new features of Windows 2000.

Change is a constant in the IT world: Buy a new printer and it comes with new printer drivers. Buy a new NIC and it comes with new drivers. Have a problem with a piece of hardware—what's the first thing you do? Download the latest and greatest drivers. Every component of your network is a potential change-management client. Controlling the process of change is critical to a stable environment. Do it well, and your days are filled with spare time. Do it wrong, and you (or your peers) end up having to solve the same problems over and over again.

From a design perspective, your analysis of the change-management process should accomplish two tasks:

- It will provide you with a list of persons who are currently responsible for IT tasks.

- It will give you an idea of the current state of the environment.

The results of both tasks will be helpful during the planning and implementation of the Windows 2000 rollout.

Who Is Responsible?

During the early stages of the design process, you need to determine which persons should be assigned to each task. Starting with a list of current responsibilities will make the choices easier. It also helps you to build a list of current skill sets available and determine the amount of training that might be required before implementation. As we'll discuss later, one of the first goals of a design project is to build a design team with the correct mix of skills.

What Is the Current State of the Environment?

Documenting the standard procedures that are employed to manage changes can help you determine the general condition of the network and its components. If, for instance, you ask what version of software is installed on the router and no one knows, you can begin to make assumptions about network components. One of the first rules of a design process is to make the current environment stable before introducing change. At this point in the design process, you should ensure that the latest drivers, fixes, and service packs are installed across your network.

Exam Essentials

In this section we analyzed management concerns for the IT department of a company. While IT is "just another department" to the business, it is also unique in two respects—it is not only a consumer of network services, it is also the provider; and the IT staff will have to implement and maintain the AD environment.

Be able to describe the differences between a centralized and a decentralized IT philosophy. Don't just know the technical differences; be able to describe the advantages and disadvantages of both environments. (See the "Critical Information" section for details.)

Understand ROI and how to calculate it. Microsoft knows that most companies will not make a move to a new operating system without justification. Being able to present a reasonable ROI is critical to "selling" the idea of a migration to Windows 2000.

Understand the advantages and disadvantages of outsourcing services—especially DNS! Microsoft has always positioned its software as the easiest to administer. In most cases, Microsoft would rather see a company be self-sufficient than for a company to outsource services.

Key Terms and Concepts

Centralized Management A philosophy of management in which a small administrative staff in a central location manages and makes all decisions.

Decentralized Management A philosophy of management in which responsibility for IT resources is held by local support staff.

Return on Investment (ROI) A calculation of the length of time it will take for a new technology to pay for itself in reduced costs.

Outsource To have an outside company assume responsibility for an IT service.

Change-Management The process used to manage changes within the IT environment.

Sample Questions

1. In a centrally managed IT environment, which of the following are true?

   A. The AD structure will generally have fewer OUs.

   B. The AD structure will generally have more OUs.

   C. The IT staff relies upon local personnel to support each site.

   D. Automation can be used to reduce IT management overhead.

   Answer: A, D.   In a centrally controlled IT environment, all IT decisions are made by a small group of individuals who are also responsible for implementation. Because there is less delegation of tasks, there are usually fewer OUs in the AD structure. To avoid repetitive management tasks, scripts and other automation techniques can be used.

2. In a decentralized IT environment, which of the following are true?

   A. The AD structure will generally have fewer OUs.

   B. The AD structure will generally have more OUs.

   C. IT responsibility is delegated to local staff members.

   D. The headquarters staff dictates all IT policies.

   Answer: B, C.   An AD structure that contains more OUs also provides a more granular environment for delegation of management tasks.

3. ROI refers to _____

   A. Repeat Over Interface messages

   B. Return on investment

   C. An aspect of DNS

   D. Router Oscillation Time

Answer: B.   One of the best ways to justify the expense of moving to a new operating system (such as Windows 2000) is to prove that the move will pay for itself over time. ROI refers to the amount of time this will take.

4. Change-management policies define which of the following?

   A. The process of hiring new departmental managers

   B. The processes used to maintain system components

   C. A text file used to automate the installation of Windows 2000 Server or Advanced Server

   D. A database used to track network utilization over time

   Answer: B.   Change-management refers to the management of ongoing maintenance of IT resources.

5. How NIC drivers are updated on local machines is primarily part of which if the following IT considerations?

   A. Funding

   B. Centralized vs. decentralized management model

   C. Change-management

   D. Outsourced services

   Answer: C.   Change-management refers to any updates, fixes, or other changes made to components of the IT environment.

Chapter

2

Analyzing Technical Requirements

MICROSOFT EXAM OBJECTIVES COVERED IN THIS CHAPTER:

▶ **Evaluate the company's existing and planned technical environment.** *(pages 77 – 105)*
- Analyze company size and user and resource distribution.
- Assess the available connectivity between the geographic location of worksites and remote sites.
- Assess the net available bandwidth.
- Analyze performance requirements.
- Analyze data and system access patterns.
- Analyze network roles and responsibilities.
- Analyze security considerations.

▶ **Analyze the Impact of Active Directory on the existing and planned technical environment.** *(pages 105 – 109)*
- Assess existing systems and applications.
- Identify existing and planned upgrades and rollouts.
- Analyze technical support structure.
- Analyze existing and planned network and systems management.

▶ **Analyze the business requirements for client computer desktop management.** *(pages 110 – 140)*
- Analyze end-user work needs.
- Identify technical support needs for end-users.
- Establish the required client computer environment.

n Chapter 1, "Analyzing Business Requirements," we discussed the analysis of the business into which Active Directory will be installed. Understanding the business model, management philosophy, and the myriad of other business considerations can help to create an Active Directory structure that is stable, easy to manage, and easy to use. Providing an Active Directory–based business solution depends on an intimate understanding of the business environment.

An analysis of the business is only half the battle. The next step is to evaluate the technical environment—both the existing system and the effects that Active Directory will have upon it.

In this chapter we will begin with an analysis of the existing network—the number of users, computers, servers, and other resources; the distribution of resources; the WAN; and numerous other physical attributes of a network. From there we'll look at the effects of moving to AD on the existing environment. We'll end with an objective that is concerned with the management of the user's desktop.

Evaluate the company's existing and planned technical environment.

- **Analyze company size and user and resource distribution.**

- **Assess the available connectivity between the geographic location of worksites and remote sites.**

- **Assess the net available bandwidth.**

- **Analyze performance requirements.**

- **Analyze data and system access patterns.**

- **Analyze network roles and responsibilities.**

- **Analyze security considerations.**

The information described in the next few sections acts as the foundation upon which the rest of the design process relies. As such, it is imperative that you spend the time to collect, collate, and analyze the physical and business environment before implementing Windows 2000 and Active Directory in any but the most basic of networks.

Critical Information

This objective focuses on your ability to gather pertinent information about the physical environment and use that information to provide workable business solutions.

Evaluate the company's existing technical environment.

The next step in any design project is to look at the business processes that use the physical structure of the network. This involves a lot of what we call "face time." You'll need to sit down with the IS staff and discuss their current environment. Be sure to include these topics in your discussion:

- IP addressing

- Use of Dynamic Host Configuration Protocol (DHCP) servers: Are they being used? Where are they? To whom do they lease addresses? Who manages them?

- Current Domain Name System (DNS) implementation: Has a domain name been registered on the Internet? Who manages DNS? What software is being used?

- Network and local operating systems in use: What are their versions? What service packs have been applied? Who manages them?

- Software distribution and update management processes

- What server-based applications are currently being used? What are their versions? Who manages them?

- What client-based applications are being used? What are their versions? Who manages them?

- Current support staff, their experience and training levels

- Review of all troubleshooting logs to determine current problems

- What hardware standards are in place for client computers, servers, and other peripherals (including network components)?

In other words, find out what technology is currently in place, how it is managed (and by whom), and if it is working to their satisfaction. This is where you learn the environment. Take your time to get a good picture of what's currently in place.

TIP Exam (and Real-Life) Hint: At this point, *fix all existing problems*! Microsoft—and our experience—suggest that you make sure everything is working before you make any major changes to a network.

Evaluate the company's planned technical environment.

For the MCSE Design exams, Microsoft stresses your ability to analyze an environment and provide the best solution to the business needs of the company. Listening to what the company plans for the future can make this task quite a bit easier. If your client plans to open an e-commerce site on the Internet, for instance, you should certainly take that into account when planning network bandwidth needs, the number of servers, and security policies.

This is one of the more difficult tasks in a design project. You must not only listen to their ideas, you must come up with ideas of your own that can improve their business. If, for instance, your client or company is currently using statically assigned IP addresses, you might want to suggest (and then justify) a move to DHCP services. If your client or company has a limited budget for hardware upgrades, you might want to suggest using terminal services to save money on client computer upgrades.

Unfortunately, there is no crystal ball approach to this process. Because every situation is different, you will have to take a different approach to each project. This is where your interpersonal communication skills will come into play. The most successful consultants we know are the ones who can sit down and talk to a client for a while and walk away with an idea of where the company wants to be three years in the future.

For the MCSE exams, you will be presented with case studies. The real skill needed for successfully answering these kinds of questions is the ability to separate the important information from the fluff. The case study will describe a company and have quotes from various key personnel. Your job is to extract from the text the business needs of the company and decide which technologies you would implement to fulfill those needs. (Basically, this is the same job that any good consultant does every day.)

Analyze company size and user and resource distribution.

At a minimum, you should know the following information about each location within the company infrastructure:

- Number of users

- Number and configuration of servers

- Number and configuration of client computers

- Specification of computers

- Network services utilized

We usually put together two sets of documents at this point in the design process: a general information sheet and a detailed listing for each location. A sample general information sheet is shown in Table 2.1.

T A B L E 2 . 1 : General Information for Company XYZ

Location	Number of users	Number of Client Computers	Number of Servers
Grand Rapids, MI	200	148	4
Tampa, FL	145	152	3
St. Paul, MN	53	40	1
Reno, NV	27	5	0
Payson, UT	12	17	3

We then put together a detailed analysis of each location. The following example, Table 2.2 and the notes below it, shows the kind of information we include. Provide this kind of detailed list for each site in the company.

Current implementation   This site represents a resource domain in the company's Windows NT 4 network. All user account information is managed by the central IS department in the corporate headquarters.

TABLE 2.2: Specific Information for Grand Rapids, MI

Category	Value
Users	200
Client computers	148
Servers	4

Users The Grand Rapids location consists of a manufacturing plant and a distribution warehouse. Most of the staff is made up of non-knowledge workers. Any changes to the environment will be have to made slowly with adequate training to prevent downtime. There is no on-site IS staff for support during the migration process. The office staff (approximately 25 users) is connected to the Internet through an ISDN router.

Computers Two basic configurations: manufacturing line and office staff. The manufacturing computers are older Pentiums with an average of 32MB of RAM. The office staff has newer, but not high-end, equipment. The average computer is a Pentium 166MHz with 64MB of RAM. All are currently using Windows 95 as their operating system and Office 95 as their productivity suite. No specialized software in is use.

Servers 1 BDC (Backup Domain Controller)of the master domain, 1 PDC (Primary Domain Controller) of the local resource domain, 2 database servers that provide services to both manufacturing and administrative departments.

Other issues The site has 5 HP5 printers, shared using Windows 95 printer sharing. Recently the target of a hostile workplace lawsuit based upon inappropriate material downloaded from the Internet. The database servers place a heavy load on the WAN link to corporate headquarters every evening. Backups are sporadic at best.

Suggestions for Grand Rapids before the upgrade:

- Ideal:
    - Upgrade all client computers to a minimum of Pentium 233 with 128MB of RAM.
    - Increase bandwidth on wide area link.
    - Purchase direct connect cards for all printers.
    - Provide one-day training to all users regarding the migration and its effects.

- Minimum:
    - Upgrade clients to Windows 98 for added stability. Begin purchasing higher-end computers that will support Windows 2000 Pro.
    - Merge resource domain with the master domain.
    - Apply latest service packs to all servers and applications running on them.

From a design perspective, this information lays out the tasks that will be involved in implementation—how many workstations, how many servers, how many printers, and so on. It also serves as the basis for analysis later in the project. Knowing how many workstations are at a site, for instance, can help you estimate the amount of network traffic that will travel on the WAN link to and from that site.

NOTE   For the test, you'll probably see this information provided for you in the case study. (It would be hard for Microsoft to test your ability to gather the number of workstations at a location in a testing room!) This means that the real objective here is to know *which* information to gather.

Assess the available connectivity between the geographic location of worksites and remote sites.

One of the biggest issues facing wide area networks is limited bandwidth. The costs of connecting two or more locations can be outrageous. Knowing the physical limitations of your network infrastructure is the first step in a good ADS design. Many, if not most, of the decisions you will make later will be based upon your knowledge of the wide area infrastructure.

The first step in learning the environment is to put together a wide area network map. This map should show all of the locations in your company or your client's company and the links between them. Find out which vendor provides the lines, how much they cost, and how reliable they have been in the past. Talk with the network gurus to determine which vendors have provided the best service. A major change to the network, such as upgrading or migrating to Windows 2000, might be the perfect opportunity to optimize the network infrastructure.

When you are done, you should have an overall picture of how the network is laid out, as shown in Figure 2.1.

FIGURE 2.1: Infrastructure map

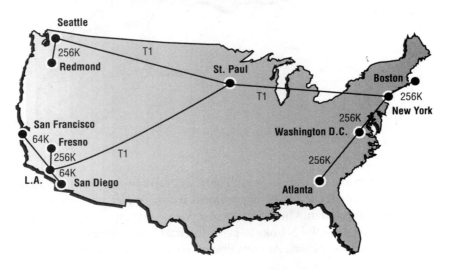

Over the years, we've all used all kinds of maps—everything from electronic atlases to hand-drawn "cocktail napkin" versions. The most intuitive for most people are probably paper-based maps. Almost every major city in the world has a map store—we buy new maps for every project and hand-draw the links on them. This is an opportunity for us to learn the environment (unlike using the auto-mapping software that does the work for you).

Once you have an overall picture, break the network into regions, if it's appropriate. On the regional maps, label each link as shown in Figure 2.2.

FIGURE 2.2: Detailed WAN map

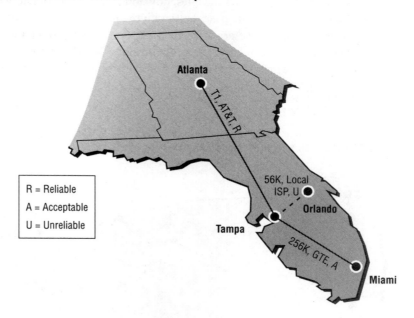

A map like the one shown in Figure 2.2 can sometimes lead to an optimization of the WAN environment before implementation of the migration plan. One of the best services you can offer a client is to redesign the WAN links to provide better performance, more reliability, or lower costs. As consultants, we've found that it is in our best interest to have a general idea of the costs of various links from different providers in various regions.

NOTE   Once again, it would be difficult for Microsoft to test your ability to gather this information. For testing purposes you should concentrate on *what* you would gather, not how you would gather it.

Assess the net available bandwidth.

Once you've created your maps, the hard work starts. The next step is to determine the available bandwidth on each link. *Available bandwidth* is the amount of bandwidth remaining after current traffic has been taken into account. There are many tools available on the market that can be used to measure the amount of traffic actually being placed on a network. If you are upgrading from an earlier version of Windows NT, tools such as Performance Monitor and Network Monitor are available. If you are migrating from some other operating system, you will have to determine what tools that operating system (OS) has available. In some cases, you will need to purchase or lease hardware and software to gather this information. The easiest method by far is to use the services of your connectivity vendor. Almost every major provider in the market has the ability to give monthly, weekly, or daily reports that detail the network traffic crossing its lines. The biggest mistake you can make, though, is to trust this information implicitly. When you are measuring bandwidth, make sure that you do the following:

- Measure bandwidth at different times of the day. Bandwidth utilization often fluctuates throughout the business day. A wide area link that is carrying minimal traffic at 9:00 A.M. might be saturated during the across-the-wire backup being performed at 7:00 P.M. each day.

- Measure bandwidth at different points in the business cycle. A network that is saturated during the month-end reports might be underutilized during the rest of the month. Add information about network bottlenecks and periods of congestion to the detailed maps you made earlier, as shown in Figure 2.3.

FIGURE 2.3: Detailed Information

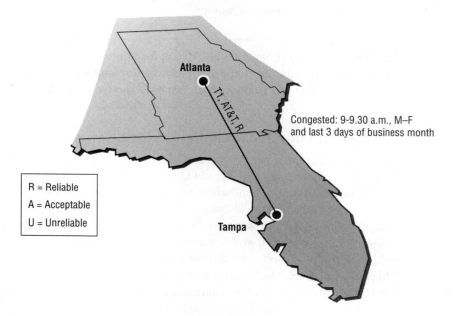

R = Reliable
A = Acceptable
U = Unreliable

Atlanta

T1, AT&T, R

Congested: 9-9.30 a.m., M–F
and last 3 days of business month

Tampa

The information you gather during this design phase will help you make decisions about server placement, ADS replication, ADS sites and site bridges, and other services that the network will provide.

NOTE Once again, this topic is difficult to test. Your case study questions will provide this information. The questions will often provide you with more information then you really need. The trick is to cut through the text and pull out only the information that will help you make choices later.

Analyze performance requirements.

For the most part, today's networks are both reliable and secure when configured properly. This allows you the luxury to consider performance in your AD design. Performance is one of the trickier topics in any design discussion because *performance* is a relative term. What is considered great performance in one environment might be considered unacceptable or unnecessary in another.

During your interviews with key personnel, you should include questions that draw out comments about the current state of the network. Surprisingly, these comments can often lead you to critical design decisions. If everyone complains about the network "being down," you should spend some time determining what is causing this condition. Is it faulty hardware? Unreliable WAN links? Operating system instabilities? Or are the downtimes due to faulty business processes?

NOTE   There are many instances where people complain about the network when the real culprit is some other entity. Bob had one client, for instance, where the entire production department staff complained about the network being "down." What they really meant was that the sales order database, which was stored in a server at another site with a replica on the production plant server, wasn't always synchronizing completely overnight. This left the production department with no direction as to which product to manufacture, thus resulting in downtime. To the users, it seemed as if the network was to blame, when in reality, the database replication process was at fault.

The first step in analyzing performance needs is to ascertain expectations. In today's world, when many individuals have computers at home, it is not uncommon for users to have unrealistic performance expectations for the business network. Think about it—for under $1,000.00 it is possible to purchase a fairly high-end consumer computer. (We recently purchased a computer for our home lab that had an Intel 550MHz processor, 64MB of ram, a 13GB hard drive, a built-in 10/100 NIC, and a 16MB AGP graphics card for under $600.00 from a *major* vendor. Add $300.00 for a decent 17-inch monitor and modem and you've got a great home machine!) At home, the user sees blazing fast response; their games run well, Microsoft Word loads in seconds, and their tax software runs without a hitch. Then they are disappointed when they get to the office expecting the same performance from the SQL database that is supporting hundreds of users simultaneously.

Just recently, Bob was working at a company that had about 20 users who shared a T1 link to the Internet. The CEO complained about performance. He said that even when he was the only one in the office on weekends, Internet performance was not acceptable. After their meeting, Bob sat down at a computer and accessed some graphic-intensive Web sites, and he was pleased with the Internet response times. He had the CEO come in and had him access a few of his favorite sites. To Bob, the performance looked fine; to the CEO, it was unacceptably slow. Bob started doing what he should have done in the first case, asking questions. When it was all said and done, he found out that the CEO had just had a cable modem installed in his house. He expected the same performance on a shared T1 line as he was getting from his cable modem at home.

The point here is that the analysis of performance needs is both a physical task *and* a social one. You need to determine what is acceptable in a given environment and then lower your users' expectations to match. That is not to say that you *can't* improve performance; however, there are times when the costs of raising system performance to match users' expectations outweigh the benefits.

Before you can set expectations, though, you need to determine the current performance conditions on each component of the network. This is a *big* task! You will need to master (or bring in someone who has mastered) tools to test the performance on many different types of hardware and software. You should always start with the basics and work up, so you begin your analysis at the workstation level. You can visit typical workstations throughout the company and talk to the people who use them. Have the employees access the tools they use in their everyday jobs—word processors, spreadsheets, shared databases, printers, everything! (This is a good time to start evaluating the users' perception of network performance.) Find out what works well and what doesn't. Find out if there is anything that doesn't work.

The components you'll have to test include the following:

Workstations Compare disk space, total memory, and operating system configuration against your software list and security needs analysis.

Servers   Use the tools included with Windows 2000 (Performance Monitor is a great place to start) to document the current level of performance (and any bottlenecks) on each existing server.

Routers, switches, and other network components   Just about every connectivity component on the market today comes with (or works with) some management software. Check for times of peak usage and check network performance at those times. Ensure that the actual throughput is not exceeding the thresholds of each component—in other words, try to find the bottlenecks on your network.

Software   Compare the performance of workstation-based software on various hardware configurations. Determine the minimum hardware requirements to achieve acceptable performance. For server-based software (e-mail server, distributed database, and so on), determine the hardware necessary to provide acceptable performance.

Wiring   Check LAN segments to determine if network utilization is too high, causing bottlenecks.

Training   Determine if users need training to increase their comfort level with the tools they use to perform their business tasks. We've found that properly managed training can often dramatically increase perceived performance.

There are two considerations to keep in mind during your analysis of performance. First, remember that perception is reality. Just because *you* believe that a component is performing at its optimum, unless your users also believe that, you have not done your job. Second, and probably most importantly, remember that sometimes good enough is good enough. There is always a point of diminishing returns on optimization. Once you reach this point, the cost of continuing to increase performance (by adding hardware or tweaking configuration) outweighs the benefits gained.

Analyze Data and System Access Patterns.

In Chapter 1, "Analyzing Business Requirements," we discussed the importance of both information and communication flow within the company. At this point in the design process, you will use the information gathered earlier to help you analyze the efficiency of the current network infrastructure. Knowing who accesses what data and services and who talks to whom within the company gives you clues to the traffic produced on the network as well as the networks (from an infrastructure perspective) across which that traffic will travel.

Earlier in the design process, you gathered information about the physical infrastructure of the network. At this point, you'll begin to use the maps you created. For example, you might have produced a map similar to the one shown in Figure 2.4. This map shows the infrastructure of the network and the gross (as well as net) bandwidth of each connection and gives an overall reliability rating to each WAN link.

FIGURE 2.4: **A typical network map**

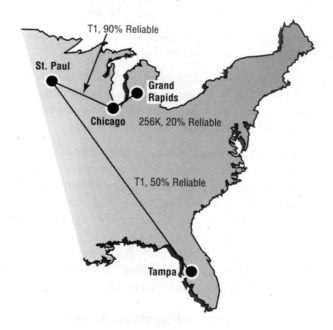

Combine the physical map with your spreadsheets of data and service access (created during your business analysis of the company), and you can begin to get a clear picture of where, and how much, traffic flows through the network. Your physical analysis already provides you with available bandwidth figures, but now you can correlate those figures with the business functions that generate the traffic. This type of analysis takes time, patience, and practice, but once you get accustomed to the process, it provides a fairly complete picture of the IT environment.

There are many methods to document the correlation between traffic and infrastructure. Our method is to first take the physical map and give each WAN link a unique identifier (that's a fancy way to say we number them), as shown in Figure 2.5.

FIGURE 2.5: **Uniquely identified WAN links**

The next step is to build for each data source a spreadsheet that shows which groups of users access it and where they are located, as shown in Tables 2.3 and 2.4. As you can see, we also include a general indication of the amount of access: H for heavy, M for medium, L for light, and N/A for no access.

TABLE 2.3: Inventory Data Access

User Group	St. Paul	Tampa	Grand Rapids	Chicago
Accountants	H	L	L	M
Sales	H	H	H	H
Production	H	N/A	N/A	H
Purchasing	H	N/A	N/A	M
Order Fulfillment	H	H	N/A	H
Upper Mgmt	L	L	N/A	L

TABLE 2.4: Sales Data Access

User Group	St. Paul	Tampa	Grand Rapids	Chicago
Accountants	L	H	L	L
Sales	M	H	M	M
Production	L	N/A	N/A	L
Purchasing	N/A	H	N/A	N/A
Order Fulfillment	H	H	N/A	H
Upper Mgmt	M	H	N/A	M

From this information, we can begin to plan for the placement of the data. For instance, from our examples, we can see that the inventory database will be accessed the most from users in St. Paul and the sales database will be accessed most from Tampa. Given this type of analysis, we can begin to make suggestions about where the data should be physically located.

The next step is to determine the amount of traffic that will be generated by remote data access across each WAN line. We build yet another spreadsheet that cross-references the WAN link identifier with the amount of traffic, as shown in Table 2.5. When looking at this table, remember that the inventory database was placed in St. Paul and the sales database was placed in Tampa. We take all of the access that will cross the link between two sites and average the lights, mediums, and heavies (a process called access weighting) to come up with a final rating for how much traffic each site will place on each connection.

TABLE 2.5:   WAN Traffic Analysis

Link	Traffic
1 (SP to T)	M
2 (SP to Chi)	H
3 (Chi to GR)	L

The weighting process becomes much more complex in a larger environment. For our simple exercise—with only one data source in St. Paul and another in Tampa and only three WAN links—all we had to do was look at who accesses the two databases. The Tampa users will produce a medium level of traffic on their link to St. Paul. The Chicago users access the inventory database heavily, and the Grand Rapids users won't place much of a load on the network in accessing either database. The tricky part of this analysis is to remember to include secondary traffic in your calculations. In our example, you would have to remember that *any* Grand Rapids traffic to St. Paul or Tampa would also travel on the link to Chicago.

Once you've mapped out by user access the overhead placed on the network, you can begin to formulate some design strategies. In our example, for instance, we already determined that the inventory database should be placed in St. Paul and the sales database should be placed in Tampa. We can also see that Chicago will generate a lot of traffic to St. Paul in accessing the inventory database. We should take careful note of the available bandwidth on that link—if it is approaching saturation, we might want to either upgrade the line or place a replica of the data on a Chicago server (limiting traffic to a nightly synchronization).

On top of the traffic generated by data access, your network must support the traffic generated by various services. Given a good analysis of the traffic on each link, you can now determine whether each site will need a domain controller to limit logon overhead on the line. You should also be able to consider the traffic generated by other network services such as DNS, WINS (Windows Internet Name Service) synchronization, and messaging systems (such as Exchange Server). Just keep adding traffic notes to your spreadsheet until you have a good idea of the types and amounts of *all* traffic that will cross each link.

Remember that at this point in our design project, we are still dealing with the original environment. The types of traffic on the wire will vary depending upon what operating system is currently in use.

Analyze network roles and responsibilities.

During your analysis of the physical infrastructure, the business environment, and the IT department, you will talk to many individuals. From a design perspective you can divide these people into three groups:

People with little or no technical knowledge   These individuals use a computer to accomplish their day-to-day work but have no IT skills (nor do they have the need for these skills).

Departmental gurus   These people are often used for departmental IT support. Usually, they either have a little knowledge about computers in general or have in-depth knowledge of one of the software packages used within the company. Every large organization has at least one of these people. They're the ones who always seems to know how to get a coworker's word processor to perform a certain function, or they know how to write macros for spreadsheets, or maybe they just understand the relationship between the order entry system and the inventory database.

IT professionals   These are the true computer geeks of the company. They have knowledge and/or experience in key areas of the IT environment.

There are certain skill sets that are necessary to design, implement, and maintain any larger IT environment. Very few consultants (no matter what they might claim) have all of the skills necessary to do the job alone. From the first day of the design project, you should begin gathering the design team. The design team is made up of individuals with the *skills* necessary to design and implement an AD structure *within a given environment*. The makeup of the design team is critical to the overall design project. If the design team doesn't have the appropriate skills, the end design might not take all of the environmental variables into account. On the other hand, too many people on the team can make it more difficult to finalize the details. (It is especially important to avoid a situation where the team is divided along strict political boundaries; members can have strong opinions, but they need to be open-minded.) The best consultants we've ever known have all had the ability to interview key personnel and, from the information they gather, pull together a design team for a given project. That's not to say that all of the skills *have* to be found internally. Often your interviews with key personnel will highlight skill-set weaknesses. When you find that you are missing a necessary set of skills, you are faced with the choice of training internal staff or bringing in an outside expert.

You will need to determine what skills are necessary for your design project. Unfortunately, we can't give you a definitive list. The skills needed will vary depending upon the environment. There are, however, some general roles that usually need to be filled. We're going to present each role as a separate function, but you should be aware that multiple roles are often filled by a single individual (and occasionally, a single role will be split among several people). In general, your design team should have people to fill the following roles:

- IT management
- Windows 2000/AD expert
- Server support

- Workstation support

- Application support

- Printing support

- Wide area connection support

- Implementation testing

- Education Coordinator

The people fulfilling these roles will need a certain amount of expertise in order to provide valid information and suggestions to the team during the design process. Each person will probably also have their own priorities that might be at odds with the priorities of other team members. These differences are what promote the dynamic environment necessary to create a stable AD structure. You will want to define each person's function within the design team, their priorities, and the level of technical knowledge necessary to fulfill their role in the design process.

IT Management

Any design project must have the support of upper management. It is usually the job of the IT manager to garner this support. The IT manager does not usually have a hands-on role in the design process or in the actual implementation. Instead, they are responsible for ensuring that the project stays on schedule and on budget. In many cases, the IT manager makes the decision to move to Windows 2000 and then leaves the actual implementation to the IT staff. Given the limited role of IT managers in the actual work involved in a project, they need a specific set of skills, which include the following:

- An ability to see the advantages of one technology over another without that vision being clouded by brand loyalty or technical prejudices.

- Project management experience. The design process in a large environment is a big project utilizing a large number of people, large budgets, and a lot of person-hours. The IT manager *must* be able to keep the team on track!

- Budgeting experience. The IT manager will be responsible for justifying to upper management the costs of the migration. The ability to create and justify a budget are mandatory.

- Presentation skills. The IT manager will often have to "sell" the proposed changes to upper management and to other departments.

Because the IT manager does not necessarily take a hands-on role in the design and implementation, this person does not usually need a heavy technical background. If necessary, the IT manger should attend a few "big picture" overviews of the Windows 2000 operating system. It is more important that the person filling this role have true management skills than it is for them to have technical skills.

Windows 2000/AD Expert

In many cases, the role of Windows 2000/AD expert will be filled by an outside consultant. No matter who takes on this role, there are certain skills that are necessary for a successful design. The Windows 2000/AD expert must understand the entire Windows 2000 operating system—both its strengths and its weaknesses. This expert must have experience installing and configuring all of the components involved in a Windows 2000 network—everything from DNS to AD, from DHCP to printer services, from user accounts to Group Policy. The expert's major responsibility will be to direct the design of the actual AD structure. As such, this expert will (at a minimum) need the following skills:

- An in-depth understanding of network directories and AD. Because they will lead the design of the AD structure, they must be familiar with how AD works and the various object classes that exist.

- An in-depth understanding of AD security.

- An understanding of the effect that AD will have on the network infrastructure. They must be proficient in the design of AD sites and site bridges and understand how network traffic is generated by AD.

- An understanding of the business needs of the company as a whole, as well as the needs of each department.

This is the person who must know the most about AD and its function in the network. Because their area of responsibility will have an impact on all other aspects of the network, they must also be experienced in all other facets of the network. They will act as the center of the design team, ensuring that the overall recommendations will work together in a single AD structure. Our opinion is that this should be an experienced network professional with numerous network design projects under their belt. If you are relying upon internal staff, ensure that they receive adequate training—at least the full MCSE track to start. You might also consider training on specific aspects of your environment. This person should also have a background in business.

Server Support

The service support person should have experience working with the current servers on the system *and* knowledge of the idiosyncrasies of Windows 2000 Server. They will be responsible for the actual upgrade or migration of existing servers and will be aware of the services currently being offered to the network by server-based components of the environment (everything from DHCP to a server-based e-mail package). They will need the following skills:

- An understanding of the impact of each server on network traffic and the ability to document that impact

- An understanding of the upgrade/migration process

- In-depth knowledge of the server hardware currently in place as well as the hardware requirements for the new environment

- Working knowledge of Windows 2000 Server

This person will be responsible for determining whether the current hardware can support the move to Windows 2000 Server. If not, this person will also be responsible for determining the physical changes made necessary by the move. Their training and/or experience should at least be the equivalent of an MCSE. They should also have any vendor-specific hardware training available for the server hardware in use on the network.

Workstation Support

The workstation support person will be responsible for the configuration of all workstations on the network. Extensive hardware and operating system experience is mandatory. They will work hand in hand with just about every other member of the design team, so communication and documentation skills are also necessary. At a minimum, the workstation support person should possess the following skills:

- An in-depth understanding of the operating systems in use on the client computers

- Experience in maintaining the client software

- Working knowledge of PC architecture, with an emphasis on the specific hardware in the environment

- Working knowledge of the Group Policy Objects in AD

- Experience in automating the client upgrade process

This person is usually the jack-of-all-trades of the computer industry. They need to understand the local operating systems, hardware, and client software used at each computer on the network. Although an MCSE is not necessary in this role, this person needs to be an experienced IT professional. Vendor-specific training in operating systems and hardware will be a great benefit.

Application Support

The application support person is often the least respected member of the IT department—after all, they are *really* geeks, aren't they? The reality is that the application support specialist usually knows more about how to make computers work than the average network person. People are always fumbling around trying to get their word processor to format a sentence or their spreadsheet to calculate an average. The application person knows most of the capabilities of every piece of software in use on the system. They also usually know the best way to install each software package. Once you move to Windows 2000 and start using Group Policy Objects to distribute applications, this person will take on a whole new importance in your department.

The application support person will be responsible for migrating all end-user applications to the new operating system. The application support person needs to know what updates, patches, and fixes are necessary; which software packages are not compatible with Windows 2000; and whether applications will be accessed locally or from the server.

Training for the application support person will consist of vendor-specific courses and seminars (on the software in use in the company). They should also have an understanding of AD because much of their function will be the management of Group Policy Objects. We would suggest that this person be at least an MCP (Microsoft Certified Professional) and certified for any applications they will manage.

Printing Support

The same person who acts as the applications expert usually fills the printing support role. Printing is a critical piece of the network and has become a complex process. This person must understand the specific hardware in use and the printing components of a Windows 2000 network. In most cases, the printing support person will also need to understand third-party management software. If you are using printers that are connected directly to the network (currently the most common configuration), they will also need to understand protocol-level addressing, print drivers, and network bandwidth issues. Because printing is so critical, we would suggest that this person be vendor-certified to support the brands of printers in your network. We would also suggest that they have Windows 2000 administrative training so that they can understand the concept of printing in an AD environment.

Wide Area Connectivity Support

The most technical role to be filled on the design team is that of the connectivity expert. This person must understand routing, switching, protocols, and the cost structure of leased lines (as far as we're concerned, understanding all this is the hardest part). They will direct the team's efforts to connect all sites—always with an eye on bandwidth control. They will determine which protocols are used on the network, which connectivity technologies will be implemented, and what routes will be available. They *must* understand all of the protocols in use, the hardware in use, and the wiring in place at each location. This person plays a central role in designing a stable network. (Notice that we didn't even mention AD in their skill set—they'll have to be competent in all network operating systems and networked applications in the environment.)

Training for a good wide area connectivity specialist includes vendor-specific certifications on both the network hardware in place and the operating systems in use on the network. At the very least, this person should be an MCSE, with a background in TCP/IP implementation. They'll also need to understand the various services (DNS, WINS, DHCP) in use on the network, at least from a bandwidth perspective.

Implementation Testing

The person in charge of implementation testing will work closely with all of the other members of the design team. The main responsibility of this role is to set up a test environment in which ideas, suggestions, and implementation techniques can be tested and perfected *before* they are attempted in the production environment. Our experience shows that overall costs of a major upgrade (such as the move to Windows 2000) can be reduced by 20 percent or so by performing adequate tests before implementation. Working out the bugs in your procedures prevents unnecessary downtime in the production systems. The most important skills that this person must have to work through problems are the ability to document processes and an analytical orientation.

Although this person does not necessarily need to be an expert on any particular component of the IT environment (they can always ask the other team members for assistance), they should be familiar with a wide range of software and hardware. In the past, we have used promising college interns to fulfill this role. They get a few dollars for college and some needed field experience, and we save a few bucks in salary—it's a win-win situation.

Education Coordinator

The education coordinator must be involved in the employee interviews from day one. They must compile a list of skills necessary for each employee after the upgrade and then provide the necessary training to fulfill those needs (and often on a limited budget). Unless your company has a well-developed internal training department, our experience has shown that bringing in an outside training coordinator is usually the best bet. (Most training companies, such as Progressive Education Services—the company Bob works for—are willing to put together a complete training package for a reasonable price.) Because they usually have access to the latest courseware and a direct line to Microsoft education, this is usually the most effective way to provide training for your staff.

Analyze security considerations.

There's an old adage in network design that the three most important factors in a good design are reliability, security, and performance—in that order. Reliability is a touchy topic. We've already discussed the reliability of the network infrastructure (during the physical analysis of the network) and can assume that Windows 2000 itself will be more reliable than earlier Microsoft network operating systems (namely, Windows NT).

Earlier, you gathered a list of network components, data sources, and network services. The next step in your design process is to determine the security needs of everything on your network *and* an overall security ranking for the environment. Some networks, such as Bob's home office network, need little to no security (heck, for quite some time, his Internet Web server had a blank password for the administrator account). Other networks, on the other hand, have a need for complex security schemes. Bob recently spent a little over a year teaching Windows NT networking courses to military personnel in Europe. Every class was filled with questions about Windows NT security (and, unfortunately, comparisons of Windows NT to other legacy operating systems). Those two environments—his home network and the networks on a military base—are the two extremes when it comes to network security. Most networks will fall somewhere in the middle.

Your list of resources and their security needs will be used to help design the AD tree *and* the overall implementation of Windows 2000. For more information about designing a security strategy, please see *MCSE: Windows® 2000 Network Security Design Study Guide*, by Gary Govanus and Robert King (Sybex, 2000).

Exam Essentials

The following topics will most definitely be touched upon (either directly or indirectly) in your MCSE exam:

Know which information should be gathered when analyzing the physical environment. For each location gather the number of users, workstations, servers, and networked peripherals.

Understand the importance of having a complete map of all WAN links. Knowing what connections are available will help you to design an AD structure that distributes network traffic evenly.

Understand the concept of available bandwidth. Available bandwidth is the amount of traffic that a network segment can accept *after* current network traffic has been taken into account.

Understand the importance of documenting data and system access patterns. Knowing how, when, and by whom resources are accessed can help you design a system that distributes network traffic evenly across the environment.

Know the skill sets that might be needed on an AD design team. See the Critical Information section, "Analyze network roles and responsibilities," for details.

Key Terms and Concepts

Bandwidth   A description of the amount of traffic that a network segment can accept.

Available bandwidth   The amount of traffic that a network segment can accept *after* current network traffic has been taken into account.

Sample Questions

1. Analyzing data access patterns will provide information that will be used in which of the following design decisions? (Choose all that apply.)

   A. Server placement

   B. AD site boundaries

   C. Data replication policies

   D. WAN design

   Answer: A, B, C, D.   Analyzing the traffic generated by system access can help in any decision that might affect the network infrastructure.

2. You discover that the wide area link between two locations is currently running at 75 percent of its capacity. Which of the following is true?

   A. You need to determine what process is putting traffic on this line.

   B. This line is overutilized and you should not plan to add more traffic to it.

   C. You should immediately upgrade this line to a faster dedicated link.

   D. This number is fine. You should be able to run with a line at 100 percent of its potential.

   Answer: A.   Although this number *could* represent a problem, you will need to determine if this is a peak usage or if it is constant and what processes are placing this traffic on the wire. Without this knowledge, you cannot make any realistic assumptions about the line.

3. What is the first step in the analysis of performance?

   A. Run a series of benchmark utilities to measure throughput.

B. Compare the environment with the performance statistics you achieved on your last consulting job.

C. Determine the expectations of the users.

D. Create a baseline to use for comparison after you have optimized the environment.

Answer: C.   The first step when analyzing performance issues is to determine what level of performance is expected by the users of the system.

4. Which of the following IT positions usually requires the least amount of technical skill?

A. AD expert

B. Server specialist

C. Application expert

D. IT manager

Answer: D.   In many companies, the IT manager is more responsible for the budget and the use of resources than for technical know-how.

Analyze the impact of Active Directory on the existing and planned technical environment.

- **Assess existing systems and applications.**
- **Identify existing and planned upgrades and rollouts.**
- **Analyze technical support structure.**
- **Analyze existing and planned network and systems management.**

Critical Information

In most cases, the migration to Windows 2000 and an Active Directory environment should provide more benefits than costs. That is not to say, however, that everything will continue to function as it did before the rollout of Windows 2000. Each and every component on your network might (and probably will) be affected by the upgrade. Before you begin the actual design of your AD structure, and certainly before you begin implementation, you need to assess the impact of the change and determine which processes or procedures will remain basically the same and which will need to be overhauled. No two migrations are exactly the same, but there are certain aspects of the IT environment that will warrant a close look:

- Applications
- Technical support processes
- System and network management
- The upgrade process and rollout procedures
- The network infrastructure

When considering each of these areas, keep your focus on what the environment looks like now and what you expect it to look like after the migration.

Assess existing systems and applications.

Of all the new or improved features that are available in Windows 2000 and Active Directory, those that pertain to application management might have the biggest overall impact on IT management techniques. By this time in your MCSE education, you should be quite familiar with the application management features of the Group Policy Object (GPO) in AD. The ability to publish applications easily and efficiently, and the built-in ability of the GPO to correct common application problems such as the accidental deletion of files, could conceivably change the way network administrators look at end-user applications.

Earlier in your analysis of the environment, you built a list of the applications that are in use on the network and the users who access them. At this point in the design process, you need to take a closer look at that list. First, use the expertise of the application support person on the design team to document the current application management process. Then, document ways in which AD can change this process to make it easier and more efficient.

Once you've created a list of proposed management changes, you will need to present this list to the rest of the design team. Each member should look at the list and analyze the impact on their area of responsibility. The server support person, for instance, will probably want to think about the server storage required to hold application packages. The AD expert will want to consider the effect of GPOs on the overall AD structure. Even the training coordinator will want to include end-user training on the installation of published applications.

NOTE This process of proposing solutions and then having your proposals critiqued by the rest of the team should be a common procedure for the entire design process. We often develop tunnel vision when working on one aspect of the design and forget to consider the ramifications of our suggestions on the overall network. Having input from the rest of the team can bring those consequences to light.

Identify existing and planned upgrades and rollouts.

As a general rule, you should have as stable an environment as possible *before* moving to any new operating system. Microsoft recommends that all servers have the latest patches and fixes installed, the latest versions of all drivers be in place, and all applications be brought to the latest version. Above all else—fix any existing problems before the upgrade to Windows 2000!

During your interviews with the IT staff, document any upgrades that are planned during the Windows 2000 implementation. While it is best to either finish them or put them off until after the migration, if an application *must* be upgraded during the time period in which the Windows 2000 implementation is taking place, ensure that all ramifications of the simultaneous actions have been tested in a lab.

Analyze technical support structure.

No matter what Microsoft might say in its marketing material, Windows 2000 is a complex environment. Your technical support staff must be trained in the intricacies of the operating system *and* given an opportunity to work with the features before they are expected to support end users in a production environment. You should schedule a rollout of Windows 2000 Pro to all technical support personnel long before it is rolled out to the rest of the company. Technical training should also be high on the priority list for the support personnel.

Once again, you'll want to analyze the features of Windows 2000 and AD and compare those features with current support processes. If, for instance, your support personnel spend a lot of time at client computers (supporting those pesky end users), you might want to investigate remote control features or terminal server services. As always, present your ideas to the rest of the team before finalizing any decisions.

Analyze existing and planned network and systems management.

The same story holds true here as for the earlier topics—analyze the current methods and philosophies used to manage the environment, and document them. Then compare those processes with the features of Windows 2000 in order to propose changes. The biggest aspect of this topic is that you might want to consider the "why" of the management philosophy as well as the "how." If, for instance, certain functions have been outsourced due to a lack of expertise or inadequate staff, you might want to consider having those functions taken over by in-house staff. DNS comes to mind—because DNS is critical to the proper functioning of AD, it might be better to manage your DNS environment rather than outsource that task. You might also want to look at the centralized-versus-decentralized management philosophy question. If, for example, a company uses a decentralized management philosophy (and hires outside consultants to handle management at remote sites) due to a lack of staff, you might want to consider the ease with which remote management of servers and workstations is accomplished in Windows 2000. As a matter of fact, many tasks are inherently easier in Windows 2000—this might free up some time for your staff to take on additional responsibilities.

> **TIP** If you are going to lend this book to anyone in management, we suggest that you tear out this page (or at least scribble over the last paragraph). There's no use in letting them know you are going to have more free time after the upgrade is complete. ☺

Exam Essentials

From a testing perspective, this is an interesting set of objectives. The goal of this section is to use the information gathered in the earlier steps of the design process to predict the effects that Active Directory will have on the company's environment.

Understand the implications of on-going upgrades and rollouts. Before beginning your implementation of Windows 2000, it is best to ensure that your existing environment is stable.

Key Terms and Concepts

There were no key terms or new concepts presented in this section.

Sample Questions

1. The migration to Active Directory can have an effect on numerous aspects of a network. Which of the following can be affected? (Choose all that apply.)

A. Applications in use on the network.

B. The processes used to support IT resources.

C. Plans for upgrading software on the network.

D. The network infrastructure.

Answer: A, B, C, D.   The truth is that every aspect of an existing network could be affected by a migration to Active Directory.

Analyze the business requirements for client computer desktop management.

- **Analyze end-user work needs.**
- **Identify technical support needs for end-users.**
- **Establish the required client computer environment.**

Windows 2000 Server introduces a whole new level of central control over user environments. The Group Policy Editor, a new utility for Windows 2000 Server, extends the functionality of the System Policy Editor and enhances the ability of administrators to configure user and computer settings by fully leveraging the Active Directory database.

NOTE This is an interesting set of objectives. While the main objective is fairly important, the subobjectives are really a rehash of information discussed in earlier sections. In a real design project, end-user needs analysis is dependent upon the information gathered early in the process. The bottom line for this section is your ability to plan, configure, and justify the use of Group Policy Objects (GPO) within an Active Directory environment. You'll see this reflected in the content—we spend most of this section discussing GPOs.

Critical Information

In this section, we'll discuss the components of AD Group Policy Objects, the areas that they can influence, how they are executed, and how to secure them. Based upon that discussion, we can then discuss the creation of a desktop-management policy.

What Is Desktop Management?

It's funny how the IT industry seems to go in cycles. In the days of the "big iron," or mainframes, there was no such thing as a personal computer. Each station was just a dumb terminal that connected to, and used the power of, a large, centrally controlled and managed mainframe computer system. From an administrative perspective, those environments didn't really even have a workstation component—there was little to manage at the terminal because all the processing occurred at the central computer. "Workstation management" (though the phrase didn't really exist at the time) was at best a physical function—it entailed the skills and techniques necessary to ensure that the dumb terminals were connected to and communicating with the central system. The user's interface was created, managed, and run from the central system. There were no concerns over screen savers, color schemes, wallpapers, or any of the other user interface components that are common today. Users had no input into the look and feel of their computer interface—all of those components were created by a group of programmers who were (in most cases) insulated from the day-to-day work of the average user. This really wasn't a big deal, though, because most of the terminals could display only text (usually green text on a black background).

As PCs entered the business environment, we saw a switch from central control to a distributed model. Users were given a certain amount of control over their environment—they were allowed to pick out color schemes, increase the size of the text, and even add custom components such as screen savers and wallpaper. The business world embraced the idea of *personal* computers (notice the emphasis on personal!). Management was euphoric over the perceived cost savings—a few PCs certainly cost a *lot* less than a mainframe, and users felt empowered by the freedom they were given to create a personal workplace (virtual though it is) that fit their needs.

All good things come to an end—and so did our days of wild abandon with the PC. Somewhere along the way, someone started to look into the total costs involved in supporting a PC-based environment. Sure, multiple PCs at a couple of thousand dollars were cheaper than mainframes, but business costs don't stop at acquisition. Business costs include the maintenance, upkeep, and replacement of components, and management started to notice that those costs were getting out of control. Numerous cost analyses were run, and the bottom line was that PCs were a lot more expensive than originally thought.

Costs of Support

Putting a definitive dollar figure on the total costs involved in supporting a network can be a tough job. Many of the costs are easy to quantify:

- Initial cost of equipment
- Initial cost of software
- IT staff salaries

Other costs *can* be quantified, but they're harder to budget for because they are not consistent:

- Software upgrades
- Hardware upgrades
- Hardware maintenance
- Software installations
- Training costs
- Help desk costs

Then there are the costs that are even less tangible, and therefore even more difficult to quantify:

- Lost productivity due to inefficient software, failed workstations, down servers, down WAN lines
- Training/retraining employees
- User error
- Lost revenue due to customers' inability to access support

The process of estimating costs becomes even more difficult when you realize that many costs change over time. When you upgrade to Windows 2000, for instance, you can expect that training and help desk costs will increase for the first few weeks or months (depending upon how good your design is) and then (it is hoped) drop down to less than they were before the upgrade as users and administrators become more familiar with the environment.

As you can see, the costs associated with supporting a complex network are themselves complex. Part of your job during the design process is to quantify costs that are static, estimate costs that are variable, and minimize associated intangible costs. All in all, this might be one of the most difficult phases of a design project.

One of the areas in which we hope to reduce costs is workstation management. The process of keeping a workstation up and running is one of the larger costs in most IT budgets. Hardware and software costs are actually minimal in the overall budget for maintaining workstations—and they are fairly static. You can easily estimate the costs of replacing broken components, upgrading hardware, and purchasing software. Harder to estimate are those intangible costs associated with the PC—lost productivity and IT support costs.

One of the basic precepts of support is that software cannot fix hardware. There's not much we can do to reduce the hardware-related costs of PC maintenance (except through proper purchasing practices). What we *can* control are the costs of PC configuration by limiting the amount of time we actually spend at each workstation and by limiting the control that users have over their PC environment.

Group Policies Overview

Group policies are used to define user or computer settings for an entire group of users or computers at one time. The settings that you configure are stored in a *Group Policy Object (GPO)*, which is then associated with Active Directory objects such as sites, domains, or organizational units. Many different aspects of the network, desktop, and software configuration environments can be managed through group policies.

What Are GPOs?

The following list describes, in general terms, the different types of policies that can be created—and enforced—using Windows 2000 Server's Group Policy Editor:

Application deployment policies   These policies affect the applications that users access on the network. They are used to automate the installation of software in one of two ways:

> **Application assignment**   The group policy installs or upgrades applications automatically or provides users with a shortcut that they cannot delete.

> **Application publication**   The group policy advertises applications in the directory. The applications then appear in the Add/Remove Programs list found in Control Panel. This gives users the ability to install and remove programs using a process with which they may already be familiar.

File deployment policies   These policies allow the administrator to place files in special folders on the user's computer, such as the Desktop or My Documents folders. For example, an employee telephone directory could be placed in the My Documents folder each time a user logs on to the network.

Script policies   These policies allow an administrator to specify scripts that should run at specific times, such as logon/logoff or system start-up/shutdown.

Software policies   These policies work much like system policies did in earlier versions of NT. Administrators can use them to globally configure most of the settings in user profiles, such as Desktop settings, Start menu options, and applications.

Security policies   These policies are some of the more important ones that you will configure. Using security policies, an administrator can restrict user access to files and folders, configure how many failed login attempts will lock an account, and control user rights (such as which users are able to log on locally at domain servers).

TIP   Exam hint: Know the various areas of function for the types of policies!

As you can see from this list, you can make policies do more than you could in earlier versions of Windows NT. Most of this additional functionality comes from the integration of policies with Active Directory services.

In effect, the Group Policy Objects for each container define their own folder structure, which works like a namespace. These structures are tied to one of the three places at which a GPO can exist in the Active Directory tree: site, domain, or organizational unit. Their placement will determine which users or computers will be affected by the settings in the GPO. The first rule to remember with policies in Windows 2000 is that they can be applied only to users or computers—they will have no effect upon other classes of objects in the AD tree.

At the root of the GPO structure are two nodes: Computer Configuration and User Configuration (also known as *GPO nodes*), as shown in Figure 2.6.

As the names imply, each of these subnodes contains parameters that can be configured based upon either the computer that is attaching to the network (Computer Configuration) or the user who is logging in to the network (User Configuration).

Computer Configuration

The following tasks are among the options available within the Computer Configuration settings area:

- Create policies that specify operating system behavior and the appearance of the desktop
- Assign applications
- Assign settings
- Set file deployment options

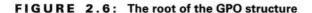

FIGURE 2.6: The root of the GPO structure

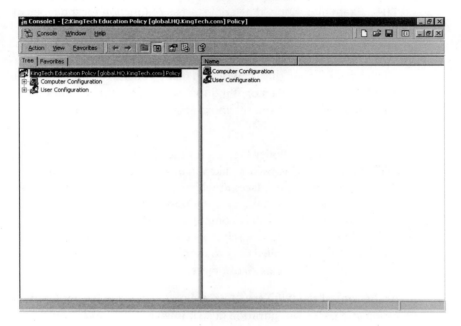

- Specify security settings
- Specify computer start-up and shutdown scripts

TIP Test hint: Computer-related policies are applied when the workstation's operating system initializes.

User Configuration

Among the options available within the User Configuration settings area are parameters that can be used to perform the following:

- Create policies that determine operating system behavior, Desktop settings, application settings, and assigned and published applications

- Set file-deployment options

- Set security options

- Assign user logon and logoff scripts

TIP   Test hint: User Configuration policy options are applied when a user logs on to the computer.

Using Computer and User Configuration

The bottom-line difference between the Computer Configuration settings and the User Configuration settings is when they are applied. For Computer Configuration options, the policy is applied as the operating system boots. This means that the configuration options set in the Computer Configuration area will affect *any* user who logs on at the specified computer. User Configuration policies, on the other hand, are applied *after* the operating system has initialized and *only* to specified users or groups based upon a fairly complex series of rules that we'll discuss later.

For example, if you were trying to lock down user Bob, you would use a policy created within the User Configuration area. If, however, you were trying to lock down a particular computer, you would create a policy within the Computer Configuration area.

NOTE   At first glance, the ability to apply a policy to a particular computer might not appear too useful. If your company has a computer located in a public area, however, these options can be very beneficial. Imagine a computer in a public library. It could have a policy set up so that all temp files are deleted at shutdown—or better yet, at logoff. This would delete any private e-mail or Internet browser temporary files that had been copied to the local machine. Using Computer Configuration settings would clean up the computer's environment *and* secure files against undesired access at the same time.

Each of these nodes—Computer Configuration and User Configuration—acts as the root of a GPO structure. Within each you will find a series of folders and subfolders. Each of these nodes contains configurable options for a specific area of your environment.

Although group policies are managed through AD-based tools, the actual policies are still specific files, just as in NT 4. These files are located in a structure called the *group policy template* in the system volumes folder, called Sysvol, of the domain controllers in the \Policies subfolder. As an object in the directory, each policy you create has a unique SID (System Identifier). Within the \Policies subfolder, you will find a series of subfolders, as shown in Figure 2.7. Each subfolder is named with the SID of the GPO that it contains. As you can see in the right side of the figure, within each GPO folder are two folders, MACHINE and USER, and a file, GPT (Group Policy Template). The GPT file contains a version number that is used to determine if the policy has been changed since the last time it was applied to a user or computer. The version number is used to prevent processing a policy when it is not necessary.

FIGURE 2.7: Policies **folders**

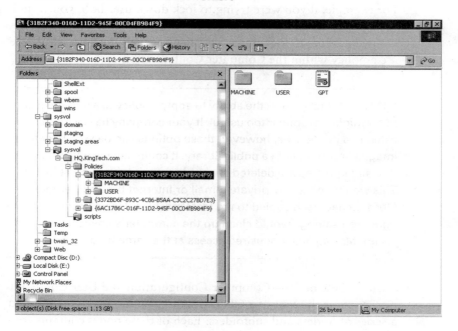

Software Settings

The Software Settings node of the GPO is the same for both the user and computer policies. This node allows you to manage the installation and maintenance of software for a user or computer. Applications can be managed in two different modes: assigned or published.

Assigned Mode

Assigned mode is used when you want all people using the policy to have an application on their computers. Suppose, for instance, that you want everyone in the education department at KingTech to have Microsoft PowerPoint on their computers. Your first step would be to create a *software package* containing all of the files necessary to install an application along with a description of all system changes needed (registry changes, file locations, etc.). Many applications now include a package when you purchase them (or have a package available for download on their Web site). If the application does not have a package, one must be created. There are many third-party products on the market that can accomplish this task. Place the application package in some shared folder available to the network.

Once you have your package, adding it to a policy is a straightforward procedure. First, decide if you wish to assign the application based on user identity or if you wish this application to be available on all computers within a site, container, or organizational unit. The answer to this question will determine whether you should work in the Computer Configuration node or the User Configuration node of the policy.

You will then have to choose how this application should be distributed. Your choices are to *assign* or to *publish* the application.

When an application is assigned, the policy will advertise it to users the next time they log in (or to a computer the next time it initializes). When an application is advertised, it is not actually installed on the computer. Only enough information is installed to make its shortcut appear on the Start menu and to create the appropriate file associations.

The first time a user tries to run the application, either by using the icon on their Start menu or attempting to open an associated file type, the application will be installed on their computer. The user can delete an *assigned application*, but because it is advertised, the icon and associations will be re-created the next time they log on.

The software installation mechanism of group policies can greatly ease administration of the applications used by your users. In our education center in Grand Rapids, Michigan, we use Windows 2000 and group policies to control the computers in our classrooms. We've created packages for each of the applications that we teach. We then assign them to whichever user accounts our students will use to access our network. Each night, we can put a new clean image down on our classroom computers (avoiding the hassle of cleaning up student work manually and greatly reducing our risk for virus infection), and when a student logs in the next day, all of the applications they need are available. The best part for us is that we don't have to worry about setting up specific machines for specific classes. We use the same clean image on all of the computers; who logs in at a computer will determine which applications are made available.

If your users move from computer to computer, you can reap the same benefits. Administrators no longer have to worry about installing applications on computers—that task will happen automatically when users try to use the tools they need. Because Microsoft has created a standard format for software packages, many applications (not just those from Microsoft) can be installed using this method. (You can also create your own packages for software that does not ship with a package.)

Published Mode

Another option available is to publish the application package. When you use *published applications*, nothing is installed automatically on the client computer. Instead, the application is added to the list of available programs in the Add/Remove Programs applet in Control Panel. This allows users to install the application on their own if they so desire. They do so by using a familiar interface—the Add/Remove Programs applet. They also do not have to have the disks (floppies or CD-ROM) at their computer—all of the files needed to install the application are part of the package.

From a design perspective, you will need to decide which software should be installed and what method (assigned or published) will be implemented. Because software distribution can also be used to maintain and upgrade installed software, you will also want to use the information you gathered earlier to build an application management plan for your environment.

Policy Inheritance

Having looked at a few of the options available, the next step is to determine why and how policies are applied to users, groups, and computers. We'll look at how policies are applied by default and then we'll look at how those defaults can be changed.

First, let us stress this one last time:

- User policies are obtained when a *user* logs on to the network.

- Computer policies are obtained when a computer boots.

TIP   Exam Hint: No other classes of objects receive policies—just users and computers.

The Order in Which Policies Are Applied

As we discussed earlier, policies can be associated with various objects in the Active Directory structure—domains, sites, and organizational units. There is also a local policy that is stored on and managed at the local client computer. Because you have the option to place policies at various points in your hierarchy, the first question that should come to mind is, "Which policy or policies will apply to which users and computers?" In a perfect world, the answer to this question would be short and sweet. Unfortunately, a simple answer would probably also imply a simple solution, and simple solutions do not often meet the needs of today's complex networks. The truth of the matter is that most of the rest of this chapter will focus on answering that "simple" question.

Default Order of Application

The default order in which group policies are applied is as follows:

1. The local policy, if one exists

2. Policies assigned to the AD site object, in an order specified by the administrator

3. Policies assigned to the domain, in an order specified by the administrator

4. Policies assigned to organizational units, starting at the top of the AD tree and working from parent to child OU until the context of the object (user or computer) has been reached. Once again, if an OU has more than one policy, they will be applied in an order set by the administrator.

This order can be influenced in numerous ways, but the default behavior is that the policies are applied in the order listed above. Each policy that is processed will override those settings made in policies applied earlier in the process. In other words, if a parameter is set to "true" in the local policy, the site policy could change it to "false," the domain policy could change it back to "true," and then various OU policies could change it back and forth so many times that it could be hard to determine what the settings will be once the process is done! The point here is that the implementation of group policies takes some prior planning to avoid these kinds of issues.

The general philosophy is that the policies should be designed so that the least restrictive are applied first. You should plan your policy strategy so that the policies are more restrictive as they work through the order. This means several things:

- Local policies should be the least restrictive. In most companies, local policies won't be used at all so that all policy management can occur within the Active Directory database.

- Site policies should be extremely generic. Perhaps you have decided that no computer should display the last logged-in user-name in the Log onto Windows dialog box. This type of overall configuration is best done in the policy that will affect the most users, such as the policy assigned to the site.

- Domain policies should contain configurations that are specific to the needs of the users and computers defined within the domain. This sounds obvious, but it is possible for a single site to contain resources from multiple domains. This option allows you to be a little more specific as to who or what will be affected by a policy. Here you might want to configure the DNS suffix that all computers within the domain will use when dynamically updating DNS.

- Organizational unit policies should contain configuration parameters that apply to a branch of your AD tree. Perhaps no users in the Sales OU (and those OUs under it in the tree) should be allowed to run programs other than those that are company approved. Here you could configure the policy with the list of approved programs.

You can use this cascading effect to reduce the number of places in which you have to manage certain parameters—sweeping parameters only have to be configured once (in the site or domain policy) rather than in each OU policy.

Placing Policy Objects

Look at the AD organizational unit structure shown in Figure 2.8. In our example, we have an education OU that contains a Michigan OU, which in turn contains OUs for each of the levels of schools that we support. This seems like a workable design—resources from each type of school can be placed within a container that represents their type (K–6, middle school, or high school). Under each container (K-6, Middle schools, and High Schools), we might have containers for each individual school—but we'll leave that level of containers out to avoid confusing the issue.

FIGURE 2.8: **The education department**

Within this type of structure, certain aspects of our users' environment will be similar. All of our students, for instance, should be able to use Internet Explorer. Other items of control, though, will differ based upon age group—first-graders should probably have a Home Page setting different from that used by high school students. This is where the cascading nature of group policies comes in handy.

Our first step will be to determine which type of policy files we wish to use—local, site, domain, or organizational. The process of assigning a policy to a site is the same as for assigning them to a domain or OU. In real life, we would sit down with the teachers and administrators and ask for their input: What types of controls do they desire, and how sweeping should those decisions be? After our research we might come up with a list that looks something like this:

- All students:

  - Advertise basic programs to all computers—word processing, spreadsheet, and database.

  - Run a script that checks for viruses each time a user logs on.

  - Do not allow printers to be published to AD.

  - Limit access to the display options in Control Panel.

- Based upon grade:

  - Add appropriate URLs to the Favorites list in Internet Explorer.

  - Assign specific applications.

  - Redirect all data, Desktop settings, and other personal information to network locations.

In a real-world scenario, the list would probably cover pages, but for our purposes here, this should be sufficient. As you can see, there are certain policies that should apply to all students and others that should be applied only to specific groups of students.

The second step in our process will be to determine which policies should be applied to computers and which to users. Some of the parameters will be available to only one or the other, but some can be configured in either manner. The next step is to determine the type of policy to use—local, site, domain, or organizational unit. Because our environment is a single domain and a single site, we could use either a site or a domain policy as our most generic. Given our single-branch scenario, we could even use a higher-level OU as our least restrictive policy—but this would be rare in a true business.

If planned carefully, the default order of cascading group policies can work fairly well. The problem is that it is often necessary to have a policy apply to one group of users but not another, even if those users exist in the same organizational unit. At other times, you might want to allow one container within your AD structure to set its own policy without having to worry about it being overwritten by a policy in a lower container. The opposite is also true—there might be a time when you want a lower-level policy to be the *only* policy applied to the users in an organizational unit.

Based upon what we've discussed so far, these cases would require very careful planning of both the placement of policies *and* the AD organizational units themselves. Luckily, Microsoft has provided us with three methods for taking control of which policies will be applied in any given situation:

- Filtering policies by security group membership

- Blocking policy inheritance

- Mandating a policy—i.e., preventing a policy from being overwritten by policies above it in the AD tree

By understanding the default mechanisms involved in *policy inheritance* and the various methods available to override those defaults, an administrator can use group policies to exert complete control over their network.

Filtering Policies by Security Group

Each GPO created has its own set of properties as an object in the AD structure. These properties refer to the *object*—not to the parameters that the GPO passes to the user or computer to which the policy itself is applied. To see these properties, right-click the GPO in the Microsoft Management Console (MMC) and choose Properties, as shown in Figure 2.9.

FIGURE 2.9: Accessing the properties of a GPO

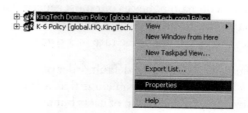

The properties dialog box of a GPO can be used to gather information about the policy, manage the policy, determine where the policy will be applied, and manage who will use the policy.

ACTIVE DIRECTORY GPO SECURITY

Like any other object in the AD database, GPOs have access control lists (ACLs). The ACL lists those objects that have been granted permissions to the object itself. GPOs have a unique permission—look at the bottom of the permissions list in Figure 2.10 and you will see the Apply Group Policy permission.

FIGURE 2.10: Security tab of the GPO properties dialog box

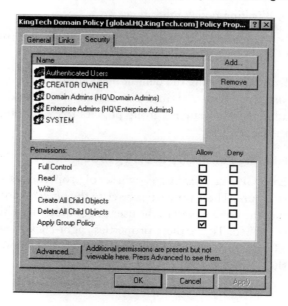

The permissions shown in Figure 2.10 are the default permissions granted when a Group Policy Object is created. Table 2.6 lists these default permissions.

TABLE 2.6: Default Permissions to a GPO

User or Group	Permissions
Authenticated Users	Read, Apply Group Policy
Creator Owner	None
Domain Admins	Read, Write, Create All Child Objects, Delete All Child Objects
Enterprise Admins	Read, Write, Create All Child Objects, Delete All Child Objects
System	Read, Write, Create All Child Objects, Delete All Child Objects

The important assignment for our discussion here is the assignment made to all authenticated users. Basically, this assignment is what creates the default rules. All users who logs in to the network and whose user object exists in this domain (because this is a domain policy) will have the policy applied to them.

As an example, let's return to the KingTech education department. The policies we've discussed so far have all revolved around the needs of the students—limiting their ability to change configurations or adding tools that they will need to their desktops and applications. The problem with the default GPO assignments is that this policy will also be applied to the teachers and administrative staff at KingTech (because they too will be authenticated users in this domain). To correct this, we could create a security group—perhaps named Students—and change the default permissions to this GPO. Remove the Authenticated Users group from the list and add the Students security group, as shown in Figure 2.11.

FIGURE 2.11: Using security groups to limit GPOs

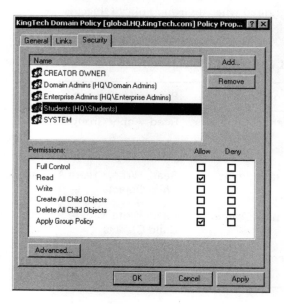

Make sure to give the Students group both the Read permission and the Apply Group Policy permission. Without the Read permission, they would be unable to read the various parameters set in the policy itself.

Blocking Policy Inheritance

At any site, domain, or organizational unit, Block Policy Inheritance can be set to block the inheritance of group policies. Because this setting is made directly to the site, domain, or OU instead of to a particular GPO, it will block *all* policies from reaching the designated area. In effect, you are creating an autonomous branch of your structure that will not inherit policies from above itself in the tree.

To block the inheritance of group policies, access the properties of the site, domain, or OU where you wish the block to begin. To do this, highlight it in the MMC, right-click, and choose Properties. You will be presented with the object's properties dialog box. On the Group

Policy tab, shown in Figure 2.12, you will find an option to block policy inheritance. Select this option, click Apply or OK, and inheritance will be blocked.

FIGURE 2.12: Blocking inheritance

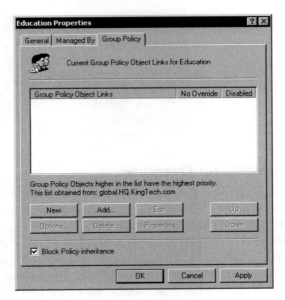

Mandating a Policy

There will be times when you want to block inheritance as we just discussed, but there will be other times when you want to ensure that a higher-level policy setting is not overwritten by a policy later in the policy list. To prevent a policy from being overwritten, access the properties of the container in which you wish to protect the policy. On the Group Policy tab, click the Options button. You will be presented with the dialog box shown in Figure 2.13.

Here you can either select the No Override option or disable the policy in this container.

As you can see, group polices can greatly ease the administrative overhead of workstation management. GPOs are a component of a larger management tool known as IntelliMirror. IntelliMirror is a big piece of the overall change in management philosophy for Microsoft—so you can bet it will be included in the MCSE exams!

FIGURE 2.13: The Policy Options dialog box

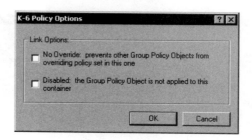

IntelliMirror Overview

IntelliMirror is a set of management technologies built into Microsoft Windows 2000 that are designed to increase the availability of services and reduce the overall costs of supporting users of Windows-based operating systems. Once configured, IntelliMirror configurations enable users' data, software, and operating system settings to follow them wherever they might need them—whether they are on- or offline. IntelliMirror provides three major areas of control:

- User data management, which consists of the files, documents, and other information that users access.

- User settings management, which allows for the customization of the operating system and applications in the user's computer environment. You can, for instance, mandate language settings, custom dictionaries, desktop layout, and other user preferences.

- Software installation and management allows the management of the installation, configuration, repair, and removal of applications and their patches and upgrades.

Although most of the functions that make up IntelliMirror can be implemented through AD group policies, AD is not a necessity. From the perspective of AD design, *IntelliMirror* is more a marketing term than a technology. All of the functionality of IntelliMirror is included in the AD group policy structure. You will, however, need to be aware of a few particulars about IntelliMirror for your exam. In this short section, we'll discuss a few of the prominent differences in how Microsoft presents GPOs versus how they present IntelliMirror.

One of the best features of IntelliMirror is the fact that it can be configured on stand-alone (non-networked) computers and that certain aspects can be configured so that they are available on or off the network.

User Data Management

Managing the vast amounts of data that exist in a large environment can be a daunting task. Designing an environment where that data is always available—given network outages, server downtime, and roaming users—has been almost impossible. IntelliMirror provides the tools to ensure data availability under any circumstances. These services can be set up manually or on a per-user basis, or they can be configured through the use of group policies.

One of the key services that IntelliMirror can provide is the ability to redirect data folders (such as the My Documents folder) to a network location. This provides all of the benefits that are inherent in a server-based storage environment—central backups, accessibility from other computers, and security. Of course, *just* moving the data to a server would leave the user at the mercy of the network—if the server (or some other component of the network) fails, the user will not be able to access their data.

To combat this single point of failure, redirected folders can be configured so that the data is synchronized back to a copy stored on the local computer. When folders are configured in this way, each time a user saves a file to the folder, the save is performed both to the network location *and* to the local drive. This configuration guarantees that data will be accessible at all times—even when the network is unavailable. If the network is unavailable, the user can work with the local copy of the data. When the network eventually becomes available, resynchronization with the network copy will occur (without user intervention). In the event that both copies (the local and the network versions) have changes, the synchronization manager will give the user the choice of saving both copies or synchronizing against one or the other.

User Settings Management

There are no capabilities in IntelliMirror that we have not already covered in our GPO discussion. This area allows you to manage the end users environment—desktop settings, color scheme, and so on.

Software Installation and Management

This component of IntelliMirror is basically just the software distribution that we discussed with GPOs—with one additional twist, software repair. If a user tries to open an application that is managed through IntelliMirror and that attempt fails due to missing or corrupted files, IntelliMirror will manage the replacement of those files automatically.

Creating a Desktop-Management Policy

Knowing the change management capabilities available in Windows 2000 is only the beginning of the design process. Now we must discuss the actual implementation of these technologies to serve business needs. From a design perspective, this means designing a desktop-management policy that will be used across the board to manage workstations within the environment.

Overview

Centrally managing any component of a complex environment requires an intimate knowledge of the particulars of that component. If, for instance, you wish to manage the traffic generated on your network, you will have to understand the types of traffic, analyze existing traffic, and estimate any additional traffic that will be generated due to changes to the environment (this is a great review of earlier chapters!). The same applies to desktop management. Up to this point in the chapter, we've been looking at the technologies available to manage the users' workstations. Now we need to move to the next step—analyzing the current environment.

Assessing the Existing Environment

The first step in designing a desktop-management policy is to gather information about the current state of your environment. You'll need to look at what hardware you have, what applications are in use, and the needs of your users. Much of the information you will need will have been gathered earlier in the design process—now you will need to look at that information with an eye toward desktop management.

Hardware

You will want to look over the hardware used within your environment to ensure that you do not specify configuration options that would conflict with the capabilities of computers on your network. You do not want, for instance, to mandate a particular display setting on computers that do not have hardware that is compatible with that setting.

Applications

Your next step to is to analyze the use of applications within your network. Earlier in the design process, you built a list of all software in use on your network and who uses it. You can use this list to determine which software should be published to which users or computers.

User Needs

You will also have to look at the needs of your users. You might, for instance, want to mandate a particular video display setting for most users within your company. You will have to determine if any of your users have a business need that is at odds with this policy. A user in the marketing department, for instance, might need a higher resolution for working with graphics files.

Looking to the Future

At this point, you will also want to think about the future of your network environment and the business that it supports. If you have an application that is constantly being upgraded, patched, or altered in some way, you might want to ensure that it is managed from a central location (through IntelliMirror) to reduce the administrative overhead of managing it.

Available Resources

You will also want to look at the IT resources that are available and how they are currently deployed. If your company has a limited number of IT professionals on staff, you will be more likely to configure central management of the desktop environment. A general rule of thumb is that there are two types of environments in which a restrictive desktop-management policy is most likely to be implemented:

A highly-managed network   In an environment where users are given little freedom, you are likely to use GPOs to control their workstation environment. GPOs allow you to exert complete control over the look and feel of their desktop as well as to limit the types of actions that users can take.

A network with a large number of computers and users relative to the size of the IT department   IT departments that are "understaffed" are more likely to limit the effect of user actions than companies with large IT departments are. Limiting user actions also limits the types of mistakes they can make, thereby limiting the amount of IT support they will need.

Design Considerations for a Desktop-Management Policy

There are four main goals for the use of GPOs within an IT environment:

- Enforce common security standards
- Enforce user and computer configurations
- Simplify the process of configuring computers
- Simplify software management

Enforce Common Security Standards

In many companies, the network has developed over time—first one department put up a server, and then another, and another, until the entire company was networked. The next step in the evolution of networks was to tie these separate environments together into a single system. The end result of this effort was the development of complex network operating systems such as Windows 2000.

As the networks become more complex and they begin to provide mission-critical services, it is imperative that a set of security standards be put in place to protect against user mistakes or unwanted access. Enforcing such standards on a user-by-user or computer-by-computer basis is cumbersome and time-consuming at best. At worst, such granular activity leads to mistakes in security configuration. Those mistakes can be exploited by unscrupulous or inept users to access confidential information or make unwelcome changes to the environment. Using GPOs to enforce security can help to reduce these risks.

Enforce User and Computer Configurations

Even though our users are becoming more and more computer literate, we still spend more time fixing user mistakes than we do improving the functionality of our networks. Most of these user mistakes could be avoided through the application of AD group policies that are configured to mandate the user preferences and limit a user's ability to make changes.

Simplify the Process of Configuring Computers

This is almost a corollary to the preceding goal—when a new computer is set up for a user, someone must spend time installing the proper software, setting up the default user preferences, and doing all of the other tasks that must be done before a user sits down to use the computer. Group policies can be used to perform this configuration as the user logs on to the network.

Simplify Software Management

One of the most exciting capabilities of IntelliMirror is that it gives you the ability to distribute and manage applications remotely. Anything that can be done to reduce the amount of time spent managing a single desktop will reduce overall IT costs and free up IT staff for other duties.

Specific Configuration Considerations

Microsoft suggests some specific GPO configurations to use in a given situation. These suggestions are valid in both your real-world system *and* in the exam room.

Optimizing GPOs for Slow Links

The hierarchical nature of the GPO structure within Active Directory lends itself to optimization of processing over slow links. You have the option of disabling processing of most of the nodes within the hierarchy. Disabling a node prevents its settings from being downloaded to the client computer. In general, you should always disable any nodes in which you have not made configuration changes.

TIP Exam Hint: Disable GPO nodes in which everything is left at its default setting. This reduces the amount of traffic that must be sent to the client computer.

NOTE A tool named GPResult.exe comes with the Windows 2000 Server Resource Kit. This command-line utility displays the group policy settings in effect on a computer and for the user logged on to the computer.

You can also configure certain nodes to not download when a slow link is detected. This allows the nodes to be implemented when a normal connection is made but reduces the amount of information that must be transferred when a slow link is used. This option is usually associated with dial-in connectivity. Table 2.7 lists various types of GPO settings, whether they are implemented over slow links by default, and whether this can be changed.

TABLE 2.7: Optimizing GPO Performance over a Slow Link

Type of Setting	Downloaded by Default?	Can Be Configured?
Security settings	Yes	No
Administrative templates	Yes	No
Software installation and maintenance	No	Yes

TABLE 2.7: Optimizing GPO Performance over a Slow Link *(continued)*

Type of Setting	Downloaded by Default?	Can Be Configured?
Logon/logoff and start-up/shutdown scripts	No	Yes
Folder redirection	No	Yes

The GPO Refresh Rate

By default, group policies are refreshed every 90 minutes, give or take 30 minutes to randomize the process (this helps to avoid a situation in which all computers are refreshing simultaneously). During a refresh, the entire GPO file is downloaded to the client computer— whether changes have occurred or not. Lengthening this interval can reduce the effect of GPO traffic on your network.

Exam Essentials

One of the most important features of Windows 2000 and Active Directory is its ability to ease the effort of managing the desktop. Microsoft is aware of this, and tests accordingly. Before you take the exam, ensure that you are comfortable with the topics presented in this section.

Within a given scenario, be able to analyze the costs involved in supporting the network. Costs include salaries, equipment, software, ongoing maintenance, and more. See the Critical Information section for details.

Know the five types of GPOs and, in general, what type of configuration options each provides. The five types of GPOs are: application deployment, file deployment, script, software, and security.

Keep in mind the events that cause policies to be processed. Computer-based policies are processed as the computer initializes; user-based policies execute when a user logs in to the network.

Know the difference between assigned and published applications. Assigned applications appear on users' desktop each time they log in (even if they delete the icon,) and are installed the first time they try to access the program. Published applications appear in the software list in the Add/Remove Programs list in Control Panel.

Know the default order in which policies are applied. The order is local, site, domain, then OUs.

Know how to change the order in which policies are executed. The inheritance of policies can be controlled through filtering group memberships, blocking inheritance, and preventing a policy from being overwritten from above.

Key Terms and Concepts

Group Policy Object An Active Directory object that can be used to control aspects of the network environment.

Desktop management A phrase that refers to the method used to control a user's PC and network environment.

Application assignment A group policy that installs or upgrades applications automatically or provides users with a shortcut that they cannot delete.

Application publication A group policy that advertises applications in the directory. The applications then appear in the Add/Remove Programs list found in Control Panel.

Script policies Policies that allow an administrator to specify scripts that should run at specific times, such as logon/logoff or system start-up/shutdown.

Software policies Policies that can be used to globally configure most of the settings in user profiles.

Security policies Policies used to restrict user access to files and folders, configure how many failed login attempts will lock an account, and control user rights (such as which users are able to log on locally at domain servers).

Filtering policies The practice of limiting who will be effected by a policy through the use of group memberships.

IntelliMirror   A set of management technologies built into Microsoft Windows 2000 that are designed to increase the availability of services and reduce the overall costs of supporting users of Windows-based operating systems.

Sample Questions

1. Which of the following types of GPO would you implement to ensure that a virus software was run each time user logs on to the network?

   A. Application deployment

   B. File deployment

   C. Script

   D. Software

   E. Security

   Answer: C.   Script policies allow you to run at specific times a script such as logon/logoff, system startup/shutdown, or virus detection.

2. Which of the following GPO types would you implement to control the Start menu options for a user?

   A. Application deployment

   B. File deployment

   C. Script

   D. Software

   E. Security

   Answer: D.   Software policies are used to globally configure most of the settings in users' profiles.

3. Which of the following GPO types would you implement to control which users can log on at domain controllers?

   A. Application deployment

B. File deployment

C. Script

D. Software

E. Security

Answer: E. Using security policies, an administrator can restrict user access to files and folders, configure how many failed login attempts will lock an account, and control user rights (such as the ability to log on at domain controllers).

4. Which of the following types of group policies would you implement to ensure that users have an updated copy of your employee phone book installed on their laptop each time they log on to the network?

A. Application deployment

B. File deployment

C. Script

D. Software

E. Security

Answer: B. File deployment policies allow the administrator to place files in special folders on the user's computer, such as the `Desktop` or `My Documents` folders.

5. Which type of group policy would you implement if you wanted users to have the option to install a program on their computer?

A. Application deployment

B. File deployment

C. Script

D. Software

E. Security

Answer: A. Application deployment policies are used to automate the installation of software.

Chapter

3

Designing a Directory Service Architecture

his objective group is where most of the actual AD design issues are covered. As such, a lot of the information presented will be critical to your success on the MCSE exam. Many of the topics will be subjective, meaning that in design issues there is seldom a "right" answer. You'll want to watch the guidelines closely, because they will hint at the correct answer on your Microsoft test.

We'll start by looking at the AD forest and domain structure and how it affects design issues. After that we'll discuss a variety of topics that pertain to AD design:

- Naming strategies

- Designing an OU structure

- Planning for the coexistence of AD with other directories

- Designing a site topology

- Planning for schema modifications

- Designing an implementation strategy

This chapter represents the core set of skills that Microsoft is testing for on the design exam. Ensure that you are extremely comfortable on each of the topics!

Design an Active Directory forest and domain structure.

- **Design a forest and schema structure.**
- **Design a domain structure.**
- **Analyze and optimize trust relationships.**

Active Directory forests and domain structures act as the foundation upon which the rest of the AD environment is based. As such, the ability to analyze a given environment and propose a stable forest is critical to a successful design—and success on the exam!

Critical Information

You might recall the definition of a *domain* from earlier versions of NT: a logical grouping of computers and users managed through a central security accounts database. According to this definition, a domain can be thought of both logically and physically:

- Logically, it is an organizational grouping of resources allowing central management of those resources.

- Physically, it is a database containing information about those resources.

Combining the logical with the physical entities gives you a management or security boundary; administrators for a domain can manage all resources in that domain by default.

The definition of a domain has not changed in a Windows 2000 environment. The only real change is that we now have to work this definition into a bigger picture—that of the entire network. In earlier versions of NT, domains were tied together by establishing trust relationships between them. In Windows 2000 Advanced Server, trusts still exist, but they are established by default and they function quite differently from before.

In Windows 2000 Server, domains act as the building blocks for an AD tree structure. The first domain created becomes the *root domain*. The root domain acts as the top of the structure and determines the beginning of the AD *namespace*. The name of this domain *must* match the top level of your desired namespace. After the first domain is created, each subsequent domain is added to the tree somewhere beneath it. In other words, additional domains are always children (though not necessarily children of the root domain), whereas the root domain has no parent. This concept is illustrated in Figures 3.1 and 3.2.

FIGURE 3.1: The root domain

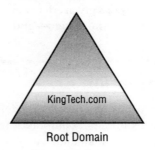

Root Domain

In Figure 3.1, the first domain for the company King Technologies has been named KingTech.com. As the first domain added to the tree, it becomes the root domain. All subsequent domains will follow the naming pattern of `<something>.KingTech.com`, as shown in Figure 3.2.

Figure 3.2 demonstrates the principle of *hierarchical naming*. Each subsequent domain adds the names of all domains above it to create a distinguished name.(We'll discuss distinguished names a little later in this chapter.)

Partitioning the Database

In large environments, the AD directory database can become quite large. The X.500 recommendations specify a method of breaking the database into smaller pieces, known as *partitions*, and distributing them across multiple servers. The X.500 recommendations also include a methodology for replicating changes to multiple copies of the same partition.

FIGURE 3.2: Subsequent domains

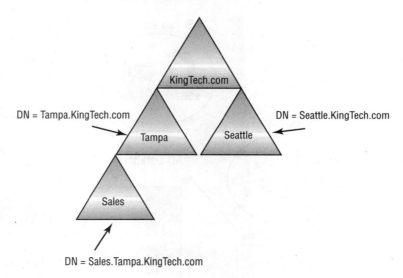

For the Active Directory database, domains act as the boundaries of partitions. In other words, each domain represents a partition of the overall directory database, as shown in Figure 3.3. (The term SAM refers to the Security Accounts Manager Database.)

Breaking the database into smaller pieces places less overhead on each Active Directory server. It also grants the administrator more control over the amount and route of traffic generated by the database replication process. Consider the environment depicted in Figure 3.4. Because there is only one domain defined, each AD server holds records for every resource in the enterprise. If a new printer is installed in Seattle, information about that printer will have to be updated on every AD server in the entire company. The same holds true for *every* change made to the database. If user Katie in Tampa changes her password, that change will have to be replicated to every AD server across the entire network. Although this design is functional, it is probably not the best design possible for the network.

FIGURE 3.3: Each domain is a partition of the AD database.

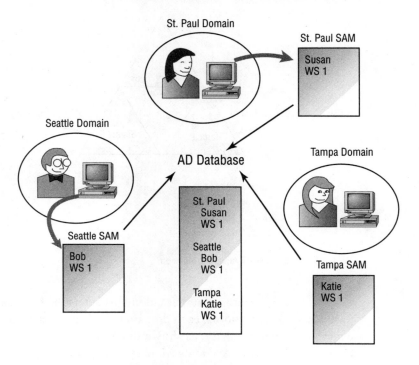

FIGURE 3.4: Company XYZ domain structure

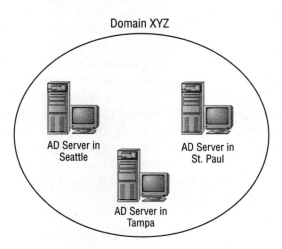

The King Technologies Company has come up with a much better design, as you can see in Figure 3.5.

FIGURE 3.5: King Technologies' domain structure

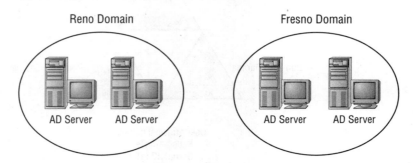

Reno Domain   Fresno Domain

AD Server   AD Server   AD Server   AD Server

In this design, each server contains only records for objects that are in its own geographic area. Notice that this design has two benefits:

- It limits the amount of traffic generated between the two locations.

- It ensures that no server is overburdened by holding records that are of no real value to its purpose.

We'll look at various design strategies in more detail later in this chapter.

What Is a Forest?

Domains and organizational units combine to form the Active Directory tree. *Domains* act as the physical divisions, or partitions, of the overall database, and *organizational units (OUs)* form logical groupings of resources within each domain. As we discussed earlier, this structure defines the namespace for the environment. In other words, every object within the AD tree has certain aspects in common with every other object. In the structure shown in Figure 3.6, for instance, every security principal object within the tree has a user principal name (UPN) that ends in KingTech.com.

FIGURE 3.6: KingTech.com AD tree

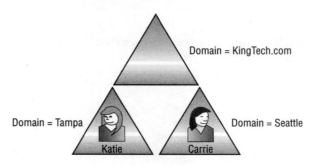

Domain = KingTech.com

Domain = Tampa

Katie

Domain = Seattle

Carrie

User principal names =
Katie@KingTech.com
Carrie@KingTech.com

Not only do the user principal names all end the same, but also all of the other types of names have a common format as well. The two users shown in Figure 3.6 both have distinguished names that end in DC=KingTech.DC=com. The user principal name is really what interests us at this point, though. Although it might not be apparent from the simple structure of the King Technologies tree, there is an inherent weakness in this single namespace design. Suppose that King Technologies were an internationally recognized brand name. Being popular has certain advantages, one of which is that it is conceivable that some other large company, let's call them MicroSofts, might want to merge with King Technologies to capitalize upon its success. (By the way, King Technologies is open to this type of arrangement—we could use the money!) What we end up with is two Internet registered domain names, both of which have brand appeal. In a single namespace environment, we would have to choose between the two names—would our e-mail addresses end in MicroSofts.com or KingTech.com? Remember, the user principal names all end in the name of the root domain. Not an easy choice, is it?

For these types of situations, or for any situation where a single namespace will not fulfill the business needs of a company, you can create an AD forest. A *forest* is two or more separate AD trees joined together by trust relationships. (We'll review the principels of trust relationships later in this chapter.) Setting aside security issues—you'll have to read the other Sybex study guide that we wrote, *MCSE: Windows 2000 Network Security Design Study Guide* (Sybex, 2000), for that discussion—this allows the sharing of resources and even administrative tasks between the two AD databases. Conceptually, the multiple trees become one big environment, but an environment that contains multiple namespaces, as shown in Figure 3.7.

FIGURE 3.7: An AD forest

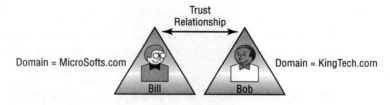

This concept can also come in handy for any situation in which your company has a close relationship with another company. This might sound cold, but in business, we've always believed that the best way to make money was on someone else's effort—often called the OPE (Other People's Effort) principle. At its most basic, this translates into passing as much of the effort involved in doing business as possible to an outside entity. As an example, let's look at the Great Style Shirt Company. Great Style makes great shirts (hence the name), but it doesn't make buttons. Any time the company designs a shirt that needs buttons, it contracts with an outside company to provide the button stock necessary for its production facility. In business, Great Shirts is in the power position over the button company because Great Shirts is the "customer" in the relationship. In a traditional environment, Great Shirts would have to call the button company every so often to order buttons—the right amount, color, and style for whatever shirt is being produced at the time. This means that, in a traditional environment, the "work" of keeping track of button needs is handled by Great Shirts.

Now let's move to an AD world. If both companies are using Windows 2000 (and AD) as their network operating system, the two companies could create a trust between the two trees, thus easing the process of sharing information. Great Shirts could then demand (we told you this might sound a little cold) that the button company access its production database and send just the right number of buttons each week. Notice that now the "work" of controlling inventory has been moved from Great Shirts to the outside vendor.

The Great Shirts example is probably a bit extreme, but it does describe the power of Windows 2000 and AD. AD is flexible enough to handle any business configuration that you might need to implement.

TIP   Exam Hint: The decision to create a forest should be fairly straightforward on the MCSE exam. In most cases, a forest is created in an environment in which two distinct namespaces need to exist— the one thing that a single AD tree cannot do!

Exam Essentials

Forests are an integral piece of many large Windows 2000 environments. As such, it is important that you understand what they are, and when they are used.

Know what a forest is.   A forest is multiple AD trees tied together to form a single unit.

Know when to use a forest, as opposed to a single AD tree.   In most cases, a forest will be created when two or more branches of the company need to use different namespaces or when company philosophy demands a complete separation of resources (such as when each division acts as a separate business entity).

Key Terms and Concepts

Domain A logical grouping of computers and users managed through a central security accounts database

Root Domain The first (and topmost) domain created in an Active Directory structure

Partition A section, or piece, of a directory services database

Forest Two or more AD trees tied together by trust relationships

Sample Questions

1. The first domain created within an AD tree is known as the

_____.

A. Master domain

 B. Root domain

C. First domain

D. Binding domain

Answer: B. The first domain created within an AD tree is known as the root domain. Because all user principal names are in the form of <username>@<root domain name>, it is critical that this domain be planned carefully.

2. A partition is _____.

A. One attribute of an object

 B. A section of the overall AD database, also known as a domain

C. A clustered-server domain controller group

D. A section of a Group Policy object

Answer: B.   Each domain represents a piece of the overall AD database, which is stored on domain controllers. Domains are tied together by trusts, which create one logical database out of the pieces. The process of breaking a database into pieces is known as partitioning and each piece is known as a partition.

3. Which two of the following are true about partitions?

   A. A partition is a section of a distributed database such as AD.

   B. A partition is an attribute of a server object.

   C. Each domain represents a partition of the AD database.

   D. A partition is a segment of wire.

   Answer: A, C.   Domains act as the boundaries of sections of the overall AD database. These sections are known as partitions.

4. Your company, XYZ (a well-known chain of motorcycle accessories outlets), is going to merge with ABC (a well-known manufacturer of motorcycles). Each company has a well-established Internet presence, will maintain autonomy, and will share sales, inventory, and marketing data. Which of the following AD designs would best fit this situation?

   A. Create a root domain named motorcycle and have a separate OU to hold the resources of each company.

   B. Create a single tree with two top-level domains, one for each company.

   C. Create a tree for each company and join them in a single forest.

   D. Merge both companies into a single domain.

   Answer: C.   Because each company has a well-established Web presence, you will probably want to retain their original registered DNS domain names. To accomplish this, you will need to create separate AD trees for each company. To ease the sharing of data, tie the two domains together in a forest.

Design an Active Directory naming strategy.

- **Establish the scope of the Active Directory.**
- **Design the namespace.**
- **Plan DNS strategy.**

In most directory-based solutions everything revolves around the development of a stable and usable strategy for naming objects within the environment. With Active Directory a proper set of naming standards is critical to the successful integration with the business in which it will be installed.

Critical Information

Much of this section is just a matter of applying common sense to your technical solutions—standardization of names for resources has been a common administrative policy for as long as networks have existed. To develop a set of naming standards you must begin by determining how much of the world your specification will affect. In other words, begin by determining the limits of your responsibilities.

Establish the Scope of the Active Directory

A few years ago a network administrator who was responsible for more than 100 computers and a couple of physical locations was working in what was termed a large environment. Today most medium-sized companies have an infrastructure that makes those old "large"networks seem puny in comparison. As the IT world has expanded, so has our yardstick for comparison. It is not unusual for even small companies to have networks that tie together multiple locations, run multiple client computer platforms, and connect to the world through the Internet.

To try to design a naming strategy for the entire infrastructure can be overwhelming unless you eliminate those areas for which you are not responsible. If, for instance, your company is connected to the Internet and has a registered DNS domain, the odds are that your responsibility for setting naming standards ends with your own domain. In other words, you are not responsible, nor do you have any control over, the names used by other companies on the Internet.

Even within your own network, there might be areas in which your design has no control. Your company might, for instance, have an internal group that is wholly responsible for its own resources. Although you might need to integrate them into your AD design, you might not have control over how their resources are named.

Lastly, using the information you gathered earlier in the design process, you will need to determine if there are any physical limitations to naming within your company. You might, for example, have some legacy operating system running on your network that has its own rules for how devices are named. You might also have some application that uses computer names as part of its process, and it might be hard-coded with naming rules (or even mandatory names).

Determining your areas of responsibility and control is known as scoping your design project. Knowing the scope of your project allows you to estimate more accurately the money and time that will be needed to complete and implement the design.

Design the Namespace

A *name* uniquely identifies an object. No matter what operating system you are currently using, everything on your network has at least one name. Names are an extremely important component of your environment. Think about it—without a unique identifier, how would users print to a specific printer? Or how would your users find the server that contains their files? Or how would you find the Microsoft Web page?

In earlier networks, it was possible to take naming for granted. Duplicate names, for instance, were handled in a slipshod manner. Bob once worked for a company for two years with the account name Bob2. Luckily, he's never suffered from low self-esteem or he could have spent two years wondering if he would ever earn the title of Bob1. A few years ago, we were doing some research and discovered a list of the most popular names given to servers on business networks. The results surprised us. The first most popular "naming standard" was to use the names of various *Star Trek* characters. This was followed closely by the seven dwarfs in second place. When networks consisted of a couple of servers (up to seven in the latter case) and 20 or so users, administrators could get away with these types of names. Today, however, networks consist of hundreds of servers, thousands of users, and numerous other resources that require unique, distinctive, and user-friendly names.

Planning a Consistent Naming Standard for Objects

One of the first considerations when building an Active Directory structure is that of object naming. The design team should sit down and develop guidelines for naming everything from user accounts to printers to servers. This naming standard should then be applied to every object created in the AD tree. Surprisingly, this discussion is often one of the most heated of the entire design process. For some reason, people can get quite emotional about how objects are referenced.

When designing your naming standard, start with the basics. Begin by creating a standard method for naming user objects. There are many industry-standard methods in use, but you should come up with a standard that fits your company. Here are a few examples, and the outcome, for user Bob King:

- First initial, full last name—BKing.

- First name, last initial—BobK.

- First initial, last initial, and some unique numeric identifier—BK1234. (Many companies will use the last four digits of the employee's company ID number or Social Security Number.)

WARNING   Our opinion is that the username should be easily identified with the user. When using a numeric or random component, this isn't the case. Also, be aware that using any component of a person's SSN can be potentially dangerous.

Once you've come up with a consistent standard, think about the possible exceptions to the rule. Your standard should define what should be done if two employees have the same name. If you had two users named Bob King, you might decide to include the middle initial or enough of the middle name to ensure uniqueness.

NOTE   Remember that *no* standard can be made to handle every contingency. We've seen design teams bog down trying to come up with the "perfect" naming strategy. When designing a standard, design for the norm, plan for inconsistencies, and be ready to intervene when it doesn't work.

Complete this same process with every object class you will utilize in your tree. Printers, servers, applications, even organizations and organizational units will need unique names. Remember that your names will be used by end users, so the names should readily reference the resources to *your* average user. We were once working as consultants on the directory design team for a company that had an office in Chicago. We had decided that all organizational units would have a three-character name and that the name would identify the object to end users. When we came to the name of the Chicago OU, the argument became quite heated—one group wanted CHI, another wanted ORD (the designator for O'Hare International), and yet another wanted CGO. The team deadlocked on this issue for over an hour. Remember, the names you choose are for your users' convenience—ensure that they make sense!

NOTE   When we were deciding on a name for the Chicago OU, we finally had to call a halt to the seemingly endless discussion. We instructed our employees to go home that evening, look over their last six months worth of e-mail, and count the number of times Chicago had been referenced with each abbreviation. CHI won by a landslide.

Planning a Consistent Usage Standard for Properties

If you have gotten far enough into your MCSE studies to be studying for the Design test, you should be quite comfortable with the various classes of objects and their properties. The user class, for instance, contains properties such as login name, first name, last name, telephone number, and even application associations and group membership. From a network administration perspective, the use of most of this data is apparent—login name is used to identify the user, group membership is a list of the security groups of which a user is a member, and so on. Some of the information stored in the Active Directory database, however, is not really network related. Strictly speaking, the title property is not used by any of the default processes of Windows 2000. (For the purists, you *could* write a script that uses this information, such as to assign permissions based upon title, but by default, it has no real network purpose.)

NOTE   If you are not comfortable with the basic format of the Active Directory database, we suggest that you read *MCSE: Windows 2000 Directory Services Administration Study Guide* (Sybex, 2000).

After you have created an object-naming standard, the next step is to take a closer look at each of the object classes to standardize property use. Active Directory might be a critical piece of the overall Microsoft network environment, but at its heart, it is only a database. If you're going to store data, you might as well spend the time to ensure that you can use that data once it has been entered. Once again, begin with the basics. You've defined your naming standard for user objects.

Now look at each of the properties available for the user class and decide if the data will be mandatory, optional, or not used in your environment. Table 3.1 gives a few examples for a user object.

TABLE 3.1: User Properties Standards

Property	Use*	Format	Description
Login name	M	First initial, Last name	User's account name.
Telephone number	M	###-###-#### X####	Telephone number and extension.
Title	O	Use only titles approved by human resources.	HR will approve all titles. Perhaps a script can be written that will check the value entered against a preapproved list.
Managed by	R		Reserved for future use.

* M = Mandatory, O = Optional, R = Reserved

There are many more properties for a user object. When defining standards for properties, you should create a list that includes all of them. Remember that the Active Directory is extensible, so the list may vary depending upon what changes you have made to your schema. You can find a complete list of objects and their properties in the Windows 2000 online help system. Perform this task with every class of object that you will utilize in your environment.

One more time, let us emphasize: Consistency is key! Remember that two of the goals of AD are to make the data it stores accessible and to make it usable. If you enter information in a haphazard manner, your database will not live up to either of these goals. Let's say that you decide to enter a title for each user. In Table 3.1, we suggest that you use the list of company titles that might be defined by the HR department. This will help to make the information useful later. On the flip side, letting anything get entered will negate some of the benefits of a central database. If, for instance, your administrator in Chicago enters

Manager and your administrator in London enters **Mgr**, you will not be able to perform an effective search for all managers in your company. If you tried using **Man*** as your search criteria, you wouldn't find any managers in London. You could use **M***, but that would also return all mailroom clerks—hardly the list for which you were looking.

Name Formats within AD

As we mentioned earlier, each object within the directory structure must have a unique name. There are four different types of names that can be used to reference an object within AD:

- Relative distinguished names (RDNs)
- Distinguished names
- Canonical names
- User principal names

RELATIVE DISTINGUISHED NAMES

The *relative distinguished name* of any object is that portion of its name that uniquely identifies it in the container within which it resides. In other words, if you create within the education container a user whose object is named Katie, and if the education container is in turn within the KingTech.com tree, as shown in Figure 3.8, the relative distinguished name of the object is CN=KATIE. (CN stands for common name.) Another way to look at this is to see the relative name as that portion of the distinguished name (described in the next section) that is an attribute of the object itself.

NOTE   If you have taken any of the Novell CNE courses, you will have been taught a different definition for *relative name*. The definition used here is not only the Microsoft definition, but it is also the definition used in the LDAP specifications. In this case, Microsoft's usage is more "industry standard" than is Novell's.

FIGURE 3.8: A relative distinguished name

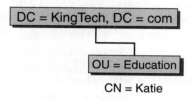

DC = KingTech, DC = com

OU = Education

CN = Katie

DISTINGUISHED NAMES

The *distinguished name* of any object is the relative name of the object plus the names of the containers that make up the path to that object. The object CN=Carrie in Figure 3.9, for instance, has a distinguished name of CN=Carrie, OU=Education, DC=KingTech, DC=com.

NOTE The *DC* in the distinguished name is the abbreviation for domain component. It refers to the DNS domain name within the AD tree. These components act as the point of logical connection between DNS and AD.

FIGURE 3.9: A distinguished name

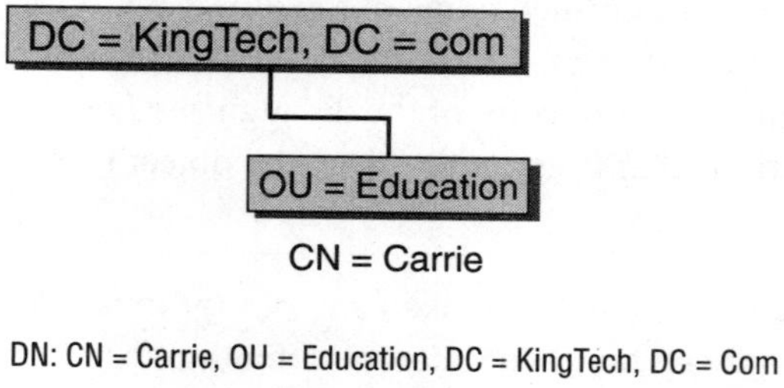

DC = KingTech, DC = com

OU = Education

CN = Carrie

DN: CN = Carrie, OU = Education, DC = KingTech, DC = Com

Notice that the distinguished name of the object identifies the nature of each container in the path.

CANONICAL NAMES

Canonical names are created in the same fashion as distinguished names—only the notation is different. In our earlier example, Carrie's canonical name, CN=Carrie, would be written as `KingTech.com/education/Carrie`. The major difference is that here we work from the top down in the directory hierarchy to create the name rather than from the bottom up.

USER PRINCIPAL NAMES

LDAP relative and distinguished names are long and difficult to remember. Rather than force users to use these inconvenient names for identification, Active Directory also assigns each security principal a more user-friendly name known as the *user principal name*. A *security principal* is any object that can be assigned permissions within the directory structure, namely users, groups, and computers. The user principal name is the object's relative name combined with the name of the domain tree in which it exists. Using our sample tree for KingTech.com, shown in Figure 3.10, user Susan's principal name would be `Susan@KingTech.com`.

FIGURE 3.10: A user principal name

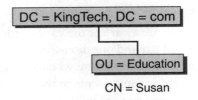

User principal names are designed to avoid some of the complexity that is inherent in a hierarchical design. If a company has a deep OU structure, as shown in Figure 3.11, a user's distinguished name might end up being too long to be convenient. User Tom, for instance, has a distinguished name of CN=Tom, OU=education, OU=Glendive, OU=Montana, DC=wildlands, DC=com. Forcing Tom to use such a long name to log in to the network would be inhumane at best. The user principal name of Tom@wildlands.com is much easier for Tom to remember.

FIGURE 3.11: A deep OU structure

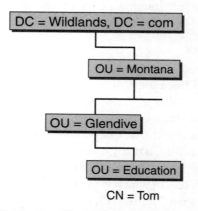

DN: CN = Tom, OU = Education, OU = Glendive, OU = Montana, DC = Wildlands, DC = com

UP = Tom@Wildlands.com

The Technical Side of Naming

Now that you are aware of the various forms of names that are used in AD, we can expand our discussion to the behind-the-scenes procedures that you will implement when you create objects. Microsoft has added numerous components to the AD environment to ensure that naming requirements are met.

DOMAINS IN AD

You should already be aware that NT domains still exist in Windows 2000. Microsoft likes to gloss over this, but the fact remains that certain limitations are inherent in this continued use of old technology. The first major aspect of domains is that, though Microsoft has added an X.500-compatible structure for management purposes, these containers are not really a part of the domain structure. In other words, OUs do not really "exist" within the domain itself. A working definition of a domain could still be "a logical grouping of computers and users managed through a central database." The format of this database has changed a little, but certain aspects have, unfortunately, stayed in place. The first of these limitations is that computers and usernames within a domain must be unique. Take a look at Figure 3.12. Within this hierarchical structure, we have two users whose common name (CN) is BKing.

FIGURE 3.12: KingTech AD structure

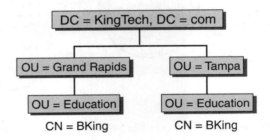

CN = BKing   CN = BKing

The distinguished names of these user objects are indeed unique: CN=BKing, OU=Education, OU=**Grand Rapids**, DC=KingTech, DC=Com on the one hand, and CN=BKing, OU=Education, OU=**Tampa**, DC=KingTech, DC=Com on the other. (The difference between the names appears in bold.) Because the names are unique, one might assume that this is acceptable. The reality is that this would depend upon the domain structure that had been implemented within this database. Look at the two domain structures shown in Figure 3.13.

In the design on the left, the two BKing accounts are in different domains; in the design on the right, the two accounts exist in the same NT domain. Because domains still act as if they were a flat database, the design on the right is invalid—computer and usernames must be unique across the domain within which they exist.

Plan DNS Strategy

The basic function of *Domain Name System (DNS)* is to resolve user-friendly domain names into IP addresses. When a client enters a Fully Qualified Domain Name (FQDN), the DNS server is queried for the IP address of the corresponding server. DNS is the tool most commonly used to find resources on large IP networks such as the Internet.

FIGURE 3.13: Two possible domain structures

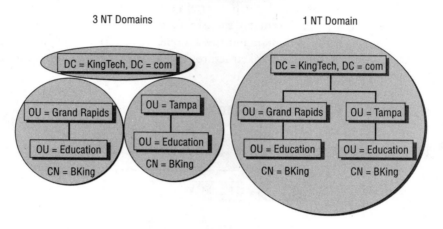

DNS is basically a text file broken into logical units known as *domains* and distributed across multiple computers known as DNS *servers*. The logical domains are organized in a hierarchical structure, much like the DOS file system. There is a very specific format, known as the *namespace* of the DNS system, for the names used in a DNS system. The concept of a namespace will be very important in understanding how AD is accessed by clients, so let's redefine the term to ensure that we are all in agreement:

A *namespace* is a set of rules governing how objects (DNS records in this case) are formatted within a directory.

On the Internet, domain names are registered with a central consortium to ensure that they are unique and that their format follows the namespace rules set forth for the Internet. This consortium, known as InterNIC (short for Internet Network Information Center), controls the last section, or "upper level," of domain names and has created a specific set for use on the Internet.

Each DNS server contains records for resources only in the domains for which it is responsible. If the DNS server receives a request for information that it does not contain, it will pass that request up or down the structure until the appropriate DNS server is found.

You could see DNS as a DOS-like structure—a series of directories (or domains) organized in a treelike format, as shown in Figure 3.14.

FIGURE 3.14:   **The DNS hierarchical structure**

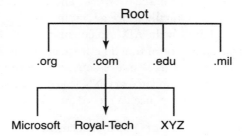

The hierarchy of domains within the DNS structure allows the database to be broken into smaller sections, which can in turn be distributed across multiple servers. This reduces the hardware required at any given server, as well as the network bandwidth required to support queries.

Imagine a system that was *not* broken into smaller pieces. First, the database would be huge (a record for *every* resource on the Internet). Few companies would be able to afford the kind of equipment that would be required: large hard drives, tons of memory, and multi-processor servers would be mandatory. With fewer DNS servers available, each would have to handle more queries from clients. This would result in more network traffic, which would in turn require more bandwidth on the link to the Internet. Without the capability to distribute the workload across multiple servers, DNS would probably not work for name resolution on large IP networks.

This ability to break the database into logical pieces and distribute those pieces across servers is critical to any network directory that hopes to serve in medium or larger environments. As you'll see in a bit, Active Directory takes this a step further.

DNS Records

Due to the various services that can be listed in a traditional DNS database, the format of each record can get quite complex, but the bottom line is that DNS is a series of text files containing IP addresses for hosts in an IP-based network. These text files must be created and maintained manually (once again, in a traditional DNS implementation; we'll discuss the AD implementation in a few pages), a task that can consume a lot of time in a large environment. If a company is forced to change its IP addressing scheme, the DNS records for each resource must be updated in DNS. If a resource is added (another mail or Web server, for instance), a record must be added to the DNS database.

The manual nature of DNS management is both a blessing and a curse. On one hand, the simplicity of a text file offers advantages in a mixed environment. On the other hand, a database that does not offer any automation will require a lot of person-hours in a large environment.

DNS Fault Tolerance

To provide fault tolerance, DNS defines two types of DNS servers:

- Primary servers
- Secondary servers

Primary DNS servers regularly copy the domain information they contain to secondary servers. Clients can be configured with the IP addresses of multiple DNS servers. If the client attempts to contact a DNS server and receives no response, the client will proceed to the next DNS server in its list, as shown in Figure 3.15. This ensures that clients will continue to function normally even if the network loses a DNS server to some catastrophe.

Although the primary/secondary arrangement of servers provides a level of redundancy, it is configured in a limited manner known as a *single-master environment*. All changes to the DNS database *must* occur at the primary (or *master*) DNS server and be propagated to the *secondary DNS server*. If the master DNS server should fail, no changes can be made to the database until one of the secondary servers has been promoted to the status of master.

FIGURE 3.15: **Primary and secondary DNS servers**

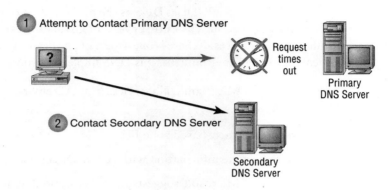

DNS in Short

The Domain Name System is a database used to resolve host names into IP addresses. The namespace it defines consists of a set of rules that is the industry standard. The database can be broken into smaller pieces (domains) and distributed across multiple servers. The service provides a mechanism for combining these separate files into a logical whole. Using a series of primary and secondary servers, the service adds a limited amount of fault tolerance to the database by replicating domain information to multiple servers.

All in all, DNS is a success. It has fulfilled its purpose in a large environment (the Internet) for quite some time. You might be wondering, "If DNS is so great, why don't we use it as our network directory instead of implementing Active Directory services?" The answer to this question revolves around functionality. DNS was designed for a specific purpose: resolving a host name into an IP address. DNS handles its intended function very well—so well, in fact, that AD incorporates DNS into its own design—but DNS could not handle the extra functions that would be placed upon it in an expanded role. DNS is based on a series of text files that are seen as a flat-file database. Adding additional functionality (holding the configuration information for a router, for instance) would stretch such technology beyond its limits.

DNS in an Active Directory Environment

Microsoft Windows 2000 uses DNS as the major means of resolving user-friendly names, such as `FileServer1` or `ColorPrinter`, into the IP address of resources. If there is one aspect of AD design that is most critical to a stable environment, it is DNS implementation.

When you deploy Microsoft DNS services in an AD environment, you have two choices:

- Use traditional, text-based zone files.

- Integrate the zone information with Active Directory.

Not surprisingly, Microsoft suggests the latter option! When you integrate DNS with AD, all zone information is stored in the AD database—a distributed, replicated, fault-tolerant database—which is then stored on all of the AD servers within your organization.

TIP   Exam Hint: Due to its importance to Active Directory, DNS design and implementation is tested heavily throughout the entire MCSE exam suite. By the time you are ready to take the AD Design exam, you should know DNS inside and out.

AD can store one or more *DNS zones*. All domain controllers can then receive dynamic DNS information sent from other Windows 2000 computers. Each Active Directory server can also act as a fully functional DNS authority, updating the DNS information stored on all of your AD servers.

In other words, once DNS has been integrated with AD, every AD server acts as a primary DNS server for all zones. In fact, *all* zones stored by AD must be primary—if you need to implement old-fashioned secondary zones (perhaps in a mixed DNS environment), you will have to stick with the old-fashioned text-file-based DNS.

TIP Exam Hint: If you are presented with a scenario that describes a DNS implementation that *must* use secondary DNS zones, you *must* use traditional text-based DNS.

In addition to integration with Active Directory, the Microsoft implementation of DNS provides the following functionality:

SRV Resource Records *SRV resource records* are a new type of record (defined in RFC 2052) that identifies the location of a service rather than a device.

Dynamic Update Microsoft DNS is more properly called DDNS: *Dynamic* Domain Name System. It is capable of allowing hosts to dynamically register their names with the zone, thereby reducing administrative overhead.

Secure Dynamic Update Windows 2000 Server security is used to authenticate hosts that attempt to dynamically register themselves within the zone.

Incremental Zone Transfer With *incremental zone transfer*, only changed data is replicated to other AD servers.

Interoperability with DHCP A server running *Dynamic Host Configuration Protocol* (DHCP) services can register host names on behalf of its clients. This allows non-DDNS clients to dynamically register with the zone.

Active Directory uses DNS to locate domains and domain controllers during the logon process. This is made possible by the inclusion of SRV-type records in the DNS database. Each Windows 2000 domain controller dynamically registers an SRV record in the zone. This record represents the domain Netlogon service on that server. When a client attempts to log on, it will query its DNS server for the address of a domain controller. The bottom line here is that, even if you are not going to use DNS for anything else, you will have to install and configure it for the logon process to work properly. Let us stress this one more time—DNS is critical to an AD environment!

NOTE The process of installing and configuring DNS is covered in *MCSE: Windows 2000 Network Infrastructure Administration Study Guide* (Sybex, 2000).

Dynamic DNS (DDNS)

One of the biggest weaknesses of traditional DNS configurations is that the text file must be manually updated. Every time a host is added to your environment, you must create a DNS record for it. With DDNS, Windows 2000–based computers can automatically add their name to DNS as they initialize and remove themselves when they are shut down.

AD Integration with DNS

As discussed earlier, previous versions of DNS were based on text files. For Windows 2000, the DNS service has been integrated into Active Directory. This integration results in two major changes in DNS deployment:

- DNS is required for locating Windows 2000 domain controllers. The Netlogon service uses the DNS database to register the domain controllers on your network. Clients then use DNS when requesting a list of domain controllers during the logon process.

TIP Exam Hint: This means that the Netlogon service relies on DNS to find a domain controller—remember this fact!

- The DNS database is stored within the Active Directory database. This allows you to take advantage of several AD features to improve the performance, reliability, and fault tolerance of DNS.

Microsoft strongly advises using an AD-integrated DNS system on all Windows 2000 networks. Doing so will provide many benefits:

- Multi-master replication
- Enhanced security

- Automatic replication and synchronization with new domain controllers as they are added to the domain

- Faster and more efficient replication

Let's examine each of these advantages in more detail.

MULTI-MASTER REPLICATION

In a traditional DNS implementation, DNS updates use a single-master model in which a single authoritative DNS server is designated as the source of all updates for the zone. This represents a single point of failure. If this server is not available, update requests cannot be processed. You would think that secondary copies of a zone stored on another server could take over this functionality. The reality is that, if the master copy becomes unavailable for a specific (it varies with vendor) amount of time, all secondary DNS servers for the zone consider themselves to be out-of-date and also stop providing name resolution services to clients.

In an AD-integrated environment, a multi-master update model is used for DNS changes. Because the DNS database is stored within the AD database (which is replicated to all domain controllers), the zone information can be updated by the DNS service running on any domain controller in the Windows 2000 network. In this case, all Windows 2000 Active Directory servers that have DNS services installed act as the primary source and can accept client requests for changes and replicate (through AD) those changes to all other DNS servers. It also means that, in the event of a DNS sever going down, all other AD DNS servers can continue to service client DNS queries.

ENHANCED SECURITY

Once the DNS database is moved into the AD database, its information can be protected using all of the security tools available for any other data in the AD database. The DNS data is stored in a dnsZone object container (named after the DNS domain that it represents), which has an access control list (ACL). This ACL can be used to control which users or computers can make changes to the DNS data. This is known as a *secure update environment* and is the default configuration for AD-integrated DNS environments. This prevents unauthorized servers from adding their information to your environment.

AUTOMATIC REPLICATION AND SYNCHRONIZATION WITH NEW DOMAIN CONTROLLERS AS THEY ARE ADDED TO THE DOMAIN

Directory-integrated zones are stored on all domain controllers, so replication and synchronization are not additional resources on the servers. In other words, there is no additional overhead placed on a domain controller to facilitate zone transfers. Using a built-in replication process reduces administrative overhead. (You don't have to configure a second replication service.)

This has the added benefit that less time must be spent planning for replication. As you configure AD replication, you are also planning DNS replication.

FASTER AND MORE EFFICIENT REPLICATION

In traditional DNS replication (the single-master model), all updates involved the transfer of the complete zone file, so if one record was added or changed, the entire file had to be replicated. With AD-integrated DNS, DNS updates are handled in the same manner most other changes to the database are handled—on a per-property basis. If you change the IP address of a particular host, only the changed information will be replicated.

Designing a Zone Structure for DNS

DNS is critical to the functioning of an Active Directory network. As such, a good DNS design can greatly improve the performance of your network and reduce the negative effects of DNS on the network. In reality, coming up with a good DNS zone design is not difficult if you follow a few guidelines and understand a few of the basics of DNS.

The Difference between a Zone and a Domain

A zone starts out as a file that contains the information for a single DNS domain name, such as KingTech.com. Think of the zone as the physical storage of the data and the domain as the logical organization of that data. This concept is easier to see than it is to explain. Assume that you are installing and configuring DNS services for the KingTech domain. When you create the first zone, your environment will look like that shown in Figure 3.16.

FIGURE 3.16: **A single-domain DNS structure**

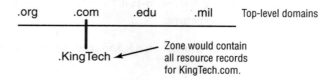

All of the resource records for the KingTech.com domain are stored within a single zone. In a traditional DNS implementation, this would be a single text file. In an AD-integrated design, these records would be stored in a single dnsZone object container (named KingTech.com).

If the environment required a subdomain named Education.KingTech .com, you would have the choice of adding the subdomain to the original zone, as shown in Figure 3.17, or creating a new zone (usually on another server) for the Education.KingTech.com domain, as shown in Figure 3.18. In a traditional DNS implementation, the resource records for the education subdomain would be stored in a separate text file. In an AD-integrated implementation, a new dnsZone object container would be created.

FIGURE 3.17: **The domain and subdomain in the same zone**

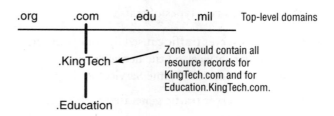

FIGURE 3.18: **A multidomain, multizone configuration**

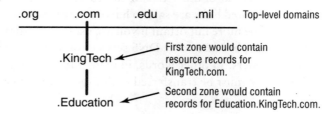

Zone Planning Guidelines

There are only two hard-and-fast rules when it comes to planning your DNS zone structure:

- There can be no more than 65,553 resource records within a single zone.

- Do not place more than 1,000 zones on a single DNS server.

Staying within these two guidelines should be easy for all but the largest companies. After you have ensured that you have not exceeded the maximum limits for a DNS server, the remainder of your planning will be a bit more subjective.

The first step to take when deciding upon zone boundaries is to analyze the traffic patterns on your network. (If you are designing a new network, this will take a bit of experience.) DNS is designed to limit the amount of broadcast traffic placed on networks, but it does create some traffic that must be taken into account during planning.

NOTE To review DNS traffic, you can use the DNS server statistics or DNS performance counters provided with System Monitor.

DNS generates two types of traffic:

- Server-to-server traffic caused by zone transfers and by interaction with other services on the network, such as performing a WINS (Windows Internet Name Service) lookup

- Client-to-server traffic generated by both dynamic updates and DNS queries

In general, this traffic is negligible, but it can have an adverse effect on slow WAN links or links that are saturated with other types of traffic. (Such saturated links are said to have low available bandwidth.) This issue will be more important if you are using a mixture of DNS implementations, because some DNS services do not support incremental zone transfers. In other words, in many older DNS products, the entire zone must be transferred each time there is a change.

Microsoft AD-integrated DNS will, however, produce more traffic than earlier versions of DNS. Because clients can dynamically add themselves to the DNS zone, each time a computer comes online (or offline), a change will be made to the DNS database. This change (the new record or the deletion of the record) will have to be replicated to all DNS servers in the zone.

Choosing and Placing DNS Servers on Your Network

Once you have finished planning your DNS zone structure, you must move on to planning for DNS server placement. There are two issues to consider:

- Server placement
- Server capacity

Server Placement

The exam objective for this section asks you to consider performance, fault tolerance, functionality, and manageability when considering the placement of DNS servers. Most of these considerations will focus on the WAN links in the environment.

TIP   Exam Hint: Remember that DNS is critical to the Netlogon service. It will always be better to have too many DNS servers than not enough.

PERFORMANCE

During your analysis of DNS traffic on your network, you should have developed a good feel for the effects DNS will have on your infrastructure. Planning server placement will be a subjective decision based upon this "feel." Consider the effects of DNS query traffic and compare those effects with those of zone transfer traffic. For example, if you have two physical sites connected through a WAN link, you will have to determine whether you should place a DNS server on each side of the link or whether one central server will suffice. It is easy to trace the traffic generated by both processes and determine which will have a bigger effect on performance (zone transfer or DNS client query). Unfortunately, we can't give you a hard-and-fast rule about which will have the bigger effect—which function will generate more traffic is based upon too many variables.

FAULT TOLERANCE

You must consider the effect of the WAN link going down. In such a situation, will your users still be able to log on to local resources? Remember that DNS is used by the Netlogon service to locate domain controllers. Without DNS, clients will not be able to log on to the network. The bottom line here is that a DNS server on both sides of most WAN links is the safest design.

FUNCTIONALITY

Here you will need to make a more subjective decision. Consider the distribution of computers across your various physical networks. As with most services, it is best to place DNS servers as close as possible to the users who will access them. If you plan on one DNS server and your office has a backbone wiring scheme, place that server on the backbone. If you can limit the number of DNS queries that cross routers, do so. Analyze the traffic patterns and place DNS servers on subnets that will generate the most DNS traffic.

MANAGEABILITY

Like functionality, this is a more subjective consideration. If your company uses a distributed management model (you have site administrators), you should consider placing DNS services on local servers. If, however, you follow a centralized management model, keep the DNS servers on centrally controlled servers. Consider staffing—do you have a local person who is capable of managing the DNS service?

TIP Exam Hint: For most of these types of questions (where should I place this or that?), Microsoft has a history of describing the management philosophy during the scenario setup. For the Design tests, this is critical information!

Server Capacity

Because each DNS server loads its configured zones into memory at initialization, you will usually see the biggest performance boost from adding RAM to your server, rather than upgrading the processor or buying faster hard drives. The amount of RAM needed in any server is based upon many variables:

- How many services does the server provide to the network?

- How many clients does the server support?

- Is the server used for file and print services?

- How many DNS queries will the DNS server need to service simultaneously?

Because RAM recommendations are notoriously inaccurate, we'll stick with just the RAM necessary to implement DNS. (You'll have to deal with the other variables yourself.) In a typical environment, DNS consumption is as follows:

- Approximately 4MB of RAM for the service itself (without any configured zones)

- Approximately 100 bytes of server memory for each resource record within each zone configured on the server

For example, if a server is configured with one zone that contains 1,000 resource records, that DNS service needs the following:

4.0MB	for the DNS service
+ 100KB	for the zone (100 bytes × 1,000 records)
4.1MB	of RAM

Naming for Both AD and DNS

The mix of DNS and Active Directory names can be a bit confusing within a Windows 2000 forest. When you add domains to an AD structure, they are arranged in a hierarchical structure, as shown in Figure 3.19.

FIGURE 3.19: A hierarchical relationship of domains

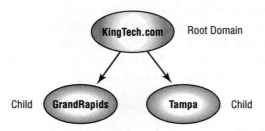

The first domain created in Active Directory is known as the *root domain*. The root domain begins the namespace that is defined with the tree. Only one name can be given to the root domain, and Microsoft recommends that, if you plan to connect to the Internet, the domain name be the same as the domain name you have registered on the Internet. In our case, for example, our root domain was named KingTech.com because this is the domain that we have registered on the Internet. You cannot change the name of the root domain without removing AD (thus destroying your tree) and creating a new tree. For this reason, it is critical that you take time to plan your structure.

NOTE   Our opinion is that you should register a domain name on the Internet, even if you plan no Internet presence, and use this name for your root domain. That way, if you later change your mind about joining the Internet, you won't have to re-create your forest, but this opinion can vary from company to company due to security considerations.

Each domain added to the structure will derive its DNS name from the domains above it in the AD domain structure. In Figure 3.20, we have added the DNS name for each domain in our tree to the example environment.

FIGURE 3.20: DNS names for NT domains

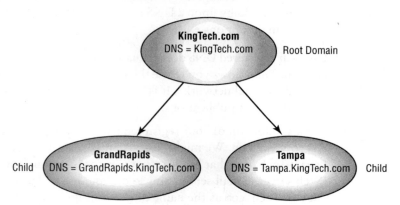

Naming Guidelines

When naming your Windows 2000 domains, you should keep the following guidelines in mind:

- The Active Directory root domain must be unique within any DNS hierarchy with which it will interact. This means that, if you are connected to the Internet, you should register a domain name and use it as the name of your root domain.

- If you are not connected, or if you are not planning to connect to the Internet, you are free to use just about any names you chose. If you plan to have an Internet presence, however, you must conform to the Internet naming standards. For more information on DNS standards, see RFCs 1034, 1035, 1039, and 2052. Microsoft is recommending that you use a naming standard that has been set aside for this purpose—end your DNS domain with the extension .local. For example, if King Technologies, LLC did not plan on developing an Internet presence, we would name the first domain KingTech.local.

- Domain names should be meaningful to end users, stable (not subject to change), and chosen with an eye toward expansion. (Using long but meaningful names might seem like a good idea, but as you add domains to your structure, the overall DNS names can become unwieldy.)

DNS Strategies

When you're deciding upon a DNS naming strategy for your environment, four main options exist:

- Use your registered DNS domain name as the name of the AD root domain. This allows you to use the same DNS name for your internal and external networks. It is also the method recommended in most Microsoft publications.

- Use a subdomain of your registered name as the name of your AD root domain. We might, for instance, use a DNS zone for Royal-Tech.com that holds resource records for our public hosts (Web server, e-mail server, and so on) and use GrandRapids .Royal-Tech.com as the name of our root domain.

- Use a different DNS name for your AD structure and a registered name for your Internet presence. This maintains complete separation of your public and private resources.

- Use the same name for both your internal and external DNS system, but separate the two systems with a firewall and manually maintain the appropriate records in each DNS server.

We'll discuss each of these options in turn.

Using Your Registered DNS Name

This is usually the easiest strategy because most companies will already have a working DNS system that uses the registered name. The only real drawback to this strategy is that you must ensure that your DNS implementation supports SRV records. SRV (service) records identify the location of a service; most important to the AD tree, SRV records are used to identify domain controllers. If you are currently using a DNS system that does not recognize SRV records, you will need to either upgrade it or install at least one Windows 2000 DNS server.

Current implementations of Bind DNS (Bind is a version of DNS) services that are version 4.9.6 or greater support SRV records. If you decide to stick with a non–Windows 2000 DNS solution, you must ensure that your DNS system meets at least this version of Bind compatibility. You will probably also want to ensure that your DNS system supports the following:

- Dynamic updates
- DNS change notification
- Negative caching
- Incremental updates

For this to be the case, you must be using a Bind DNS system that meets version 8.*x* or greater. Currently, Microsoft is suggesting version 8.2.1 or better.

NOTE   For the die-hards, you can read more about these capabilities in RFCs 2136 (dynamic updates), 1996 (DNS change notification), 2308 (negative caching), and 1995 (incremental updates). Just be warned— we've always found the RFCs to be the perfect cure for insomnia.

Using a Subdomain of Your Registered Domain

In this case, you have a registered domain name but want to keep your internal resource records in a different zone. You will configure AD and DNS with the subdomain name and use another DNS zone to look further into the overall DNS structure. For example, in Figure 3.21, Royal-Tech.com is registered on the Internet, but we decided to go with GR.Royal-Tech.com as the name for our root domain. Our ISP handles queries for Royal-Tech.com, and our internal servers just need to worry about internal records (GR.Royal-Tech.com).

FIGURE 3.21: Using a subdomain as the root domain

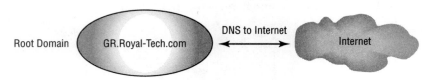

This DNS configuration allows you to continue to use your existing DNS servers without upgrading or updating them. It also allows for a complete separation of AD data in the DNS structure. On the other hand, your AD DNS names are longer because the names actually start at the third level (rather than the second), and you will need a working DNS server that the root domain can use for queries outside of the local domain structure.

TIP Exam Hint: This solution is handy for small to medium-size companies that already have an outside service handling their DNS functions.

Using Different Names for Internal and External DNS Systems

This deployment completely separates your internal DNS from the outside world. This arrangement should be used if you do not have a registered DNS name, never foresee connecting to the Internet, or want to clearly differentiate external from internal resources. The biggest problem with this arrangement is that, if you change your mind and want to connect to the Internet, you will need to completely reinstall your AD forest.

Using the Same Name on Internal and External DNS Systems

This is the most difficult scenario to manage because it requires manual manipulation of the DNS database on the external DNS server, but it is also the most secure environment due to the complete separation of internal and external DNS services. As shown in Figure 3.22, this model has two DNS servers—one for external use and one, on the other side of a firewall, for internal use. The external DNS server has only those resource records that should be made available to the public. (This DNS server will have to be managed manually.)

FIGURE 3.22: **Same name—two DNS systems**

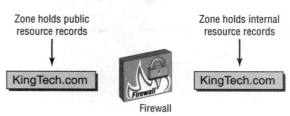

Zone holds public resource records

Zone holds internal resource records

KingTech.com

Firewall

KingTech.com

Firewall

So How Do I Decide?

We've discussed some of the variables in planning your DNS naming strategy, but so far, we really haven't given you much direction. Unfortunately, most of these decisions will be made based upon business needs.

TIP Exam Hint: Most of the DNS design questions will be found in case studies. When answering case studies, always remember that Microsoft's new philosophy is that the business needs, not the technology, should drive the design. The only time that technology should drive your design is when that technology can provide a more efficient business solution. Review the business goals of the case study when making your decisions!

With that said, Figures 3.23 and 3.24 provide decision flowcharts to use when your company either has or does not have an existing DNS solution.

FIGURE 3.23: A DNS design flowchart for existing DNS solution

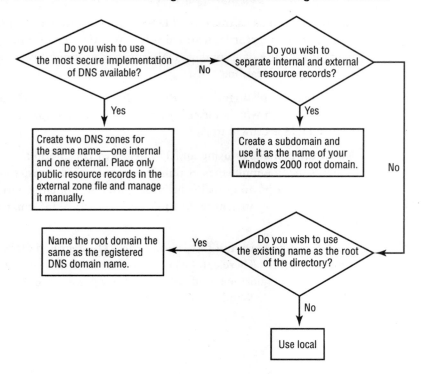

FIGURE 3.24: DNS design flowchart—no existing DNS solution

> Create a subdomain for the newly registered DNS name.

Exam Essentials

Know the following for the Active Directory design exam:

Be able to choose an appropriate set of naming standards for a given scenario. Remember that object names should be meaningful and consistent.

Be able to identify the correct relative distinguished, distinguished, and user principal names for an object. See the Critical Information section above for more information.

Know when to use a traditional DNS implementation as opposed to an Active Directory integrated solution. If an environment demands the use of secondary DNS zones, you should use a traditional implementation.

Know that the Netlogon service uses DNS to locate domain controllers through which a user logs on. A working implementation of DNS is critical to AD.

Know the benefits of using an AD-integrated DS solution. Benefits include multi-master replication; enhanced security; automatic replication and synchronization with new domain controllers; and faster, more efficient replication. See the Critical Information section for details.

Know the two hard-and-fast rules for an AD-integrated DNS zone structure. There can be no more than 65,553 resource records in a single zone, and you should not place more than 1,000 zones on a single Windows 2000 DNS server.

Know the two types of network traffic generated by DNS. The two types are server-to-server traffic caused by zone transfers and interaction with other services on the network, and client-to-server traffic generated by dynamic updates and DNS queries.

Know the formula used to determine the amount of RAM needed on a Windows 2000 DNS server. 4 Mb for the service and 100 bytes for each resource record.

Know the differences between the four proposed DNS strategies. The four proposed solutions are:

- Using your registered DNS domain name as the name of the AD root domain

- Using a subdomain of your registered name as the name of your root domain

- Using different names for your AD structure and your registered name for your Internet resources

- Using the same name for both your internal and external resources, but separating the two systems with a firewall.

See the Critical Information section for details.

Review the DNS strategy flowcharts. At the end of the Critical Information section you will find two flowcharts that can be help you decide which strategy will work best in a given situation.

Key Terms and Concepts

Scope A description of the area of responsibility for a design project. This term is also used to represent the overall complexity of a project.

Relative Distinguished Name That portion of an object's distinguished name that is a property of the object itself.

Distinguished Name The relative name of an object plus the names of all of the containers that make up the path to the object.

Canonical Name   Basically the same as the distinguished name, with different notation. These names are used for X.500 and LDAP compliancy.

User Principal Name   For any security principal, the user principal name is the object's relative distinguished name followed by an "@" symbol and the name of the root domain for the tree in which the object resides. (Such as `Bking@Royal-Tech.com`)

Security Principal   Any object within the Active Directory that can be assigned permissions within the directory structure.

Namespace   A set of rules governing how objects are formatted within a directory.

Primary DNS Server   The DNS server that acts as the repository of the master copy of the DNS database.

Secondary DNS Server   A DNS server that holds a read-only copy of the DNS database.

Dynamic DNS (DDNS)   A version of DNS that allows the host to dynamically update the DNS database with resource records.

Incremental Zone Transfer   A DNS transfer in which only changed information is replicated.

Multi-Master Replication   A system in which all copies of a database (such as Active Directory) can accept changes and replicate them to all other copies.

Sample Questions

1. Which of the following best defines "relative distinguished name"?

   A. The portion of an object's distinguished name that is not a part of your current context

   B. The portion of an object's distinguished name that is an attribute of the object itself

C. An object's location in the directory structure relative to the root of the tree

D. An object's location in the directory relative to the closest AD server object

Answer: B.   The relative distinguished name is the name you give the object when you create it. It is an attribute of the object itself rather than a part of the path to the object.

2. Which of the following would be a properly formatted distinguished object name?

A. CN=Bking\OU=education\O=kingtech.com

B. CN=Bking, OU=education, DC=Kingtech, DC=com

C. DC=com, DC=Kingtech, OU=education, CN=Bking

D. Bking@Kingtech.com

Answer: B.   DNs identify the object by using its relative distinguished name and each of the containers to the top of the tree. Each component is separated with a comma.

3. Select all that are true. User principal names _____

_____.

A. Are the user's relative distinguished name added to the DNS domain of their AD tree

B. Are designed to be more user friendly than distinguished or canonical names

C. Can be duplicated with the domain because the DN is actually used to find the user

D. Are used only when an AD-enabled e-mail service has been installed

Answer: Answers: A, B.   The UPN is the relative name plus the DNS domain name of the object, such as Bking@Royal-Tech.com. No usernames can be duplicated within either a DNS or NT domain.

4. Within Microsoft's implementation of DNS, an incremental zone transfer is _____.

    A. An update of all DNS servers in which the entire zone is transmitted in 64K segments

    B. An update of a DNS server in which transmission is controlled using the GTSP (Global Timing Sequence Protocol)

    C. An update of a DNS server in which only the changed data is replicated

    D. The process of moving DNS services from one server to another

    Answer: C. One advantage of Microsoft DNS is that the entire zone file does not have to be replicated each time the content of the DNS database changes.

5. Which of the following is the primary reason that DNS is required in an AD environment?

    A. The Active Directory database is stored within the traditional DNS database.

    B. AD uses the DNS zone transfer protocol during replication.

    C. Netlogon uses DNS to find domain controllers.

    D. DNS is *not* required in an AD environment.

    Answer: C. The Windows 2000 Netlogon service uses DNS to find domain controllers during the logon process.

6. Which of the following are benefits of using an Active Directory–integrated DNS configuration?

    A. Single-master environments are simpler to administer.

    B. Multi-master environments are more fault tolerant.

    C. It offers enhanced security.

    D. It offers more efficient replication.

    Answer: B, C, D. Multi-master replication allows changes to be made to any copy of the data, thereby eliminating the single point of failure in a single-master design. Updates are controlled by AD security, and, because AD replicates only changes (rather than the entire database), replication is more efficient.

Design and plan the structure of organizational units (OU).

- **Develop an OU delegation plan.**
- **Plan Group Policy object management.**
- **Plan policy management for client computers.**

Domains act as the building blocks of an Active Directory tree—each domain represents a distinct grouping of users, groups, and computers, and acts as a security boundary within the overall tree. They provide the important function of breaking the AD tree into smaller pieces (partitions) as well as tying it together into one logical environment for management through trust relationships.

Domains do not, however, really provide any new management capabilities over those available in Windows NT. In other words, if domains were the only component of Windows 2000 that provided the ability to group objects, there might not be enough justification to upgrade from earlier Microsoft products.

Using an X.500-compliant design, Active Directory also includes organizational units (OU) as a tool for grouping objects to ease management. The use of OUs allows for a much more granular approach to network administration.

Critical Information

In just about every article we've read about Windows 2000 and Active Directory, the authors seem to want to ignore NT domains and concentrate on the OU structure. That's understandable because OUs are new and exciting (for some of us anyway) and domains have been around for quite some time (and have garnered a fairly bad reputation). The reality, though, is that NT domains are a critical piece of the AD environment—and, more important to network administrators, a critical piece of the AD design. As you'll see later, domains are physical in nature and OUs are logical. They both have their place in your design, but knowing which to use (OU or domain) is key to a stable design.

What Is an OU?

Domains act as administrative boundaries: it is easy to give one administrator control over all resources within a domain. In many cases, though, using domains as the boundary for administrative privileges does not offer enough granularity of management. Administrators would often like to be able to limit an assistant's authority to a particular group of users or a particular geographic area. For these needs, AD includes the *organizational unit* (OU) object class. OUs form logical administrative units that can be used to delegate administrative privileges within a domain. Rather than add another domain to an existing structure, it is often more advantageous to just create another OU to organize objects.

Organizational units can contain the following types of objects:

- Users
- Computers
- Groups
- Printers
- Applications
- Security policies
- File shares
- Other OUs

NOTE   Remember that the AD schema is extensible, so the list of types of objects that OUs can contain might change if you change the schema of your tree.

NOTE   There is only one type of object that an OU cannot contain, and that is any object from another domain.

Easier Access, Easier Management

You could define an OU as a container object designed to allow organization of a domain's resources. An OU is used in much the same way a subdirectory in a file system is used. There is an old adage about creating subdirectories in DOS:

There are only two reasons to create a subdirectory: to ease access or to ease management.

You might, for instance, create the DOS structure shown in Figure 3.25. Most of us would find this type of layout comfortable and familiar. If you take the time to analyze why this structure works so well, you'll find that all subdirectories were created for one of two reasons: management and access.

FIGURE 3.25: A typical file structure

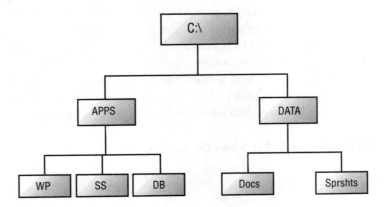

Here are two examples of how directories help ease access and management:

APPS   Naming a directory APPS lets a user know exactly where to find applications, making access easier. It also lets an administrator know where to place any applications stored in the file system, making management easier.

DATA   Again, the name helps both access and management. Placing both the APPS and DATA directories directly off the root of the drive makes navigation easier for users. Separating the data from the applications also simplifies setting up backup programs. (You can back up everything under DATA rather than all .doc files in \APPS\WP and all .xls files in \APPS\SS, and so on.)

The same reasoning applies to every directory in the file structure shown in Figure 3.25. This philosophy also works when designing the structure of your AD tree. OUs should reflect the business structure of your company. Do not create containers for political reasons or just for the sake of structure.

NOTE   The bottom line is, if you can't justify a container for either management or user convenience, then you probably don't need that OU.

Designing an Organizational Unit Structure

Organizational units provide structure within a domain. This structure is hierarchical in nature, just like the structure built by adding domains together. Each OU acts as a subdirectory to help administrators organize the various resources described within the directory. The structure must be meaningful to users and administrators alike for it to be of any value to the network. A structure designed without people in mind can do more harm than good, as demonstrated in Figure 3.26.

FIGURE 3.26: A bad OU structure

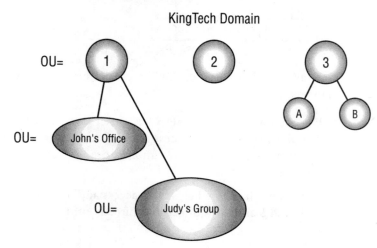

There are a couple of problems inherent in this design:

- Many of the OU names are not user friendly. A name of 1 might mean something to the administrator who created it, but it will probably mean nothing to the system's users.

- Naming containers after people *might* make things easier for a while, but as soon as there is a change in personnel or business structure, all such containers will need to be renamed.

What Makes a Good OU Model?

There are various *models* of good OU structures. A model defines categories of OUs and the relationships between them. The model you create for your tree should follow the business practices of your company. More than in any other form of network, a directory-based network demands that administrators understand the business practices and workflow of their company before designing the system.

Creating an OU model can be a difficult task—especially on your first attempt. Because a good design makes your life (and the lives of your users) easier in the long run, you would like to come up with a good, stable design the first time! With this in mind, some "cookie-cutter" models have been designed to act as guides during the planning stage of your own design.

Microsoft suggests seven different basic models for OU structures:

- Geographic model
- Object-based model
- Cost-center model
- Project-based model
- Division or business-unit model
- Administration model
- Hybrid or mixed model

In the sections that follow, we will take a look at the advantages and disadvantages of each design model.

Geographic Model

In a geographic model, OUs are structured by geographic location, as shown in Figure 3.27. The KingTech Corporation has created a first level of OUs to represent continents and a second level to represent countries. This type of configuration is helpful if each country has its own administrator; you can easily grant administrative privileges to a local user account.

FIGURE 3.27: A geographic model

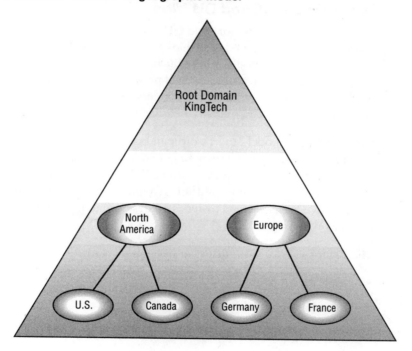

A geographic model offers a number of advantages:

- OUs will be fairly stable. Most companies sometimes reorganize internal resources, but the locations of their offices are usually stable.

- Corporate headquarters can easily dictate domainwide policies.

- It is easy to determine where resources are physically located.

- A geographic naming standard is easy for both users and administrators to understand.

A geographic model also has some disadvantages:

- This design does not mirror the business practices of KingTech in any way.
- The entire structure is one large partition (single domain). This means that *all* changes to all objects must be replicated to all AD servers worldwide.

NOTE   In most cases, the replication traffic on the wide area links will outweigh any of the benefits of using the geographic model.

Object-Based Model

The design of an OU structure can also be based on object types, as illustrated in Figure 3.28. A first-level container would be created for each class of object that exists in the tree. Below this first level, a geographic layout might make administration easier.

FIGURE 3.28: An object-based model

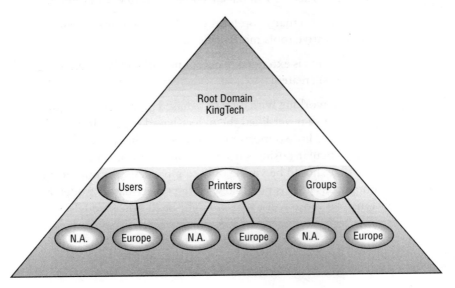

Here are some advantages of the object-based model:

- Resource administration is easier because each OU represents a specific class of object.

- Permissions are based upon OUs. It's easy to create OU-wide permissions, such as "All users should be able to use all printers."

- Administration can easily be delegated by resource type. For example, you can create a printer administrator who has permissions to add, delete, and modify all printers in the enterprise.

- A company reorganization should have little effect on the design. The same resources (with the possible exception of users) should exist no matter how the company is organized.

- Distinguished names are consistent for all objects in a class.

- It resembles the DNS structure, so it may lessen the learning curve for some administrators.

Disadvantages of the object-based model include the following:

- It is harder to define OU-based policies because all users are in the same containers.

- This flat structure will have to be created in each domain.

- There are too many top-level OUs. This can make navigating the administrative tools more difficult.

- If the schema is extended to accept new object types, new OUs will have to be created.

We've been working with directory-based networking for quite some time and we've never liked the object-based design. It offers the administrator little opportunity for customizing the environment to meet a particular business need. We might, for instance, have a printer that should be visible only to a particular group of users. Although this goal is possible with the object-based model, accomplishing it is more work than it might be in other models.

Cost-Center Model

A company may decide that the OUs within its AD tree should reflect its cost centers, as shown in Figure 3.29. This model might be used in a company where budgetary concerns outweigh other considerations. A nonprofit organization, for example, might have separately defined divisions, each of which is responsible for its own management and cost controls.

FIGURE 3.29: A cost center model

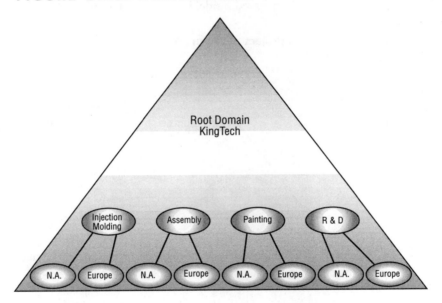

The cost center model has one main advantage: Each division or business group manages its own resources.

This model also has some disadvantages:

- Users might not be grouped together in a way that reflects their resource usage. A color printer, for instance, might belong to one department but might also be used by other departments as needed.

- Delegation of administrative privileges can be confusing.

The cost-center design does not really take full advantage of the power of Active Directory. Most companies have departments, and each department might have its own budget, but there is usually some overlap of resources.

Project-Based Model

Some companies might prefer an OU structure that is based on current project teams. A manufacturing firm, for instance, might want to create an OU for each resource group in a shop floor manufacturing process. The project-based model is shown in Figure 3.30.

FIGURE 3.30: A project-based model

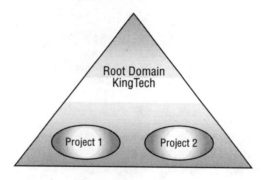

For certain environments, the project-based model offers some definite advantages:

- This model works well in an environment where resources and costs must be tracked.

- Because each project group is a separate OU, security between groups is easy to maintain.

Project-based design also has a couple of disadvantages:

- Projects often have a finite lifetime, so many OUs will have to be deleted and the resources redistributed.

- If projects change frequently, this type of structure will require a lot of maintenance.

We've found that a project-based structure will work for smaller companies with a limited product line. As a company grows (along with the number of active projects), the workload of maintaining a project-based design gets out of hand.

Division or Business-Unit Model

The OU structure can also reflect a well-known business structure if such a structure exists. A typical well-known structure would be the various departments within a law enforcement agency. You can see an example in Figure 3.31.

FIGURE 3.31: A division or business-unit model

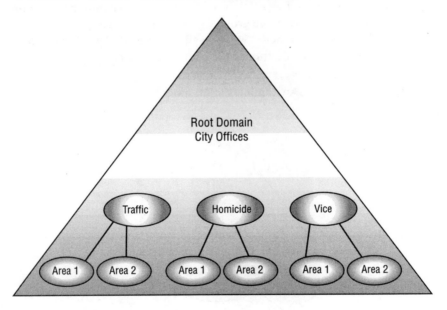

Here are some advantages of the division or business-unit model:

- This structure is very user friendly because it is based upon a structure with which users are already familiar.

- For the same reason, it is easy to locate resources.

And here is a disadvantage: Although the structure is based on a well-known environment, there is always the chance that the business divisions will change. Any such change would force a redesign of the OU structure.

NOTE The division or business-unit model works well in environments that are defined in a very rigid fashion, such as police departments and government offices.

Administration Model

One of the more frequently used models is a structure based upon common administrative groupings within a company, as shown in Figure 3.32. This model works well because it is based upon the actual business structure of the particular company.

FIGURE 3.32: An administration model

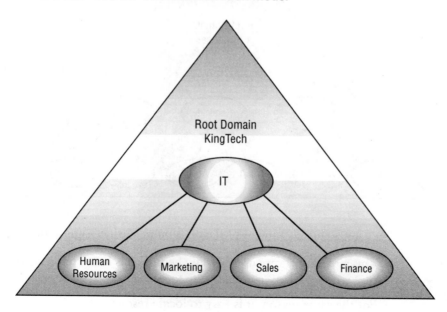

The administration model offers these advantages:

- This model is designed from the perspective of the network administrator and makes the administrator's job easier.

- Because most companies are departmental—from both a physical and a logical perspective—this model fits most enterprises.

It also has these disadvantages:

- This model is division oriented, so all resources from a single division or department will be grouped under a single OU. This might be confusing for users.

- In companies where many resources are shared among departments, this model might not reflect the business model of the company.

This is one of the more commonly implemented OU models. It works reasonably well for most companies.

NOTE   Probably the biggest advantage of the administration model is that in most companies this design matches the organizational chart. In other words, the design has already been created—all the network administrator has to do is implement it!

The administration model also matches the way many NT 4 networks were created. First, one department would install an NT server, creating its own domain and user accounts. Later, another department would see the benefits enjoyed by the first department and would in turn install its own NT server. In the process, this department would create its own domain and Security Accounts Manager (SAM) database. Next, the two departments would see the potential benefits of sharing resources and would create trusts. The end result is a network already modeled on the administrative groupings within the company.

During the upgrade to Windows 2000 Server, the administrator has the option of redesigning the structure, but because the users are already familiar with the "departmental" concept of multiple domains, it makes sense to keep the structure as it is. This results in less confusion for end users, less retraining, and less productivity lost due to confusion.

Hybrid or Mixed Model

Most companies will settle on a hybrid structure that combines two or more of the standard models.

NOTE Remember that a structure will be more stable and need fewer adjustments if it accurately reflects the business structure of your company. The standard models are often too rigid to do this.

A typical hybrid structure is shown in Figure 3.33.

FIGURE 3.33: A hybrid model

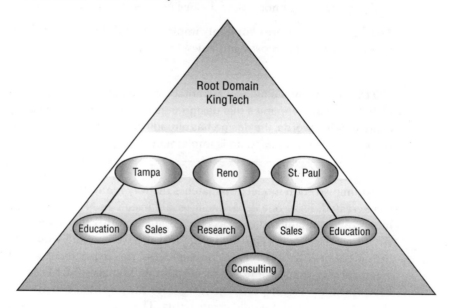

Advantages of a hybrid model follow:

- The structure can be customized to closely match the way in which the company conducts business.

- Employees are usually comfortable with the design because it reflects the way they actually work.

This model does have one disadvantage: It requires a greater understanding of the company for which it is intended than the other models do. For this reason, many outside consultants will avoid hybrid models.

Because of its flexibility, the hybrid model is probably the best overall design. It does, however, require more planning before implementation than the other models. Administrators of a hybrid model AD will have to create a set of rules governing when, why, and where new containers will be created. Here are some questions to ask yourself during this process:

- Which resources are departmental?
- Which resources are regional?
- Which resources are dedicated to a specific project?

Once you have answered these questions, you can start designing a structure that closely mirrors the way in which your business is structured.

NOTE The biggest problem with the hybrid model is that most businesses are dynamic. In other words, the way they do business changes as the market changes. Such changes could result in a design that no longer meets the needs of the organization.

Other Aspects of Planning an OU Model

After you have chosen the overall structure that you will use for your OU model, there are a few other things to consider before you start implementation. Most of the following topics are administrative concerns. Proper planning of these details will make administering your network easier down the line.

Name Standards

The names you give to OUs are used internally within the domain and can be seen when searching for particular objects. As such, it is important that the names you choose are meaningful *both* to your users and to your administrators.

NOTE OU names are not part of the DNS namespace. Users do not use DNS services to find an OU. This makes sense because OUs are not physical resources—they are logical structures used to organize the objects in your database.

OUs are identified by a distinguished name—also known as a *canonical name*—that describes their location in the hierarchical structure. Basically, this is the X.500 name for the object in the tree. An OU named Tampa that is located in the KingTech container would be known as Tampa.KingTech. These names are used most often for administrative tasks.

OU Ownership

Each OU in the structure has an object that acts as its owner. The owner of an OU can do the following:

- Add, delete, and update objects within the container.

- Decide whether permissions should be inherited from the parent container.

- Control permissions to the container.

- Decide whether permissions should be propagated to child containers.

NOTE By default, the user who creates an OU is its owner.

Develop an OU Delegation Plan

One of the most important features of Active Directory (and one of the most marketed features) is its management flexibility. You can expect to see a few questions on the MCSE exam that require you to analyze an environment with a focus on delegation of management tasks. During the design of your OU structure, you will want to consider the management philosophy of the IT department—if they use a decentralized management model, you will want to create an OU structure with containers for each area of management responsibility. (Note that, depending upon other factors, this can also be accomplished through the creation of multiple domains.) If, for instance, a company has local administrators for each site, you will want to ensure that your structure includes containers for each site so that the proper permissions can be assigned.

For every OU in a domain, there is a set of permissions that grant or deny read and write access to the OU. This allows for the delegation of administrative privileges down to the lowest level of your structure. Any permissions assigned at the OU level pertain to all objects within that OU.

There are various levels of authority you might want to delegate to other administrators:

Changing Container Properties   Administrators can change OU-wide properties, such as OU policies and other attributes.

Creating, Deleting, and Changing Child Objects   These objects can be users, groups, printers, and so on.

Updating Attributes for a Specific Class of Object   Perhaps your help desk personnel should be allowed to change *only* users' passwords (but not any other attributes of a user account).

Creating New Users or Groups   You can limit the class of objects that an administrator has the permission to create.

Managing a Small Subgroup of Objects within the Tree   You might want an administrator to manage only objects in a particular office.

Plan Group Policy Object Management

As you should already be aware, *Group Policy objects (GPOs)* are used to control the environment of users or computers (or both) within your network. To put it mildly, there are many configuration options available within the GPO structure. Luckily, the topic of this book does not demand that we list them all. For more information about the capabilities and configuration of GPOs, see *MCSE: Windows 2000 Directory Services Administration Study Guide* (Sybex, 2000). Our focus in this book is on creating a domain and OU structure that facilitates the use of GPOs as a management tool. For this, there are a few basic concepts with which you must be comfortable.

Where Are GPOs Assigned?

You can create GPOs that will affect users and computers within the AD structure at the levels of site, domain, or organizational unit. In other words, you can create a set of rules for user or workstation environments that will affect objects—that is, those users and computers—within a given site, within a specific domain, or within an organizational unit. From a design perspective, this allows you to create a single GPO that will be applied to an entire domain, or create different GPOs for each OU within the domain. A third option is to create a GPO for each site defined within your AD structure. During the design of your domain and organizational unit structures, you will have to determine which of the three options (or which combination of the three options) will best fit the business needs of your company or client. To do this, you will use (once again) the information gathered about the company and IT management philosophies.

You might, for instance, be working with a company in which all users are presented with a common interface to the network. In such an environment, you could create a single GPO for each domain and it would be applied to all users within that domain. On the other hand, you might be working with a company where a person's interface depends on his or her job function. For example, accountants get to change only their screen saver, whereas the engineers can change actual display settings. In this type of environment, you might want to create OUs for each different level of control so that GPOs could be created appropriately.

Plan Policy Management for Client Computers

If you decide to go with multiple types of GPOs—site, domain, or organizational unit (or a combination of types)—you will need to consider how those GPOs will be assigned to the users or computers. Remember that GPOs are executed in a specific order—first the site GPO is executed, then the domain, and finally the OU GPO—and that the effects are cumulative. In other words, the configurations defined within the site GPO can be overwritten by those of the domain GPO, which in turn can be overwritten by the settings in the OU GPO.

Being the flexible operating system that it is, Windows 2000 and Active Directory allow you to control the inheritance of GPO settings. You can define a domain that cannot be overwritten by OU

GPOs, or you can create an OU GPO that stops the execution of site and domain GPOs. No matter what technique you finally decide to use, your AD structure will have to reflect your desired outcome. If you want GPOs that are different for each department, you will need to create departmental sites, domains, or OUs.

How Do I Decide—New Domain or New OU?

The MCSE exam will contain questions that are worded so that you will have to make this choice—OU or domain. There are standard justifications for creating one or the other.

New OU

Here are some of the reasons to create an OU rather than a new domain:

- To delegate administrative control, giving an individual the ability to add, delete, or modify objects in a limited portion of the tree.

- To ease management by grouping like objects. You might, for instance, create a container to hold users with similar security requirements.

- To control the visibility of objects.

- To make administration more straightforward, assigning permissions once to the OU rather than multiple times for each object.

- To make administration easier by limiting the number of objects in a single container. Even though the limit on the number of objects within a single container is large (well over a million), no one wants to page through a huge list every time a single object needs to be managed.

- To control policy application. We'll discuss changes to the system policy process later, but for now, just be aware that policies can be set at the OU level.

- To be used as a holding container for other OUs. This would be the same as the APPS directory in the DOS example earlier. The APPS directory does not really hold any files; it just acts as an organizer for other directories.

- To replace NT 4 domains. In earlier versions of NT, the delegation of administration was achieved by creating multiple domains.

New Domain

Some reasons to create a new domain rather than an OU are listed here:

- To decentralize management of users or resources where administrators do not want to share control of a domain

- To make delegation easier in cases of diverse environments, such as a network in which different languages are spoken

- To create unique domain-level security policies, if they are mandated

- To control directory replication traffic (for instance, across a WAN link with limited bandwidth)

- To upgrade from an earlier version of NT that was configured as a multidomain environment

- To prepare for future changes to the company

- To modify the default trust relationships, if they do not meet your needs

---

TIP Exam Hint: Know these exam reasons inside and out! Most of this exam will focus on the actual design issues that you will face, based upon a series of case studies. One of the choices will be to create a multi-domain environment—you'll need to know when it is appropriate.

Exam Essentials

Without Active Directory and the OU objects it contains, Windows 2000 would be nothing more than an updated version of Windows NT. (Okay—that's probably an exaggeration, but it helps to drive home the following point.) Microsoft is aware of this, and they test accordingly! You must understand the uses of OUs and how those uses influence an AD design.

Remember the two reasons to create a new OU. The two reasons to create a new OU are to ease access or to ease management.

Know the advantages and disadvantages of the seven OU models. The seven models are: geographic, object-based, cost-center, project-based, division, business-unit, administrative, and hybrid. See the Critical Information section for details.

Be able to design an OU structure that facilitates the delegation of administrative responsibility. In most cases, OUs act as administrative boundaries within a domain.

Know when it is appropriate to create a new OU rather than a domain, and vice versa. See the list at the end of the Critical Information section for details.

Key Terms and Concepts

Organizational Unit (OU) An X.500 container object that acts as a logical administrative unit within a directory.

OU Model A design template that describes the categories of OUs within a directory and the relationships among them.

Sample Questions

1. Which of the following are reasons to create an OU rather than a domain?

   A. To ease delegation of management responsibilities

   B. To ease management by grouping like objects

   C. To control the visibility of objects

   D. To control directory replication traffic

   Answer: A, B, C. Directory replication traffic is based upon domain membership of Windows 2000 servers. OUs are logical objects, *not* physical, so they do not affect network traffic in any way.

2. Which of the following are reasons to create a new domain rather than an OU?

○ **A.** When administrators are adamant in their desire to control specific areas of a structure

○ **B.** To make delegation easier in diverse environments

○ **C.** To control directory replication traffic

○ **D.** When the default trust relationships do not meet your needs

Answer: A, B, C, D.   In most cases, the creation of a new domain will be in response to a physical aspect of the network as, for example, to control replication traffic or to facilitate management in a multilanguage network. Occasionally, though, a domain will be created for a political reason, such as complete separation of administrative responsibilities.

Plan for the coexistence of Active Directory and other directory services.

Throughout your studies for the MCSE examinations, you have been hearing about how Windows 2000 networking and Active Directory are based upon "open standards" and "industry-standard protocols." By now you should know LDAP, X.500, DNS, and even WINS, inside and out! But until now, probably no one has talked about how the use of industry-standard components is going to make managing a heterogeneous environment easier.

Critical Information

In this section, we are finally going to discuss how AD can be configured to talk to, share information with, and even manage other directory services that you may have implemented in your environment. This is accomplished by installing and configuring a software component called an AD connector. For this exam objective topic, we've got some good news and some bad news. The good news is that this appears to be a very low-priority objective on the MCSE test. (That's not to say that you *won't* see a question about connectors—just that it appears that there are not a lot of questions on them.) The bad news is that, at the time that this manual is being written, there is only one viable connector to use in our discussion—the connector to the Exchange Server 5.5 directory service database.

We'll begin this section with a brief overview of what connectors do, their structure, and a few of the configuration options that should be common to all connectors (when they are released). After laying that foundation, we'll move to a discussion of the Exchange Server 5.5 connector—mostly as an example of how connectors will affect your overall Active Directory design.

NOTE   As we write this, Microsoft has included on TechNet Plus a beta version of a connector for NDS (NetWare Directory Services), named MSDSS for NetWare. It is also available through the Microsoft Certified Solution Provider (MCSP) program. Because our focus here is on how connectors will affect your AD design, we feel that we can avoid the whole beta issue and still cover the concepts in enough detail for our purposes by concentrating on the Exchange Server connector.

What Are AD Connectors?

An *AD connector* is a software component that allows synchronization between dissimilar directory services. *Directory synchronization* is a process that keeps the information in two separate directories synchronized; that is, changes made to information in one directory will be propagated automatically to the other. You should remember that one of the most important features that Microsoft is marketing about Windows 2000 and Active Directory is the concept of a single point of management for all network resources. If you have an environment in which multiple directories exist, you could conceivably have multiple points of management for a single resource. As an example, look at Figure 3.34.

FIGURE 3.34: **Multiple directories**

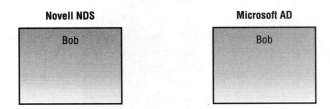

In this example, user Bob has accounts in both the Novell and Microsoft environments. Without some method of synchronization, Bob's two accounts would have to be managed separately—if Bob were to leave the company, for instance, his information would have to be deleted in both locations. Even management of less-critical changes would require multiple administrative steps. For example, if Bob were to change his telephone number, someone would have to make the change in both directories to keep the information current.

Adding an AD connector to this example, as shown in Figure 3.35, would alleviate the redundant management tasks. Bob's account information could be changed in the AD database and the changes would be propagated to NDS.

FIGURE 3.35: **Adding an AD connector**

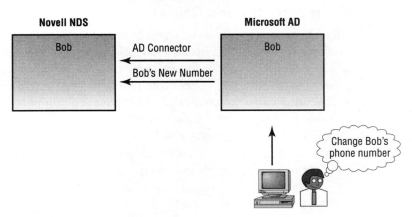

Managing Connectors

Just about every network directory on the market today, including Microsoft Active Directory, is based upon the X.500 recommendations. Most are also capable of using LDAP as a method of connecting to, searching, and managing the content of their directory database. Even though almost all vendors tout their compliance with industry standards, they don't mention that there is a lot of room for interpretation within those standards. AD connectors manage the communication between diverse directories, using the proper syntax and form to allow translation of requests from one directory to another.

When installing and configuring an AD connector, there will be certain tasks that are common no matter which vendor's directory the connector is designed to communicate with. Many of these configuration options will have a bearing on your overall AD design—if for no other reason than that they produce overhead on the network that will complete for bandwidth with other AD processes.

Connection Agreements

Installing an AD connector adds a service to a Windows 2000 server. This service becomes a component of the AD subsystem. Once this software has been installed, you must build a relationship between AD and the target environment. A *connection agreement* defines this relationship. The connection agreement holds the communication configuration between the two environments. These configuration options can include the following:

- The directory (or directories) involved

- The names of servers to be contacted for synchronization

- The object classes to be included in the synchronization process

- The direction in which synchronization should occur

- Any scheduling information for the synchronization process

- How deleted objects will be dealt with

- A list of attributes to be synchronized (and a description of how attributes map to each other)

- A method of creating new objects

- Authentication methods

- A list of which containers will be involved in synchronization and how they map between the directories

Only one instance of a particular AD connector can be installed per Windows 2000 server—but that connector can have multiple agreements defined. You might, for instance, install an NDS connector on a server but create connection agreements to multiple NDS trees, as shown in Figure 3.36.

FIGURE 3.36: Multiple agreements for a single connector

A few of the configuration options for AD connectors merit a more detailed discussion because these options can have a large effect on your overall AD design.

Configuring Bridgehead Servers

Bridgehead servers receive and forward the changes between the directories. As such, your bridgehead servers should have adequate resources to handle the additional overhead if they are performing this function. Because each connector will place a different amount of overhead on a server and the amount of information to be sent will differ from system to system (based on the number of changes made to the directories involved), there are no hard-and-fast "numbers" that can be used as a basis for comparison. (We'll actually look at the overhead placed upon a server acting as a bridgehead for an Exchange Server connector later in this chapter. You can use that information as a guide when planning for your own needs.) There are, however, certain conditions that you will have to consider when choosing which servers will act as the bridgeheads for any environment:

- The bridgehead server should have adequate resources (CPU and memory) to support the overhead of handling synchronization traffic.

- It should be well connected to the network. In general, the bridgehead servers should be highly available—usually this means placing them on your backbone or in the center of the physical environment.

- If at all possible, the bridgehead server should also act as a global catalog server. If this is not possible, then the bridgehead server should at least be on the same network segment as a global catalog server. (During the creation of a new object in AD, the connector contacts a global catalog server to ensure that an object with the same name does not already exist.)

TIP   Exam Hint: That last bullet item is a big design consideration!

Source and Destination Containers

AD connectors use the X.500 directory structure (containers within containers, which hold leaf objects) as the basis for synchronization. (A leaf object is a record that represents an actual physical resource such as a server, user, or printer.) When objects are updated between directories, the process occurs between containers in the directories. In other words, if a new user object is created in the Tampa container in one directory, the synchronization process will attempt to create that user in the Tampa container of the target directory.

In the case of the Exchange Server connector, for instance, if a recipient's container of the same name does not exist in the target directory, it will be created during the synchronization process. For instance, suppose you have a recipient's container named Persistent Image in your Exchange directory. If you were synchronizing mailboxes from it with an AD environment and a container with the same name did not exist in AD, it would automatically be created.

You have the option of configuring which containers will be polled for changes, to which container the changes should be written, and what types of objects should be synchronized.

Synchronizing Deletions

By default, an object that is deleted in one directory is not automatically deleted in any other directories to which a connector has been configured. Instead, a file that lists the objects that have been deleted is created on the server running the AD connector. This prevents accidental deletion of objects that need to be removed from only one directory or the other. This might come in handy if, for instance, you had configured a connector to your NDS directory to allow management of both environments during the migration process to Microsoft Active Directory. In this case, as you deleted objects in the Novell directory, you would not want those objects to be deleted in Active Directory.

You have the option, though, to configure your connector so that deletions are indeed synchronized across the connector. If you have installed the Exchange Server connector, for instance, and you delete a user object in Active Directory, you would probably want the corresponding mailbox to be automatically deleted from the Exchange directory.

The Exchange Server 5.5 Connector

The only real connector available at this time is the connector for Microsoft Exchange Server 5.5. We'll use this connector as an example of how connectors will affect your overall Active Directory design, to show you some of the considerations that you will need to take into account during the configuration of a connector, and to present some connector design examples for different types of environments.

Planning a connector strategy can be a full-blown design project in and of itself. Microsoft actually suggests that, for the Exchange connector, you create a completely separate design team whose sole responsibility will be creating an operational plan that describes your strategy for connecting Microsoft Active Directory with your Microsoft Exchange Server organization.

NOTE If it's this complex when connecting two Microsoft directories, imagine what it will be like when you try to connect directories from multiple vendors!

An Overview of the Exchange Server Connector

Like any other AD connector, the Exchange connector is designed to allow synchronization between two different directories—in this case, Active Directory and the Exchange Server directory. In the long run, this connector is used to manage both AD and Exchange objects in a single step, as shown in Figure 3.37.

FIGURE 3.37: A single-point administration

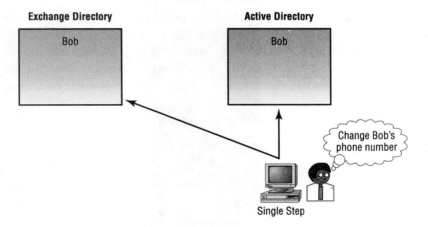

You can configure this connector for one-way or two-way synchronization. You might, for instance, want all changes to be made through Active Directory, so you would configure the connector so that changes are propagated only from AD to Exchange and not from Exchange to AD—this would be an example of one-way synchronization. Two-way synchronization would allow changes made in either environment to be synchronized to the other.

For this connector, there are two special uses that might have a big effect on the implementation phase of your design project:

- The Exchange connector can be used to populate a new Active Directory database with information from an existing Exchange directory. If, for instance, you are already using Exchange Server and have recipients created for all of your users, you can configure the connector and let the connector create AD user objects for each Exchange account.

- The Exchange connector can be used as middleware to populate your AD database with objects from any other foreign system that you can synchronize with Exchange, as shown in Figure 3.38. To do this, you configure an Exchange connector to the foreign system (such as Lotus Notes or Novell GroupWise) and let the synchronization occur so that the Exchange directory is populated with the accounts from the foreign system. Then configure the AD-to-Exchange connector and let it populate your AD database with objects corresponding to the Exchange accounts. In this way, you can use what we call "pass-through" synchronization to populate your AD database with objects from most other directories.

FIGURE 3.38: Pass-through synchronization

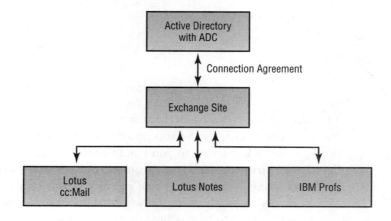

TIP We've used the latter technique a few times, and it can save you a lot of time and effort. We've gone so far as to put up a temporary Exchange server and connect it to a client's current e-mail package. Let the accounts synchronize and then use an Exchange connector to bring those accounts into Active Directory. You can then uninstall the Exchange connector and bring down your temporary Exchange server—after the user accounts have been created for you!

The key features of the Exchange connector are as follows:

Bidirectional Synchronization When configured, this allows you to make changes in either directory and have those changes synchronized to the other.

Selective Attribute Synchronization You can specify which attributes of Active Directory and Exchange objects should be synchronized through the connector.

Change Synchronization Only those objects that are changed will be processed by the synchronization software (as opposed to all objects whether they are changed or not).

Attribute-Level Changes Only those attributes that have changed are replicated across the connector. If you change Bob's telephone number, *only* his telephone number will cross the link. This seems like common sense, but you would be surprised at the number of directory synchronization products that actually do a complete copy of the entire object if any changes are made.

NOTE This last item brings to mind one of the biggest advantages of managing your directories through AD. Active Directory allows you to design a more granular management model than the Exchange directory allows. In AD, you can give an individual permissions to a particular attribute (as opposed to the container-level management delegation available in Exchange).

Planning for the Exchange Connector

Planning for AD connectors should be considered a subproject of your overall design process. Although connectors can have an effect on your overall AD design, in many ways, planning for connectors requires its own design process.

Microsoft has suggested the following process be used when planning for directory synchronization:

- Form the deployment planning team. It is important that the AD design team be represented on this team, but in most cases, the majority of its members will be from your Exchange support staff. Whoever is on this team *must* have knowledge of both Exchange and Active Directory.

- Examine your domain structure and Exchange site topology. Because the Exchange site topology does not always match the business structure of the company, you will have to analyze where the two structures differ.

- Determine your management strategy. Decide where the objects will be managed—always from one of the other directories or always from a single directory.

- Decide which object classes and attributes will be synchronized.

- Create your connection agreement plan.

- Test your connection agreements in a lab or other controlled environment.

- Determine the schedule for synchronization.

- Develop (and implement) a backup and restore strategy.

A few of these steps need a more detailed discussion.

Form the Deployment Planning Team

No other component of your overall AD design project has as many codependencies as the implementation of an AD connector. Your team must contain members from IT management, the Active Directory administration staff, the schema management staff, and the network services group. Each of these people will have knowledge and skills that will contribute to the overall connection implementation strategy.

During the initial installation of the Active Directory connector (ADC), there will be changes made to the AD schema. For this reason, someone on the connector implementation team must be a member of the Schema Administrators group—at least during the installation of the first ADC.

Examine Your Domain Structure and Exchange Site Topology

You will need to gather information about your Exchange sites—how they are managed (and by whom), which accounts exist in which recipients' containers, and the objects that will need to be synchronized. If your AD users exist in multiple Windows 2000 domains, you will have to build a list of where each mailbox recipient's AD account is located. The easiest scenario (as we'll see in a bit) is when all mailboxes for an AD domain reside in the same Exchange site. If this is not the case, you will have to configure multiple connection agreements from each Exchange site that has mailboxes to the appropriate Windows 2000 domains. This is probably the biggest hassle in setting up this connector—and in some cases, it can take almost as long as the full AD design process.

At this point you should begin to plan the placement of your bridgehead servers. Remember that the bridgehead servers must have enough available resources to handle the additional overhead of supporting synchronization traffic, be well connected and highly available to the network, and either be global catalog servers or be physically located near one (preferably on the same network segment).

Although there are no definitive numbers that can be applied to the overhead of hosting the ADC, acting as a bridgehead *will* affect overall performance of a server. Microsoft has released the following guidelines to give you a starting point when planning for the ADC.

On a Pentium-class (200MHz) server with 128MB of RAM, adding the ADC should add an average of 8 to 24 percent to the CPU usage. For domain controllers that might be contacted during the synchronization process, expect 6 to 66 percent more CPU utilization, and at the Exchange Server 5.5 bridgehead, expect up to an additional 91 percent CPU utilization. These numbers are not written in stone (and there is a wide range of possible increases), but they can be used as a starting point when determining which servers should accept each role. You should, of course, test this in a lab environment before implementing it in a production environment.

As a comparison, those same functions on a more powerful computer—Pentium II (450MHz) with 256MB of RAM—are as follows:

- On the server running the ADC, 1 to 12 percent higher CPU utilization

- On the domain controller contacted during the synchronization process, 0 to 30 percent more CPU utilization

- On the connecting Exchange Server 5.5 bridgehead, 20 to 36 percent more CPU utilization

---

TIP For a large environment in which you expect a large amount of synchronization traffic, you might even want to dedicate servers to these tasks.

One general rule of thumb—place the server hosting the ADC on the same subnet as the Exchange server and the bridgehead servers if at all possible. If not, try to avoid synchronization across slow or heavily burdened WAN links.

Determine Your Management Strategy

You have the option of controlling the direction in which information is synchronized. You can manage all objects through the Exchange Server administrator program or manage all objects through Active Directory and its tools. After wracking our brains and reading hundreds of pages of Microsoft documentation, we can think of many reasons why you would want to manage your entire environment through Active Directory, but we can't think of a single reason why you would want to limit yourself to managing objects through the Exchange

Server 5.5 directory. Nevertheless, you will need to know that the option is available should you desire to set yourself up this way.

The biggest reason to manage all of your objects through Active Directory is its ability to delegate administrative tasks down to the attribute level of individual objects. You can, for instance, grant an individual the ability to change his or her password *without* granting any other permissions. On the Exchange Server side, however, you are forced to grant permission at the container level; those permissions then pertain to all objects within the container.

The most common practice is to keep the ability to manage objects from both directories and let those changes synchronize in both directions. This allows your Exchange administrators to continue their current functions without much additional training, but it also allows your AD administrators to set up complete accounts (as in complete with e-mail mailboxes).

Decide Which Object Classes and Attributes Will Be Synchronized

One of the biggest decisions you will have to make when configuring the Exchange Server connector will be to determine which objects and attributes will be synchronized from directory to directory. You might not want, for instance, your Exchange custom recipients (placeholders that contain the e-mail address of a foreign mailbox and appear in the global address book for convenience) to be synchronized to your AD database—this would effectively create AD contact objects for nonemployees. You might, however, want your AD distribution groups to be synchronized to your Exchange directory, thus automatically creating e-mail distribution lists out of AD objects. These decisions will have to be considered carefully: as you synchronize more types of objects, you potentially add more network traffic to the process.

When deciding which objects will be synchronized, you should have two primary goals:

- Synchronize only the objects that have a purpose in both environments. In other words, if you are not going to use AD distribution objects within your AD structure, do not include AD or Exchange distribution list objects in the synchronization process.

- Make sure the objects end up in containers that make finding them (the objects) easy for both your users and your administrators.

Microsoft recommends that you accomplish the second goal by mirroring your Exchange OU and AD OU structures. You might, for instance, create the following recipient containers within your Exchange sites:

- Custom Recipients
- Mailboxes
- Distribution Lists

In your Active Directory OU structure, you would then create the following containers:

- Contacts
- Users
- Groups

This organization ensures consistency across both environments.

WARNING We are not all that impressed with the implementation Microsoft suggested. First of all, because the Exchange directory is not as adaptable as the AD structure, you will end up limiting your options for your Active Directory design. Second, and probably more relevant, mailboxes cannot be moved from one recipient container to another in Exchange Server 5.5. The end result is that this plan *might* work if you are implementing both directories at the same time, but it is probably not going to work if your Exchange organization exists before you design and implement Active Directory.

There are three ways to configure the synchronization between AD and Exchange in Microsoft's recommended implementation:

- The easiest way
- The most complex way
- The middle ground

The Easiest Way

If all of the mail recipients within a single Exchange site exist within a single Windows 2000 domain, you have the option of using the simplest connector configuration. In this case, on the Exchange Server side, you configure the Exchange site as both the source and the target of the synchronization process. At the same time, configure the Windows 2000 domain as both the source and target for the other end of the connector. In effect, this means that all objects within the Exchange recipients hierarchy will be synchronized to the Windows 2000 database and all security principals within the Windows 2000 domain will be synchronized to the Exchange Server site.

The secret to this configuration is to move all of the Exchange Server objects to one container within the Active Directory OU structure. After these objects have been synchronized, you can move them to other OUs, and AD will track them for future synchronization.

The Most Complex Way

Create three connection agreements that map each of the Exchange containers to the matching AD OUs. Configure one agreement in which the Exchange Custom Recipients container maps to the AD Contacts OU. This will result in all objects from each container synchronizing to corresponding objects in the other. Configure a second agreement that maps the Mailboxes container in Exchange to the Users OU in Active Directory, and finally, configure a third agreement that maps the Exchange Distribution Lists container to the AD Groups OU. This configuration is shown in Figure 3.39.

FIGURE 3.39: Three separate connection agreements

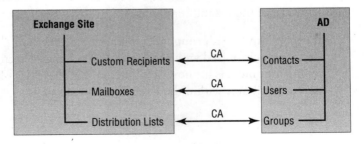

CA = Connection Agreement

The Middle Ground

Instead of configuring three separate connection agreements as suggested in the preceding example, you could configure one connection agreement that maps between the parent containers in both environments, as shown in Figure 3.40.

FIGURE 3.40: A single connection agreement

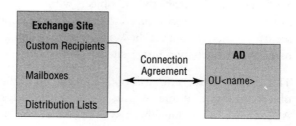

In this configuration, the first time you synchronize the directories, the AD connector will automatically create within the AD structure containers that mirror those in the Exchange hierarchy.

Active Directory Connector Object, Attribute, and Schema Mapping

Once the AD connector has been installed, an ADC policy object is created with Active Directory. This policy object contains a default mapping of objects and attributes between the Exchange Server directory and Active Directory. These *mappings* define which object classes within AD are functionally the same as object classes with the Exchange Server schema. It is possible to change the default lists, but most environments will not require this action. You should, however, be aware of the default mappings.

In general, the user, group, and contact objects within Active Directory are synchronized with objects in the Exchange directory. The following four models list how attributes within these AD object classes map to attributes within the Exchange environment.

Some attributes do not synchronize through the connector by default:

- Windows 2000 attributes

  - All individual account information, such as Account Logging and Account Password

  - Profile information

  - Routing and Remote Access dial-up permissions

  - Access control lists (ACLs)

- Exchange attributes

  - Advanced Security Settings

  - Access control lists (ACLs)

  - Home information store

Determine the Schedule for Synchronization

You can set up individual connection agreements to synchronize at specific times throughout the day. You will have to use the infrastructure information you gathered earlier in your AD design project to determine what times would work the best in your particular environment. You will also have to determine what level of synchronization is acceptable to your company. The two directories can best be described as "loosely synchronized." That basically means that, at any given point in time, changed information from one directory might not have been synchronized to the other. You will have to determine how up-to-date the information must be based upon the business needs of the company. In some cases, changes made in one directory must be made in the other very quickly; in other cases, there is an acceptable amount of delay. Microsoft makes two suggestions that you should keep in mind during your test:

- If you expect large numbers of changes, you should configure multiple agreements that synchronize at different times.

- If it is acceptable, you should configure your agreements so that synchronization occurs at night.

Microsoft-Defined Solutions

Microsoft defines four different model environments that you should follow when planning your AD connector implementation. From a design perspective, one of these "cookie-cutter" solutions will work in every environment that you can imagine. From an exam perspective, you should be able to identify these environments and describe the proposed AD connector solution.

Model 1: A Single Windows 2000 Domain and a Single Exchange Server Site

Basically, this is the simple solution we discussed earlier. In general, smaller companies with a single physical facility and under 5,000 users will use this connector strategy. Figure 3.41 depicts a Model 1 environment.

FIGURE 3.41: A Model 1 environment

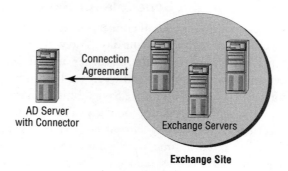

TIP Exam Hint: Microsoft will probably add multiple servers to the graphic for questions regarding this model. Remember that every AD server within a domain and every Exchange server within a site hold the same directory database (for their environment). Unless you are asked to pick a bridgehead server, you can ignore the representation of servers—they are there to distract you.

In a Model 1 environment, you really have only one decision to make: Where do you want management to happen? You have three choices:

- Windows Active Directory only
- Exchange Server 5.5 Administrator only
- Both Windows 2000 and Exchange Server 5.5

In most cases, you will want the majority of object management to happen within Active Directory because it is the more flexible of the two directories. You might also want to limit your Exchange administrators to working within Exchange Administrator so that they do not need permissions within Active Directory.

Model 2: Single Windows 2000 Domain and Multiple Exchange Server Sites

This configuration will most likely be found in organizations with up to 20,000 users and/or multiple locations. In reality, from a design perspective, Model 2 is not much different from Model 1. Basically, you just set up a connector to each of the Exchange sites within the Exchange organization, as shown in Figure 3.42.

FIGURE 3.42: A Model 2 environment

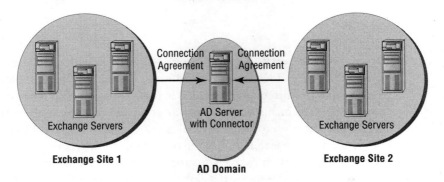

Once again, your only real design decision will be to consider where administration should take place. You have the same options as in Model 1 (Exchange only, Active Directory only, or both). You will, however, have to make this decision for each connection agreement.

Model 3: Multiple Windows 2000 Domains and a Single Exchange Server Site

It should be rare to encounter a set of circumstances in which you would have multiple Windows 2000 domains and only one Exchange Server site. In general, each AD domain can contain more objects than any single Exchange site, so the opposite arrangement (Model 4) is more likely. If, however, the original network started out with Windows NT and multiple domains *and* Exchange Server was added at a later date, it is conceivable that the Exchange Server organization would have been designed as a single site, whereas the NT environment (the older of the two) would have originally been set up with multiple domains.

Once again, this is a fairly easy environment to set up. Create an AD connector from each Active Directory domain to the Exchange Server site, as shown in Figure 3.43.

FIGURE 3.43: A Model 3 environment

Many people get confused at this point—they assume that if you synchronize the Exchange site to two different Windows 2000 domains, each Exchange object will be created in *both* domains. This is not the case. Earlier we mentioned that it was good design to place the AD connector either on or near a global catalog server. The reason that this is good design is that during the synchronization process, the connector searches for an Active Directory object with the same name as the Exchange object—using the global catalog. When it finds a match, it will synchronize changes from the Exchange side to the correct domain within the Windows 2000 environment.

Model 4: Multiple Windows 2000 Domains and Multiple Exchange Server Sites

Model 4 will be encountered only when working with very large companies. Because of the potential complexity of both the Active Directory structure and the Exchange Server organization, your connector strategy can become very complex. This is especially true if you did not follow Microsoft's recommendation (which we described earlier) of matching the two environments (having containers with the same function in both environments). You might end up creating multiple connection agreements between each Windows 2000 domain and each Exchange Server site. Your connectors have to be set up so that each Windows 2000 domain that needs to synchronize has a connector to each Exchange site with which it needs to synchronize. Sound complex? It should! Designing from a Model 4 environment can be like putting together a complex puzzle—it takes time, and you *have* to understand the relationships between the two directories. Figure 3.44 demonstrates how the connectors would be configured in a relatively small Model 4 environment.

FIGURE 3.44: A model 4 environment

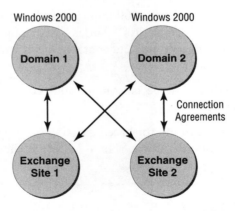

For your MCSE exam, there are a couple of points to remember:

- You do not need to install an AD connector in any Windows 2000 domains that do not have objects with corresponding objects in the Exchange directory.

- With multiple connectors, it is likely that there will be two paths through which a particular object could be synchronized. The AD connector will check the primary NT account server attribute of the Exchange Server object being synchronized. If the NT account exists in any domain to which the site has a connector, synchronization will occur with that Windows 2000 domain across the appropriate connector.

The Four Models in Review

After looking over the four models for the first time, many students are confused. In fact, we've had a few students decide to manage the two environments separately, hoping that Microsoft will make this easier in a later release of Windows 2000 or Exchange Server. After listening to our classroom lectures, though, most of these students see that this whole issue sounds complex but is, in reality, fairly straightforward.

You really have only three design decisions to make:

- Where should management take place—from the Active Directory side, the Exchange Server side, or both?

- Which Windows 2000 domains need to connect to which Exchange Server sites? (This is based upon the placement of user, distribution group, and contact objects within the AD domain hierarchy.)

- Are there any special configuration considerations for your connectors?

If you see a connector-based question on your exam, answer these three questions and you should be able to choose the correct answer!

Exam Essentials

This section is not really about the Exchange connector—it's about how to connect Active Directory to other directory-based systems.

We've used the Exchange connector as an example for the simple reason that it is the only "official" connector at this time. When you are studying for this objective, keep in mind that the concepts are more important than the details. (But at the same time remember that Microsoft would like to sell Exchange Server, so a few of the questions might focus on this specific connector.)

Keep in mind the difference between replication and synchronization.   Replication is the process of keeping copies of the same directory database up to date. Synchronization is a process that keeps information in two separate directories up to date.

Understand the purpose of a connection agreement.   Think of the connection agreement as the description, or configuration, of the connection itself. It defines the relationship between the directories.

Understand the purpose of using a bridgehead server.   Funneling synchronization traffic through specific servers allows you to control the overhead of synchronization traffic on your servers and the links that connect them.

Know the four model environments, as defined by Microsoft, that can be used as templates for designing your connection environments.   See the Critical Information section for details.

Key Terms

AD Connector   Software that allows the synchronization of information between two directories.

Connection Agreement   A description of the relationship between two directories that is used to define the synchronization process.

Directory Synchronization   The process of keeping two separate directories up to date with change information.

Sample Questions

1. Which of the following best defines the function of an Active Directory connector?

A. A software component used by the global catalog server to connect to AD servers in each domain

B. A software component used to authenticate resource requests across domains within Active Directory

C. A software component that allows synchronization between dissimilar directory services

D. A software component used to configure a redundant network connection between domain controllers

Answer: C.   Active Directory connectors allow directories from different vendors or applications to communicate and share information.

2. Which of the following best defines directory synchronization?

A. A process that keeps the information in two separate directories the same

B. A process that ensures that the date and time match on all domain controllers within a domain

C. A process that updates the information in the global catalog servers

D. A process that ensures that changes made to the Active Directory database are applied in the correct chronological order

Answer: A.   Directory synchronization is a process that keeps the information in two separate directories synchronized; that is, changes made to information in one directory will be propagated automatically to the other.

3. The relationship between two directories connected through an Active Directory connector is managed through which of the following?

A. The `ADC.ini` file

ᴃ **B.** The connection agreement

C. The translation manager component of Active Directory

D. The Exchange Server directory replication process

Answer: B.   Installing an AD connector adds a service within Windows 2000 Server. This service becomes a component of the AD subsystem. Once this software has been installed, you must build a relationship between AD and the target environment. A *connection agreement* defines this relationship. The connection agreement holds the communication configuration between the two environments.

4. The servers that receive and forward the changes between directories are known as _____.

A. S/F servers

B. ADC management servers

C. Bridgehead servers

D. ADC domain controllers

Answer: C.   Bridgehead servers receive and forward the changes between the directories.

5. Which of the following are recommended specifications for bridgehead servers? Choose all that apply.

A. They should have adequate resources (CPU and memory) to support the overhead of handling synchronization traffic.

B. They should be well connected to the network. In general, the bridgehead servers should be highly available; usually this means placing them on your backbone or in the center of the physical environment.

C. If at all possible, the bridgehead server should also act as a global catalog server. If this is not possible, then the bridgehead server should at least be on the same network segment as a global catalog server.

D. They must also act as the schema master for the Active Directory tree.

Answer: A, B, C.   There are certain conditions that you will have to consider when choosing which servers will act as the bridgeheads for any environment: They should have adequate resources (CPU and memory) to support the overhead of handling synchronization traffic, they should be well connected to the network, and they should also act as a global catalog servers.

6. In an environment with the AD Exchange connector installed and running, if an administrator changes the value of a user's telephone number attribute, which of the following actions will take place?

A. The entire object that represents that user will be sent across the connector to the other directory.

B. All objects within the user's home container will be updated in the other directory.

C. The user's new telephone number value will be sent across the connector.

D. The administrator will have to manually enter the user's new telephone number in the other directory.

Answer: C.   Only those attributes that have changed are replicated across the connector.

7. In a large environment with a lot of changes to the directories, Microsoft suggests which two of the following?

A. Configure multiple agreements that synchronize at different times.

B. Create one connector and have all traffic use that connector to take advantage of the compression capabilities built in to the connector.

▷ **C.** If it is acceptable, you should configure your agreements so that synchronization occurs at night.

D. Manage all changes through the Exchange Administrator to take advantage of its more flexible nature.

Answer: A, C.   Microsoft makes two suggestions that you should keep in mind during your design: (1) If you expect large numbers of changes, you should configure multiple agreements that synchronize at different times. (2) If it is acceptable, you should configure your agreements so that synchronization occurs at night.

Design an Active Directory site topology.

- **Design a replication strategy.**

One of the more expensive ongoing costs of a network is bandwidth. In a single-site environment, bandwidth is cheap—lay some cable and you own the world! As soon as you move to the world of WANs, however, costs start to skyrocket. Controlling the traffic placed on wide area links is one of the most important aspects of network design.

Although you cannot eliminate all of the traffic on your networks (after all, networks exist to move data), you can design your networks to eliminate unnecessary traffic and control what's left. That's what this section is all about—eliminating as much of the AD traffic as possible and taking control of what's left through the proper use of AD sites.

Critical Information

When compared to earlier Microsoft networking products (specifically Windows NT) Windows 2000 with Active Directory is more flexible, more extensible, more easily managed in an enterprise-sized environment, and is easier to administer. On the other hand, a poorly designed Active Directory structure can play havoc with your network infrastructure. Active Directory can eat up available bandwidth and bring a network to its knees. In that respect, this is the first of the objectives that forces you to think along physical rather than logical lines.

When you are taking your MCSE exam, remember that the ultimate goal when planning a replication strategy and site topology is to control network traffic.

Design a Replication Strategy

Each Windows 2000 domain has at least one server that acts as a domain controller. Unlike earlier versions of NT, each domain controller is involved in managing changes and updates to the database. Earlier versions of NT were configured in a *single-master environment*. The primary domain controller (PDC) maintained and managed the master copy of the domain database and was in charge of replicating changes to the backup domain controllers (BDCs) of its domain. In a single-master environment, the master (in this case, the PDC) is a single point of failure. If for some reason the PDC is unavailable, no changes can be made to the database.

In Windows 2000 Server, each domain controller holds a complete copy of the AD directory for its own domain. In this respect, it is much like earlier versions. The difference, however, is that each Windows 2000 domain controller can accept and make changes to the database and then replicate those changes to other domain controllers. An environment like this, where multiple computers are responsible for managing changes, is known as a *multi-master environment*. A multi-master environment offers numerous advantages over the old single-master configuration. Here are some of those advantages:

- There is no single point of failure. Because every domain controller can accept changes to the database, there is no domain controller that is critical to the process.

- Domain controllers that can accept changes to the database can be distributed throughout the physical network. This allows administrators to make changes on a local computer and let a background process (replication) ensure that those changes are updated on all other domain controllers in a timely and efficient manner.

Types of Replication

There are two basic types of replication in a Windows 2000 Server environment:

- *Intrasite replication* occurs between domain controllers within a site.

- *Intersite replication* occurs between domain controllers in different sites.

When planning your site structure and replication strategy, it is important to understand the methods used for each type of replication traffic.

INTRASITE REPLICATION

As defined earlier, intrasite replication involves domain controllers from the same site. These computers use *remote procedure calls (RPCs)* to perform the replication process.

A process known as the Knowledge Consistency Checker (KCC) generates a *ring topology* for replication among the domain controllers within the site, as shown in Figure 3.45. This ring topology defines the path through which changes will flow within the domain. Any changes will follow the ring until all domain controllers have received them.

NOTE Creating a ring topology ensures that there are two paths that changes can follow from one domain controller to another (either direction on the ring).

The KCC will also configure the ring so that there are no more than three hops between any two domain controllers within the domain. On occasion, this will call for the creation of multiple rings within a single domain, as you can see in Figure 3.46.

FIGURE 3.45: A ring topology for replication

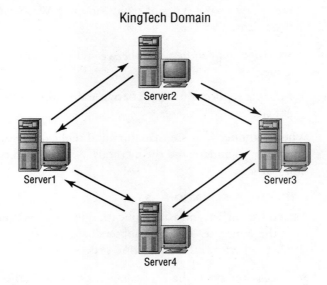

KingTech Domain

FIGURE 3.46: The three-hop rule of intrasite replication

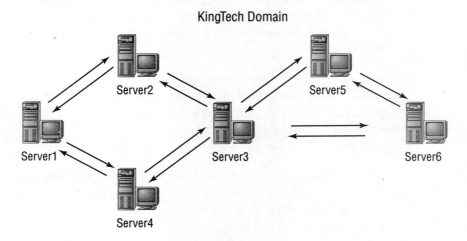

KingTech Domain

There is no master KCC server within a site. Each domain controller runs the KCC service to generate the intrasite topology for the site in which it resides. Assuming that all of the domain controllers are able to communicate and that there are no other problems within the domain structure, each domain controller should arrive at the same topology as every other domain controller. After this analysis, the KCC will create the appropriate AD connection objects on the local server. In this way, each of the domain controllers is included in the overall replication process. The KCC periodically analyzes the replication topology within a site to ensure efficiency. If a domain controller has been added or removed, the KCC will reconfigure the ring for optimum efficiency.

INTERSITE REPLICATION

The replication topology between sites is created in a completely different manner. First, within each site certain domain controllers need to be assigned the role of *bridgehead server*. Bridgehead servers are responsible for the physical act of transferring replication traffic between sites.

The KCC on one domain controller in each site is given the task of reviewing the intersite topology and creating connection objects for incoming traffic on all bridgehead servers within the site. To put that another way, the KCC on each bridgehead server does *not* create the connection objects for the local server—this task is off-loaded to another server within the site (which does not even have to be a bridgehead server itself). This server is known as the *InterSite Topology Generator (ISTG)*. The first AD server to boot within a site will assume the role of ISTG—there is no election and there are no criteria for accepting this responsibility. The same server will hold this role until it becomes unavailable for a specific amount of time, known as the KCC site generator renewal interval. (The default interval is 60 minutes and can be changed through a Registry edit.) The ISTG writes a new value to one of its properties (the KCC site generator renewal interval) every 30 minutes. Because this is seen as changed information, it is replicated to every other domain controller within the site. All domain controllers within the site monitor this attribute to ensure that the ISTG is available. In the event that a new ISTG needs to be established, each domain controller looks at the list of domain controllers within its site, using the globally unique identifier (GUID) value to determine which servers should take over the role.

NOTE All in all, the information about the KCC is of academic interest but of little use during the design process. All you can influence is how often the role is advertised—you have no control over which domain controller accepts the responsibility.

Behind the Scenes of Replication

Understanding the process of replication can give you the skills necessary to optimize that traffic and design your AD environment to minimize its adverse effect on the network. In the next few sections, we'll discuss the process of replication from an academic perspective, and then we'll use our new insights during our analysis.

UPDATE SEQUENCE NUMBERS

When a change is made to the database stored on a domain controller—either through a user action or through replication from another domain controller—the domain controller assigns the change an *update sequence number (USN)*. Each domain controller keeps its own USNs and increments the value for each change that occurs.

NOTE With respect to a single domain controller, you can think of the USN as a change counter. Each domain controller will have different values for changes that occur on its copy of the directory database. These values are not synchronized between domain controllers within a domain.

When the domain controller writes the change to the database, it also writes the USN of the change to that property. This is seen as a single transaction and will succeed or fail as a whole. In other words, AD will protect against a change being applied to the database without a corresponding USN also being recorded. This is an important feature because USNs are used to determine which changes need to be replicated to other domain controllers. This process is depicted in Figure 3.47.

If the value of the telephone number property for user Bob needs to be changed, the domain controller will check its current value for the database USN. Let's say the last USN applied to a change was 3. When the system writes Bob's new telephone number to the database, it will increment the USN and write *both* the changed data and the USN to Bob's object. The system USN will also be incremented to reflect this new value. The next change to the database will receive a higher USN.

FIGURE 3.47: **Applying a change to the database**

Object—Bob

Property	USN	Value
Telephone number	6	555-1000

MULTIPLE USNS

There are a couple of new concepts to keep in mind here. First, notice that the domain controller is keeping track of the highest USN value that it has assigned to a change. (Microsoft doesn't really have a name for this value, but we're going to call it the DCUSN for *Domain Controller USN*.) This allows the domain controller to increment the value for each change, ensuring that no duplicate USNs exist and that each USN is larger than the preceding one. Second, each property of every object really stores two values: the actual data (such as Bob's telephone number) and the USN assigned to the value the last time the attribute was changed.

TIP Reread that preceding paragraph! Its two main concepts—a domain controller USN value that represents the highest USN assigned, and the fact that *every* property stores the USN assigned at the time of change—are crucial to understanding how replication works.

The Process of Replication

Now we can discuss the process of replicating Bob's new telephone number to all domain controllers within the domain. Each domain controller stores the DCUSN from all other domain controllers at the last time of replication, as shown in Figure 3.48.

FIGURE 3.48: DCUSN tables

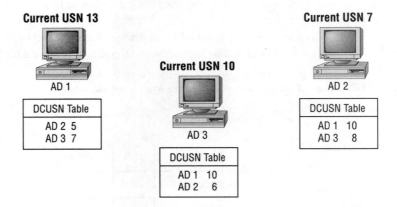

During the replication process, each domain controller sends its current DCUSN value to all of the other domain controllers in the domain. These servers compare this current value to the value that they have stored in their DCUSN table. If the current value is higher than the stored value, changes need to be replicated.

Look back at Figure 3.48. During replication, domain controller AD 2 will send its current DCUSN, which is 7, to both domain controllers AD 1 and AD 3. The last time that replication occurred with AD 1, the USN for AD 2 was 5. Because the current value is 7, AD 1 will request changes 6 and 7 from AD 2. AD 2 will search its database for the properties with these USN values and replicate them to AD 1, as shown in Figure 3.49.

FIGURE 3.49: Replication of specific changes

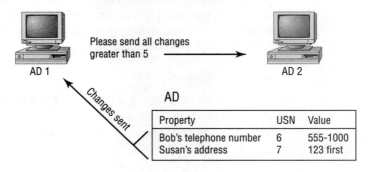

BENEFITS OF USING USNS

Using USN values to determine which changes to replicate eliminates the need for precise time stamps for changes (and for time to be synchronized among the domain controllers). Time stamps are assigned to each change, however, for tie-breaking purposes. These time stamps decide which change should be implemented if a specific attribute was changed on two or more domain controllers during the replication interval. In that event, the change with the latest time stamp is placed in the database; any other changes are discarded.

Using USNs also simplifies the recovery process after a failure. When a domain controller comes back online after a recovery, it just needs to ask all of the other domain controllers for all changes with USN values higher than the last value stored in its DCUSN table. This is true even if the replication process is temporarily interrupted (as when a wide area link goes down, for instance). When communication is reestablished, the domain controller will request all changes with USNs greater than the last change applied to the database.

Propagation Dampening

As you saw earlier in this chapter, the KCC creates the replication topology for intrasite replication. The KCC creates a loop topology so that domain controllers have multiple paths for sending and receiving updates, as shown in Figure 3.50.

FIGURE 3.50: Replication topology

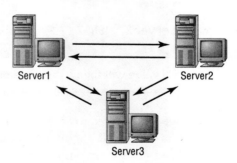

Server1   Server2

Server3

Although a loop topology increases fault tolerance and can increase performance, it can also result in a domain controller receiving the same update from two different domain controllers. To prevent this, Active Directory uses a *propagation dampening* scheme. Propagation dampening is the process of preventing unnecessary replication of directory changes.

UP-TO-DATE VECTORS

USNs can be used to determine which changes have been replicated from another domain controller, but they do nothing to prevent changes from being replicated from multiple sources. This is why, in addition to USNs, Windows 2000 domain controllers also store *up-to-date vectors*. An up-to-date vector identifies the source of the originating write to a property. The *originating write* to any property identifies the source domain controller for the change. If a user changes his or her password, for instance, and that change is made to the copy of the directory stored on Server1, on Server1 the change would be considered an originating write; the change made there is directly related to some action performed by a user. In contrast, a *nonoriginating write* would be a change that was received through the replication process. Another way to look at this is to consider the server where the change originates as the source of the originating writes.

As an example, let's look at the process of updating a change in an environment with three domain controllers: Server1, Server2, and Server3. If a user changes his or her password at Server1, the server updates the value in the database and assigns that change the next incremental value for its USN. What is actually stored in the directory will contain this:

```
Password, Server1, USN-7
```

NOTE   The USN value will follow the rules outlined earlier.

When this change is replicated to Server2, Server2 writes the change and increments its own USN. The actual record in the directory database remains the same as it was at Server1:

```
Password, Server1, USN-7
```

Server1 has also replicated this change to Server3. Server3 stores the same information, including the up-to-date vector information. When Server2 begins the replication process with Server3, Server3 will send its current USN value *and* all of its up-to-date vectors. Server2 compares the up-to-date vectors received from Server3 to its own. Server3 will not send any changes that have already been replicated to Server2.

Strategies for Replication

From a testing perspective, our discussion of the replication process can help you make decisions about server placement within a site. Given that the KCC defines and controls the replication process, and that there is a process to dampen propagation, we can concentrate on the tried and true rule for server placement—put server near the users who will access them.

Once you have an estimate of the amount of replication that will take place within a site and between sites, you can start to consider a few replication strategies. Since you really have very little control over replication within a site, your biggest decision will be the type of hardware you are going to implement. There are two schools of thought:

- Numerous less powerful (but less expensive) domain controllers.

- Fewer, but more powerful, servers.

Some experts maintain that having numerous domain controllers spread throughout a site helps to spread the workload of authentication across many servers and helps to localize traffic—users log on to the network through a domain controller that is near them. The downside to this approach is that the more domain controllers you have, the more replication traffic will be generated. This strategy is best for environments with a lot of available bandwidth on their networks (relative to the number of users accessing their servers.)

Having fewer, but more powerful, servers reduces the overall amount of replication traffic on the network because fewer replicas need to be kept up to date. Of course this also means that users are more likely to log on through a server that is not physically close to them, thereby adding a certain amount of network traffic, which might slow the logon process down. Using this strategy also implies less fault tolerance—given fewer copies of the directory. (Of course, with today's reliable servers the odds of multiple servers going down simultaneously is slight.)

Define Site Boundaries

AD sites are used to organize well-connected computers within a network to optimize the use of available bandwidth. The definition of *well-connected computers* varies from textbook to textbook, but for our purposes, we'll define it as computers that are connected over highly reliable, fast connections with adequate bandwidth. Now you can see why the definition varies—terms like *high reliability*, *fast*, and *adequate* are subjective in nature. Unfortunately, this is the best definition available. We'll define high reliability as links that have no history of connection problems, are as fast as LAN speeds (10Mbps or better), and have bandwidth that is adequate to handle your estimate of the AD traffic that will be generated. Using the tools described earlier and your knowledge of the business, you should be able to provide a fairly accurate estimate of network traffic. In general, well-connected computers are usually those that are connected by LAN technologies as opposed to WAN technology.

Computers that are connected by links that do not match our three criteria (reliable, fast, adequate bandwidth) should not be organized into the same AD site. In an environment with numerous or frequent changes to the AD database, the traffic generated by the replication process can be excessive, thereby saturating slower WAN links. Proper design of the AD site boundaries can help you control the AD traffic and optimize your Windows 2000 environment. Here are a few of the types of traffic that sites can optimize:

Workstation Logon Traffic   When a user logs on to the network, Windows 2000 computers search for domain controllers in the same site as the workstation.

Replication Traffic   When changes are made to the AD database, they must be replicated to all domain controllers for the domain where the changes occurred. Site boundaries can be used to control when and how those changes are replicated between domain controllers in different sites.

Distributed File System (DFS)   If a file is located on multiple servers, the user will be directed to a server within their own site.

File Replication Service (FRS)   FRS replicates the contents of the SYSVOL directory and uses site boundaries to determine its replication topology.

Site-Aware Applications   Third-party application vendors can easily use the site boundaries to provide a fault-tolerant environment for their applications. You might, for instance, install an application in multiple locations and let AD direct users to the closest available copy (using site boundaries as the guide).

Site Boundary Design Considerations

Planning for replication and other types of traffic requires you to balance three major considerations: performance, efficiency, and costs. Each of these will play a role in your final design decisions.

PERFORMANCE

For our discussion of AD sites, we are referring to performance strictly in terms of AD replication. The best performance would be a situation in which changes are immediately replicated to all domain controllers in a domain. As an example, if user TomS in Figure 3.51 has a connection to server FS1 and changes his password, that change would have to be replicated to all of the other domain controllers within the Montana domain (FS2 and FS3). In a perfect world, this update would be immediate. In reality, though, there will a certain delay to the actual replication of the change. This delay is known as replication latency. *Replication latency* is the time it takes for all domain controllers within a domain to be informed of a change to the AD database. The smaller the latency, the better the performance.

FIGURE 3.51: Replication latency

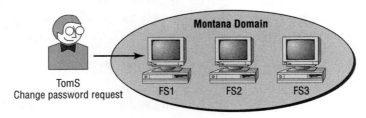

EFFICIENCY

At odds with performance is replication efficiency. In a real-world implementation, it is usually not efficient to replicate a single change. It is usually more efficient to batch multiple changes into a single transfer of data. If an administrator is creating multiple user accounts, for instance, it would be more efficient to update the other controllers with multiple accounts rather than opening a connection and replicating each change as it is made. For more information on the costs of connecting computers using IP see *TCP/IP 24seven*™ (Sybex, 1999).

COSTS

For the replication process, the cost of replication is measured in bandwidth used to accomplish the transfer. Within a LAN, these costs are negligible (in most cases), but across wide area connections, the costs can be substantial. We've stressed this point numerous times (and that should be taken as an exam hint!)—wide area connectivity is one of the most expensive components of any network. Controlling the traffic across these expensive links should be a prime design objective.

Your goal as an AD design engineer is to balance these three considerations. You are looking for a site structure that provides the most efficient and least costly replication while also minimizing replication latency. For intrasite replication, you would expect to see a low latency to ensure that users within a site are always using recent information in the database. Efficiency is maintained by batching the changes for replication. Within a site, changes will be replicated within five minutes. The originating server (the server where the change occurred) will notify its replication partners within the site of the changes and they will request an update when convenient. Replication between sites is another story: Intersite replication assumes that there is limited bandwidth available for the transfer. The process starts with a compression of the data about to be replicated, usually to about 10 percent of its original size. This optimizes the use of whatever bandwidth is available. To further optimize intersite replication, you can schedule when replication will occur between sites. Of course, this can result in a higher replication latency.

Planning Domain Controller Placement

Before planning the site boundaries for an environment, you should plan the placement of domain controllers. The bottom line here is usually performance from the users' perspective. Domain controllers must be placed so as to respond to user requests in a timely manner. This is, of course, a subjective decision. *Timely* will be defined differently in each environment. Your earlier analysis of the business will help in making these decisions. We'll discuss the placement of domain controllers within a network in Chapter 4, "Designing Services Locations."

Planning Site Boundaries

Site boundaries are defined by the IP subnetting structure of the network. *Sites* define the physical structure of the network by organizing subnets into physical groups that match our criteria for well-connected computers. If, for instance, your network consists of a location in Tampa that contains three subnets and another in Detroit that contains one subnet, you might define two AD sites—one that contains the three subnets in Tampa and another that contains the subnet in Detroit. Because sites define physical boundaries, a site may contain domain controllers from more than one NT domain.

When planning site boundaries, you should consider the estimated amount of traffic that will be generated between servers. Although the data *is* compressed when sent between sites, the compression does not occur until the amount of data exceeds 50,000 bytes. In some cases, the estimated "bursts" of traffic will be less than this amount—in such cases, there may be no reason to create a separate site because no real traffic reduction would take place. Of course, you might want to schedule the replication traffic on the link, in which case a site would be appropriate.

Site Links

The connection between sites is known as a *site link*. A site link is usually a representation of the wide area connection between two locations, though it can also represent a backbone that connects multiple locations. An example of each situation is shown in Figure 3.52.

FIGURE 3.52: Site links

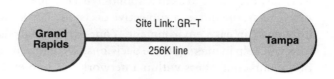

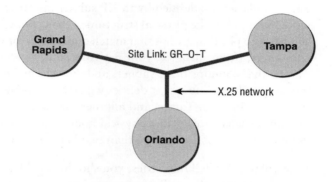

Each site link is made up of four components:

Transport The actual technology used to transfer data, such as a T1 link or 256K line.

Member Sites Those sites connected by the site link.

Cost A value assigned to the connection and used to determine the path of replication in the event that two or more paths are available. Assigning costs to site links allows you to build a fault-tolerant replication topology.

Schedule The times that replication will occur.

Schedules

Site links are used to connect physical locations for the purposes of replication. To control the adverse effects of replication traffic on wide area links, you have the option to schedule when replication can occur. Based upon your traffic analysis of each link, you should be able to determine whether a fixed schedule is needed and, if so, at what times each link has enough available bandwidth to handle the additional traffic. Obviously, you would want to schedule replication traffic for periods in which there is little traffic on the link.

When you apply a schedule to a site link, you are determining when replication can travel across the link. In environments where traffic crosses multiple site links, it is possible to set up schedules in which replication cannot function. In Figure 3.53, for instance, we have a large single-domain environment that spans multiple locations. To improve logon performance, a domain controller has been placed in each facility. Because of the limited bandwidth available to some locations, schedules have been set up for the site links.

FIGURE 3.53: Site links in a large environment

The site link S1–S2 has been scheduled to allow replication between 8:00 P.M. and 11:00 P.M. Site link S2–S3 has been set up for replication between midnight and 2:00 A.M. Given that there is *never* a time when traffic can move completely across the environment from site S1 to site S3, replication will never occur between those two sites. When designing your replication schedules, you must always consider the entire path that traffic must follow to complete the process.

Other Control Mechanisms

Using schedules is only one of the ways available to control replication traffic on site links. You can also assign costs to each site link to control the path that the traffic will follow. In Figure 3.54, for example, the company has two main locations and six remote locations. Each remote location connects to a main office with a 256K line. Most of the remote locations also have dial-up connections to other remote locations.

FIGURE 3.54: Assigning costs to site links

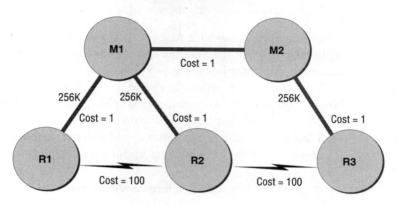

By assigning a high cost to the dial-up links between remote sites, you can ensure that replication traffic will use the 256K lines to the main offices—lines that should (it is hoped) be more reliable and have more available bandwidth. The cost of replication is the sum of the costs for all site links involved. Moving from site R1 to site R2 over the dial-up connection would have a cost of 100. The same replication process would have a cost of only 2 if the path was R1–M1 and M1–R2.

You can also control the amount of traffic placed on a line by setting the number of minutes between replication attempts on site links. By default, replication will occur every 15 minutes. Increasing this interval will not result in less overall traffic, but it will cut down on the frequency of the traffic—perhaps lessening congestion. (Remember, though, that this *will* increase replication latency.)

Site Link Bridges

Site links are considered transitive in nature—that is, if three sites are connected by site links, as shown in Figure 3.55, a replication path exists between all of the sites. (Site 1 can replicate with site 3 by using the two site links.)

FIGURE 3.55: The transitive nature of site links

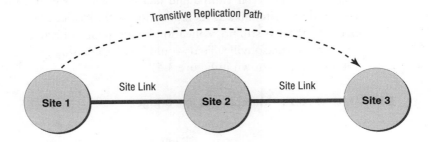

This system works well in a fully routed IP network. In the event that your entire network is not fully routed, you can turn off the transitive nature of site links and configure all replication paths manually. There will be few real-world implementations in which this ability is of value, but you will need to understand it for the MCSE exam. Once the transitive nature of site links has been disabled, you will have to configure *site link bridges* between sites that are not physically connected. In the example shown in Figure 3.56, for instance, there are site links between Grand Rapids and Tampa, Tampa and Orlando, and Orlando and Jacksonville.

FIGURE 3.56: Site link bridges

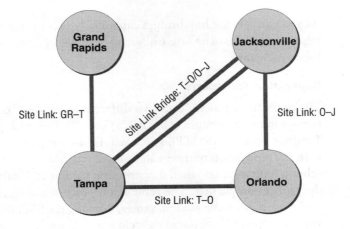

Because the site links are no longer transitive, a site link bridge has been created between Tampa and Jacksonville. This bridge uses the T–O and O–J site links as its replication path. Notice that, in the example, there is still no replication between Grand Rapids and Orlando or Jacksonville. That would involve creating two more site link bridges, as shown in Figure 3.57.

FIGURE 3.57: Multiple site link bridges

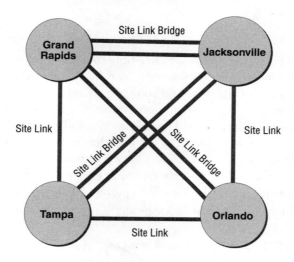

As you can see, site link bridges can quickly become confusing. Most experts agree that site link bridges should be used only where absolutely necessary.

Replication Transports

The replication process uses two different methods of communication—remote procedure calls (RPCs) over TCP/IP and Simple Mail Transfer Protocol (SMTP). RPCs will be used if a direct connection with the replication partner can be achieved. SMTP messages, on the other hand, are used when a connection cannot be established with the replication partner. The replication process will send its data in the form of simple mail messages, utilizing the SMTP capability to store and forward messages as recipients become available. SMTP is an ideal mechanism in an unreliable environment. There is a drawback, though—because the data is sent in mail format, it is encapsulated within an SMTP packet. This encapsulation can add 80 to 100 percent more traffic than RPCs.

Exam Essentials

The bottom line with this exam objective is controlling traffic across expensive WAN links. On your exam the best design will usually consist of at least one site for each physical location. One hint, though—remember that a site is meaningless unless a domain controller exists there. In other words, if you have a location with no servers, you needn't create an AD site there.

Know the advantages of a multi-master environment.
Microsoft is really pushing the fact that the directory database is (in most cases) a multi-master environment. The main advantages of this design are that there is no single point of failure and that administrative tasks can be accomplished at *any* domain controller (with a background process handling replication).

Know the difference between intrasite and intersite replication.
Intrasite refers to replication between domain controllers within a site; intersite refers to replication between domain controllers in different sites.

Know the purpose of the KCC.   The KCC generates the replication topology for intrasite replication and creates the connection objects used for intersite replication.

Understand the replication process.   See the Critical Information section for details about USNs, propagation dampening, and up-to-date vectors.

Know the two strategies for replication and the pros and cons of each.   The two strategies are having more (but less powerful) domain controllers or having fewer (but more powerful) domain controllers. See the Critical Information section for details.

Understand the implications of the phrase "well-connected computers" as it applies to site boundaries. Well-connected computers are connected over highly reliable, fast connections with adequate available bandwidth. Domain controllers within a site should always be well connected to each other.

Know the three main considerations used when designing site boundaries. The three considerations are performance, efficiency, and cost.

Know the use of site links and site link bridges. Site links act as the connections between sites. Site link bridges act as the path used to connect sites that are not physically connected.

Key Terms and Concepts

Multi-Master Environment For Active Directory, this refers to the fact that every domain controller can accept changes to the directory database.

Intrasite Replication Replication between domain controllers within an AD site.

InterSite Replication Replication between domain controllers in different AD sites.

Knowledge Consistency Checker (KCC) A process that generates the replication topology within an AD site and creates the replication connections between sites.

Replication Bridgehead Server A Windows 2000 domain controller that is responsible for the physical act of transferring replication traffic between sites.

Intersite Topology Generator (ISTG) The Windows 2000 domain controller that creates the connection objects defined during the KCC process.

Update Sequence Number (USN) A change value used to determine which information has changed and therefore needs to be replicated.

Propagation Dampening   A process used to prevent duplicate replication of changes to the AD database.

Up-to-Date Vector   A value that identifies the originating write for a change to the database.

Originating Write   An AD property that identifies the source domain controller for a change to the database.

Well-Connected Computers   Computers that are connected over highly reliable, fast connections with adequate available bandwidth.

Site Link   The connection between two AD sites.

Site Link Bridge   The logical path over which replication will take between two sites that are not physically connected.

Sample Questions

1. Which of the following best describes a multi-master environment?

A. Multiple changes are sent from the servers.

B. All servers can accept changes and replicate those changes to other servers.

C. It is a distributed management business model.

D. Two or more management consoles are run at a server simultaneously.

Answer: B.   In a multi-master environment, all replicas are peers and can accept changes and replicate those changes throughout the domain. This is the exact opposite of a Windows NT 4 domain structure, which is a single-master environment. A single-master environment has one main copy of the accounts database (which is stored on the PDC), accepts all changes, and replicates them to other domain controllers.

2. The process of one domain controller updating the copy of the domain database stored on another domain controller is known as

_____.

   A. Synchronization

   B. Replication

   C. Distributed File Copy

   D. Subnet updating

   Answer: B.   Replication keeps the copies of the domain database current with each other.

3. The service that is responsible for generating the replication topology is called the:

   A. RepGen

   B. Traffic Control Process

   C. Synchronization Consistency Checker

   D. Knowledge Consistency Checker

   Answer: D.   The KCC is a process that runs automatically and is responsible for generating the replication topology between domain controllers.

4. The function of the InterSite Topology Generator (ISTG) is to ____

_____.

   A. Generate reports on AD network traffic.

   B. Create the AD connection objects between sites.

   C. Automatically configure routers with static routes to optimize AD network traffic.

   D. Perform the authentication between domains necessary for intersite replication.

   Answer: B.   The ISTG automatically creates the AD connection objects necessary to create the replication topology designed by the Knowledge Consistency Checker (KCC).

5. Propagation dampening is used to _____
_____.

   A. Prevent unnecessary replication of directory changes.

   B. Analyze the number of domain controllers and propagate another one automatically to ensure fault tolerance.

   C. Reduce the effect of AD network traffic on a particular segment by increasing the time between packets.

   D. Reduce hard disk use by committing only changes that have been confirmed from multiple sources.

Answer: A.   The replication process uses originating write values to ensure that changes are not replicated back to the server from which they originated.

Design a schema modification policy.

The standard AD schema that ships with Windows 2000 Server will probably be sufficient for most installations, but there might come a time when you need to add to or change the schema. Microsoft has included the ability to add new object classes, add new attributes to existing object classes, and disable object classes and attributes as needed. The goal is to create an AD database that is customized for the way in which a company does business.

TIP   Exam Hint: Although we have dedicated an entire section to this objective, the Microsoft MCSE exam does not test heavily on this subject. In reality, Microsoft does not expect many network administrators to modify the schema except through the installation of additional applications. (Those applications would automatically extend the schema to meet their needs.) Although this is a low-priority objective, it does need to be covered: you just might see a question or two regarding schema customization.

Critical Information

To review, the *schema* of the Active Directory database defines the objects that can be stored there. It is the formal definition of the object classes and attributes that exist in the database. The AD database is no different from any other database that you have worked with in the past. Before you can place information within it, you must lay out a structure to define how to store that data.

What's in a Schema?

Imagine that you were going to build a database to hold the telephone numbers and addresses of your business contacts. You wouldn't just start entering names and addresses, would you? The first step would be to decide exactly what information you would like to store. Your list might include the following:

- Company
- First name
- Last name
- Nickname
- Address
- City
- State
- Zip code
- Country
- Telephone number
- Pager number
- Cellular phone number
- Fax number
- E-mail address

The next step would be to lay out the fields for each record. You would need to decide the type of data each field will hold and the maximum size of each field, as well as add any special formatting requirements that are necessary for consistency.

The Active Directory Schema

The schema of the Active Directory database is much more complex than that of our contact list database. Within the AD database, each different type of record defined is known as an *object class*. The fields, known as *attributes*, for each class might be different from those for other defined classes. The AD schema, for instance, must include definitions for the following database attributes:

Multiple Record Types in a Single Database Traditional databases had one record type defined for each file in the related system of files. In the AD database, you must define a record type for each class of object that you wish to use in your environment.

Multivalue Attributes Certain characteristics of an object class need to store more than one value. A single user's telephone number attribute, for instance, might need to store multiple telephone numbers.

A Definition of How the Various Pieces of the Database Fit Together This is necessary due to the distributed nature of the AD database. Remember that this database is divided into partitions (domains), which are spread across multiple servers. Something in the schema must define how these partitions find each other, communicate, and share information as needed.

Attributes Holding Pointers to All Other Replicas of the Same Partition There might be multiple copies of a single partition; without these attributes, the replication of database changes could not take place.

A Mechanism to Track Changes The replication process requires this of each object and each attribute of each object. This mechanism includes both the up-to-date vector and a time stamp.

Variable, Rather Than Static, Attribute Lengths Some of the data that the database will hold might be textual and the database might grow quite large—over a million objects in a single partition. In other words, each record in the database should take up only as much disk space as necessary but should have the ability to grow as more information is added.

A Hierarchy of Object Classes   To reduce redundant design, the schema is built upon this hierarchy, with subordinate classes inheriting attributes from higher-level object classes.

To make matters even more complex, the Active Directory database schema must be fully—and easily—extensible so that it can grow to meet the changing needs of a dynamic business environment. In other words, the schema must be readily accessible so that changes to the database structure can be made. Make changes to the Active Directory schema by using the Active Directory Schema Manager included with Windows 2000 Server.

At the top of any LDAP-compliant directory service (such as Microsoft Active Directory), there is a special container known as rootDSE. When referring to this container, the appropriate syntax is to refer to LDAP://rootDSE. The rootDSE container contains a number of entries, including the definition of the namespace of the LDAP structure and the schema of the database. The schema itself is stored in the subcontainer that follows this naming context:

CN=schema, CN=configuration, DC=domain_name, DC=domain_root

NOTE   For our purposes, we don't really even have to know where the actual schema is stored—the tools provided by Microsoft will find it. But it is interesting to note that Microsoft has used the industry-standard location so that other LDAP-compliant directory services can communicate (and perhaps synchronize) with AD.

Who Can Modify the Schema?

To make changes to the schema, a user must be a member of the Schema Admins group. By default, the Administrator user account is a member of this group. Although you can add other user accounts to the Schema Admins group, due to the nature of the task—which is complex and has far-reaching consequences—most companies will probably stick with the default. Whoever is going to perform the tasks associated with schema management *must* be knowledgeable in all aspects of Active Directory, the physical infrastructure of the network, and the business processes of the company.

We cannot stress this enough—the person or persons who take responsibility for schema change management must understand the technical aspects of the process, the business needs of the company, and how the two can best be integrated. There will be times when a decision must be made—whether to modify the AD schema to add functionality or to create a separate database to manage information. Take, for instance, our example of the King Technologies contact database. In reality, much of the information that we discussed is already stored within the AD database—in a couple of different object classes. We could, for example, create a user object for each of our clients. Because user objects include attributes such as telephone numbers and addresses, it would seem that this solution might be a great way to utilize the AD database to fulfill a business need. Of course, there are a few problems with this approach—first and foremost is the fact that creating a user account for each client opens a series of security issues that we would have to deal with! In some cases, perhaps even most cases, you will see more real business benefits by creating a separate database rather than adding to the Active Directory schema or modifying it.

What Can Be Modified?

When modifying the directory schema, you may perform the following tasks:

- Create new classes.
- Modify existing classes.
- Create new attributes.
- Modify existing attributes.
- Deactivate classes.
- Deactivate attributes.

> **WARNING** When you modify the schema, you are making a change that affects the structure of the Active Directory database. This is not something that should be done lightly! Before you modify the schema, Microsoft suggests that you review the existing schema to determine if an existing object class or attribute can fulfill your needs.

Modifying Existing Classes or Attributes

Once you have determined that no existing class or attribute will fit your needs, consider modifying the schema. If at all possible, try to modify an existing object or attribute rather than creating a new one.

A user object, for example, has many attributes that might not be applicable to your environment. There are numerous tabs filled with attributes for a user object. You will probably not use all of these attributes in your environment.

> **TIP** Changing a display name for an existing attribute is one of the least intrusive ways to modify the schema to meet your needs.

If schema modification becomes an AD design issue, modify an existing object class if all you need are new attributes. User objects are probably the best example of this situation. Many companies will want to store specific information about users in the directory. Often the generic definition of a user will not contain the additional attributes necessary. If your users do a lot of traveling, for instance, you might want to add attributes that store travel preferences, such as airline frequent-flyer information, and smoking or nonsmoking preferences.

Creating an Auxiliary Class

An *auxiliary class* is really just an extension of an existing object class. For example, you might have two types of users: permanent and temporary. Although the normal user object might be perfect for your permanent employees, you might wish to create an auxiliary class for your temporary workers. The auxiliary class temp workers would be based upon the user class; it would inherit all of the attributes of the user class but could be modified to fit your needs. Basically, an auxiliary class acts as a shortcut—rather than starting from scratch to create a new class, you can start with an existing set of attributes and work from there.

Adding New Classes and Attributes

Add new attributes when no existing attribute meets your needs and when they cannot be modified to meet your needs. This can be an extensive change to the directory database, and you should think carefully before you do it.

WARNING   The most intrusive and potentially dangerous change is to add a new object class. You should take this action only when no other option will fit the needs of your environment.

Can Classes and Attributes Be Deleted?

There is no way to delete an object class or attribute that is in the schema. You can, however, *deactivate* either a class or an attribute. We'll discuss deactivation in the next section.

NOTE   As you can see, there are numerous types of modifications that can be made to the Active Directory database. Although the process is straightforward (albeit *not* exactly easy), modifying the schema is not something that you should do without prior planning. Any time you change the structure of a database, you risk damaging it—not something you want to happen to your network's directory!

Deactivating Classes and Attributes

Classes and attributes are never removed from the schema. Instead, they are deactivated and marked as unused. This prevents irreversible mistakes and improves performance by not forcing a time-consuming cleanup of removed items.

NOTE Deactivating an item is functionally the same as deleting it, but deactivation leaves you the option of reversing your action at a later date.

Here is what happens when you deactivate an object class or attribute:

- That object class or attribute is no longer replicated throughout the network or to the global catalog server.

- You may no longer create objects that are part of the deactivated class or enter data into the attribute. Attempts to do so will return the same error that would be returned if the class or attribute had never existed.

- When an attribute is deactivated, you may no longer use it in definitions of new object classes or add it to an existing class.

- Objects created prior to the deactivation remain in the AD database and will appear in the various tools. You may not, however, change attributes of them; your only real management option is to delete them.

Deactivated object classes and attributes still appear in searches for two reasons:

- You can search for the deactivated information in order to clean up your directory.

- You might not have deleted those objects that were created before the deactivation (which means that you might need to search for them at some point).

You cannot create new objects or attributes with the same name, LDAP display name, or object identifier. This rule is based on common sense because the deactivated object class or attribute is still defined in the schema.

NOTE We'll discuss object identifiers later in this chapter.

What *Cannot* Be Modified?

The bulleted list at the end of the preceding section seems to imply that you can make just about any type of change to the directory that you desire. For the most part, this assumption is true. There are, however, a few notable exceptions.

There are certain attributes and object classes that cannot be disabled or changed. Any attribute whose name begins with the word *system* cannot be changed. This allows Active Directory to protect those attributes that are critical to its functioning.

NOTE   This rule also applies to object classes that you create. If at the time of creation you list *any* attribute as *system*, that attribute cannot be changed later.

Modifying the Schema

Earlier, you read about the concepts of multiple-master and single-master environments. Both *multiple master* and *single master* refer to the process used to replicate changes throughout a distributed, replicated database. In a multiple-master environment, all copies of the database can accept changes and can replicate those changes to all other copies. In a single-master environment, such as the PDC/BDC (primary domain controller/backup domain controller) relationship used in earlier versions of NT, only one copy of the database can accept changes, and the server that holds the writable copy (the primary domain controller) is responsible for replicating them to all other domain controllers.

Windows 2000 Server is a multiple-master environment when it comes to replicating changes to the information stored within the directory database, but it is a single-master environment when it comes to replicating changes to the schema. In other words, there is only one domain controller, known as the *schema master*, on which schema modifications can be made at any given time. In Active Directory, a single-master operation is known as a *Flexible Single Master*

Operations (FSMO). The domain controller that is acting as the schema master is also known as the *schema FSMO*.

NOTE The term *FSMO* (pronounced "fizzmo") has recently been replaced with the term "operations master," but we included it here because a lot of the older Microsoft documentation will still use it.

What Happens When the Schema Is Modified?

When the schema is modified, there is a delay before the changes take effect. This delay is incurred because there are actually two copies of the schema:

- One in memory
- One in the Active Directory

When a modification is made, the change is written to the Active Directory database. Active Directory waits for five minutes after the schema update before it commits the changes to the copy in memory. The copy in memory, known as the *cache schema*, is the schema that is current.

NOTE The copy of the schema used by various system processes and threads is the one stored in memory. This means that approximately five minutes will pass between the time you stop making changes to the schema and the time those changes become apparent.

The reason that the time is approximate is that there might be processes running at the time of the change. Rather than replace the old schema with the new one (in memory), the old and new schemas coexist until all current processes have ended. All new processes are pointed to the new schema, but any running processes continue to use the old. This prevents the introduction of a new schema from corrupting an active process.

During this five-minute interval, you cannot add objects that use a new or modified class or attribute. In other words, you must wait until the update has completed before making use of your changes.

Preparing for Schema Modifications

There are four preliminary steps you must complete before you can proceed with the task of modifying the Active Directory schema:

1. Obtain an OID (Object Identifier) for each new class or attribute you intend to create.

2. Verify your membership in the Schema Admins group.

3. Install Active Directory Schema Manager.

4. Set Registry settings that allow schema modifications.

So far, we've discussed the process of making modifications to the directory as if it were a common administrative practice. As you'll see, this is far from the case!

Obtaining Object Identifiers

Object Identifiers (OIDs) are globally unique object identifiers. By global, we mean that these identifiers are used to define objects and attributes as they are applied to *any* directory service, from Microsoft Active Directory to Novell Directory Services. OIDs are registered with the International Standards Organization (ISO) issuing agency. By having a central group control how object classes and attributes are implemented, the industry can avoid incompatible network directories.

OIDs uniquely define data elements, syntaxes, and various other parts of distributed applications. ISO-issued OIDs are used in many standard technologies, including Open Systems Interconnection (OSI) applications, X.500 directories, Simple Network Management Protocol (SNMP), and many other applications in which a unique identifier is important. Each object class and attribute must have a unique OID if it is to exist in the AD schema. OIDs are organized in a hierarchical structure managed by the ISO.

NOTE You probably won't need to understand the entire OID naming process, but it is important to know that the OID represents a treelike structure much like the container and subcontainer structure of AD.

Lightweight Directory Access Protocol (LDAP) is an important protocol used for accessing information in network directories, such as Microsoft Active Directory. LDAP applications use the ISO-issued OIDs to identify the objects and attributes that are available in *any* directory to which they connect. In other words, to be LDAP accessible, every object and attribute within a directory must have an OID. (The OID itself becomes an attribute of each object defined.)

As stated earlier, the International Standards Organization acts as the issuing agent for new OIDs. To create a new object class or attribute within the AD schema, the first step is to apply to the ISO for an OID. The OID will be expressed as a string of numbers delimited by decimals, such as 1.2.840.xxxxxx.w.y.z. Table 3.2 describes the purpose of each piece of our sample OID.

TABLE 3.2: Decoding OID 1.2.840.*xxxxxx.w.y.z*

Number	Represents
1	This value acts as the root of the ISO hierarchy.
2	American National Standards Institute (ANSI).
840	United States.
xxxxxx	The organization applying for the OID is given a unique identifier.
w	A location within the organization.
y	A division within the location.
z	A group within the division.

Verifying Membership in the Schema Admins Group

Before anyone attempts to make any schema modifications, verify that the person who will perform the procedure is a member of the Schema Admins group. By default, the only member of this group is the Administrator account. (The Administrator account is automatically made a member of the Administrators, Domain Admins, Domain Users, Enterprise Admins, and Schema Admins groups.) The default membership list, consisting of only the Administrator account, will be sufficient for most organizations.

WARNING   Modifying the directory schema is not something that many people should be doing, and there should *never* be multiple people performing modifications simultaneously!

Installing Active Directory Schema Manager

Administrators do not modify the schema as a matter of course, so Microsoft has not installed the Active Directory Schema Manager utility as part of the standard Windows 2000 installation. Your next step in modifying the schema would be to add this snap-in to the MMC (Microsoft Management Console). The Active Directory Schema Manager utility must then be connected to the current FSMO before modifications can take place. You can then change the server that the Active Directory Schema Manager utility points to when making schema modifications. You can also access the dialog box used to set permissions to control which users and groups can perform certain functions in the AD database.

Here are the permissions available for the schema:

- Full Control
- Read
- Write
- Create All Child Objects
- Delete All Child Objects

- Change Schema Master
- Replicate Directory Changes
- Manage Replication Topology
- Replication Synchronization
- Update Schema Cache

The default permissions assignments are described in Table 3.3.

TABLE 3.3: Default Schema Permissions

User or Group	Permissions
Authenticated User	Read
Local System	All permissions
Schema Admins	All permissions except Full Control and Delete All Child Objects
Administrators	Replicate Directory Changes, Manage Replication Topology, Synchronize Replication
Enterprise Domain Controllers	Replicate Directory Changes, Manage Replication Topology, Synchronize Replication

Setting the Registry to Allow Schema Modifications

By default, all domain controllers have read-only access to the schema. To allow modifications, you must set a Registry setting on the domain controller that will act as the FSMO. The Registry parameter must be added to the Registry under the following key:

```
HKEY_Local_Machine\System\CurrentControlSet\Services\
NTDS\Parameters
```

Add the parameter Schema Update Allowed with a data type of REG_DWORD. Set this value to anything other than 0 (zero) to enable modifications.

Only one domain controller can act as the FSMO, so setting this
parameter in the Registry automatically promotes the current domain
controller to the FSMO (and demotes the old one).

NOTE Because the Registry is a critical component of the Windows 2000 environment, be sure to back it up before making any changes. One wrong move and you'll end up having to reinstall Windows 2000 because of a corrupted Registry!

The Five Types of Schema Modifications

As you read earlier, there are five types of modifications that you can
make to the schema:

- Creating a new class

- Modifying an existing class

- Creating a new attribute

- Modifying an existing attribute

- Deactivating a class or attribute

The next few sections discuss the procedures for accomplishing each
of these tasks. All of them are accomplished through the Active Directory Schema Manager (ADSM) snap-in to the MMC.

Creating a New Class

To create a new class, you create a *class-definition object*. In effect,
this class-definition object becomes a container for the attributes that
describe the object class. Within the ADSM utility, right-click the
Class container and choose New ➢ Class. You will be presented with
the Create New Class dialog box, shown in Figure 3.58.

You will have to provide the following information:

Common Name This field is mandatory and is used as the Common Name attribute for the object class. This is an indexed field; it is
used for searches of the database.

FIGURE 3.58: The Create New Class dialog box

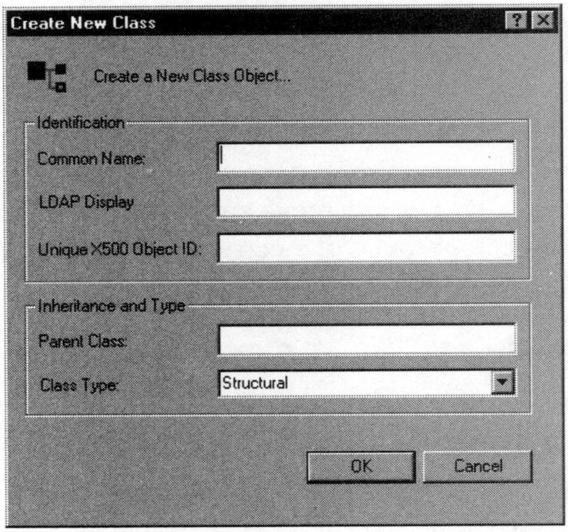

LDAP Display This is another mandatory field. LDAP tools will display the contents of this field to users when they access the directory.

Unique X.500 Object ID This is the OID you received from the ISO.

You will also have to determine whether the class you are creating should be a child to another class. Children inherit the attributes of their parents. This inheritance can be used to create a subtype of an object without having to apply for redundant OIDs or set up redundant attributes. An example would be our company's AD tree. Although we have "normal employees," we also have a subset known as "instructors." The instructors subclass inherits all of the properties of the user object class, but it also has attributes that are specific to the "instructor" type of user (vendor certifications, a list of courses taught, and so on).

There are also three types of classes:

Structural Structural object classes are those from which AD objects can be created.

Abstract Abstract object classes are templates used to build structural objects. An example of an abstract object class is the Top class.

It contains all of the attributes that are mandatory for *every* other object class.

Auxiliary   Auxiliary objects are just lists of attributes that can be added to other object classes.

Modifying an Existing Class

To modify a class, expand the Class container within the ADSM. Right-click the appropriate class and choose Properties. You will see the class Properties dialog box shown in Figure 3.59.

FIGURE 3.59:   **The class Properties dialog box**

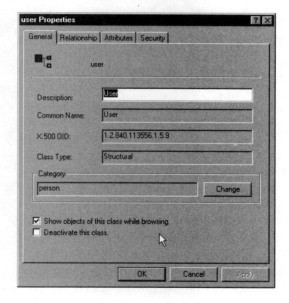

There are four tabs available:

- General
- Relationship
- Attributes
- Security

Each tab controls a different aspect of the object class.

Look at Figure 3.59 to see the General tab. Here you can change items pertaining to how the class fits into the schema.

Figure 3.60 shows the Relationship tab. Here you can assign auxiliary object classes to this structural class.

FIGURE 3.60: The Relationship tab of the class Properties dialog box

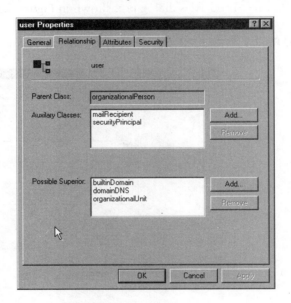

The Attributes tab is shown in Figure 3.61. Here you can add either mandatory or optional attributes to the object class.

Finally, Figure 3.62 shows the Security tab. Here you can assign default permissions to this class of object. This can be useful if you need to apply special security to a class of objects but do not want to have to repeat the assignments each time you create an object. You might, for instance, want a certain type of object to be visible only to members of the Administrators group. By applying the permissions here, they would become the default for this class of object.

FIGURE 3.61: The Attributes tab of the class Properties dialog box

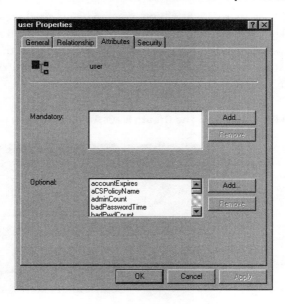

FIGURE 3.62: The Security tab of the class Properties dialog box

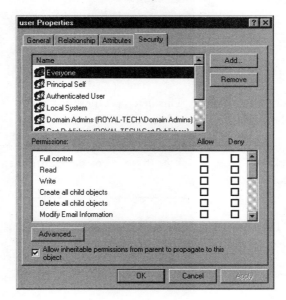

Creating a New Attribute

To create a new attribute, you create an *attribute-definition object*. The process is much like that of creating a new object class. Within the ADSM, right-click the Attributes container, then choose New ➤ Attribute. You will see the Create New Attribute dialog box, shown in Figure 3.63.

FIGURE 3.63: The Create New Attribute dialog box

Here you enter the following information:

Common Name This field becomes the Common Name attribute of the attribute.

NOTE Yes, attributes themselves have attributes—it can become confusing.

LDAP Display This is the string that the LDAP utility will display to users when they access the directory.

Unique X.500 Object ID   This is the OID you received from the ISO.

You must also configure the type of data that the attribute will hold. In the Syntax and Range area, you will decide whether the property will hold a string of data, numeric data, a case-sensitive set of information, and so on. You may also set valid ranges for the data entered to avoid incorrect information. Finally, check the Multi-Valued box if the attribute will contain more than one value (such as the telephone number attribute).

Modifying an Existing Attribute

To modify an existing attribute, follow exactly the same process for modifying an existing object class, which was described earlier. Right-click the attribute and choose Properties. The same four tabs are available:

- General

- Relationship

- Attributes

- Security

These tabs offer the same set of configuration options offered for modifying an object class.

NOTE   See "Modifying an Existing Class" earlier in this chapter for information about these tabs.

Deactivating Class or Attribute

In the ADSM, expand either the Class or the Attribute container, depending on what you want to deactivate. Within the container, find the item you wish to deactivate, right-click it, and choose Properties. On the General tab you will find a check box labeled Deactivate This <Class or Attribute>. Select this check box.

NOTE If you choose to deactivate an item that another object is dependent upon, AD will return an error describing the problem. This prevents you from deactivating an object that would interfere with the functionality of another class or attribute.

Considerations in Schema Management

So far, we've concentrated on the mechanics of schema management—the tools and techniques used to accomplish this task. Understanding how to accomplish a task, though, does not necessarily help you decide when it's appropriate to do so. Deciding whether or not to modify the AD schema is definitely something that should be considered during the design of any Active Directory environment. Although there are no explicit rules, there are a few suggestions that might help you make this choice.

Static Data Is Best

Because the AD database is replicated to multiple domain controllers within each domain, you must consider the adverse effects of any schema modifications on replication traffic. The best information to store in the AD database will be static in nature. Things like telephone numbers, addresses, travel preferences—even items like insurance coverage—work well because they do not change regularly. Avoid items such as inventory or price lists that change frequently.

Stand-Alone Facts Are Best

Don't add attributes or objects that require complex manipulation to make them useful. You wouldn't, for instance, want to add customer invoices to your AD database. Not only does this information change often, but it must also be related to multiple other items to be useful. With invoices, for example, you would have to relate the objects to client contacts, inventory, shipping, billing, and accounting functions. All of these relationships *are* possible, but there are probably more efficient ways to track such data.

Programming Might Be Required

To display objects and attributes in the management tools (specifically the MMC), you will have to write and maintain a snap-in that defines how your changes should be displayed. Although writing snap-ins is *supposed* to be fairly straightforward (we're not developers, so we can only guess), it is still programming. If you do not have someone with this skill on staff, you will have to outsource the effort—and frequent outsourcing can eat up a large portion of your budget.

Make the Least-Intrusive Changes Possible

The most important suggestion (both in real life and for your exam) is to make the least-intrusive changes possible while still meeting the business needs of the environment. There is a definite order of preference for the types of changes that can be made:

1. If you can get by with changing the display name of an existing object class or attribute, do so! This is the least-dangerous type of change you can make and involves the least amount of change to the schema.

2. If existing attributes won't fulfill your need, then consider adding a new attribute to an existing object class.

3. If necessary, create an auxiliary class object, which is basically a copy of an existing object class with a new name. It is a fairly simple change to the schema—no new attributes or classes are defined.

4. As a last resort, define a whole new object class (complete with new attributes). This is the most dangerous change you can make!

WARNING   Remember to make a complete backup of the AD database before attempting to modify the schema.

Summary of Schema Modification

Although you can make changes to the structure of the Active Directory database, this is not something you would do as part of the day-to-day administration of an AD environment. The modification process involves acquiring valid OIDs for any new classes or attributes, and because it changes the schema, it could have a negative effect on your network—such as corrupting your AD database.

Microsoft offers the following suggestions for schema modifications:

- Modify the schema only when absolutely necessary.

- Use existing attributes when creating new object classes. This allows you to avoid the process of applying for numerous attribute OIDs.

- Avoid multivalued attributes as much as possible. Large attributes are costly to store (in terms of disk space) and to retrieve (in terms of network bandwidth) and therefore should be avoided.

- Use meaningful names for any new classes or attributes to avoid ambiguity.

Exam Essentials

Keep in mind that this is not a heavily tested exam objective. Microsoft would like MCSEs to understand the concepts of schema modification and a few suggested strategies. Before you take your examination, be sure that you are comfortable with the following:

Be able to describe the function of the schema. The schema defines the structure of the AD database.

Know who has the permissions necessary to modify the schema. Members of the Schema Admins group (whose only default member is the Admin user), have the permissions needed to modify the schema.

Know the five types of modification that can be made to the schema. The schema can be modified in the following ways: Create a new class of object, modify an existing class of object, create new attributes, modifying existing attributes, deactivating classes of objects and attributes.

Be aware that no object class or attribute can be deleted from the schema. Once a class or attribute is defined within the schema, it can not be deleted. You can, however, accomplish the same effect through deactivation.

Be aware of what cannot be modified. Object classes and attributes whose names begin with the word "system" cannot be modified.

Understand why schema modifications are not immediately applied. Two copies of the schema exist—one on disk and one in memory. Changes are made to the copy on the disk. The new schema is not placed in memory until all existing AD processes have completed.

Understand what an OID is. AN OID is an object identifier that uniquely identifies an object or attribute. OIDs are issued by the International Standards Organization. This avoids LDAP incompatibilities between different brands of directories.

Know the Microsoft suggestions for creating a schema modification strategy. See the Critical Information section for details.

Key Terms and Concepts

Schema   The definition of the structure of a database.

Object Class   A specific type of record in the AD database, such as a user, group, or printer.

Attribute   A field within the AD database.

`LDAP://rootDES`   A container at the root of an LDAP-compliant directory service. This container holds the definition of the namespace of the LDAP structure and the schema of the database.

Flexible Single Master Operations (FSMO)   Active Directory operations that are processed in a single-master manner.

Cache Schema   The copy of the schema that is held in memory at each domain controller.

Object Identifiers (OID)   Globally unique object identifiers granted by the International Standards Organization.

Class-Definition Object   A container within the schema of the AD database that holds the definition of an object, such as a list of the attributes of the object class.

Attribute-Definition Object An object within the schema of the AD database that holds the definition of an attribute.

Sample Questions

1. Schema can best be described as _____

_____.

A. The planning stage of operating system implementation

B. The definition of a database design

C. The plan used to control AD replication traffic

D. The network security design

Answer: B.   The *schema* of the Active Directory database defines the objects that can be stored there. It is the formal definition of the object classes and attributes that exist in the database.

2. To modify the AD schema, a user must be a member of which of the following security groups?

A. Domain Admins

B. Forest Admins

C. Schema Admins

D. Tree Admins

Answer: C.   To make changes to the schema, a user must be a member of the Schema Admins group. By default, the Administrator user account is a member of this group.

3. At the top of any LDAP-compliant directory service (such as Microsoft Active Directory), there is a special container that contains a number of entries, including the definition of the namespace of the LDAP structure and the schema of the database. This container is referred to as _____.

A. HTTP://rootDSE

B. FTP://rootDSE

C. LDAP://rootDSE

D. LDAP://SchemaDSE

Answer: C. At the top of any LDAP-compliant directory service (such as Microsoft Active Directory), there is a special container known as rootDSE. When referring to this container, the appropriate syntax is to refer to LDAP://rootDSE. The rootDSE container contains a number of entries, including the definition of the namespace of the LDAP structure and the schema of the database.

4. Which of the following modifications can be made to the AD schema?

A. Create a new class.

B. Modify an existing class.

C. Create new attributes.

D. Modify new attributes.

E. Delete an attribute.

Answer: A, B, C, D. When modifying the directory schema, you may perform the following tasks: Create new classes, modify existing classes, create new attributes, modify existing attributes, deactivate classes, and deactivate attributes.

5. The most drastic form of schema modification is to _____
_____.

A. Create new classes.

B. Modify existing classes.

C. Create new attributes.

D. Modify existing attributes.

E. Deactivate classes.

F. Deactivate attributes.

Answer: A. The most intrusive and potentially dangerous change to the schema is to add a new object class. You should take this action only when no other option will fit the needs of your environment.

6. Which of the following actions take place when you deactivate an object class?

A. That object class or attribute is no longer replicated throughout the network or to the global catalog server.

B. You may no longer create objects that are part of the deactivated class or enter data into the attribute. Attempts to do so will return the same error that would be returned if the class or attribute had never existed.

C. When an attribute is deactivated, you may no longer use it in definitions of new object classes or add it to an existing class.

D. All instances of that object class are deleted from the AD database.

Answer: A, B, C.   Deactivated object classes remain in the AD schema to ensure that data is not lost inadvertently. No class may be completely deleted from the schema once it is defined.

Design an Active Directory implementation plan.

At this point in your design project, you should have a fairly good idea of what currently exists in your environment and what you would like your finished Active Directory structure to look like. You have poked and prodded, listened and suggested, monitored and analyzed every nook and cranny of the company. You should have an in-depth understanding of the following:

- The business management model in use
- The IT management model in use
- The network infrastructure
- The number of users, servers, and workstations
- The services currently being offered through the network
- The scope of the project

- How information and communication flow within the company
- How the IT department is structured, its personnel and their strengths and weaknesses, and the change-management processes currently in place
- The NT domain structure in place
- The types of containers you would like to create within AD
- How you plan to design your AD site boundaries to control bandwidth use on the network
- How you intend to manage the desktops within the network
- How you intend to connect to any foreign directories
- What, if any, modifications to the AD schema will be required

The bottom line here is that you should now know more about the company as a whole than just about anyone else (and that holds true whether you are an outside consultant or on staff). Most employees never know their company as well as you are now expected to. Once you are at this point, you need to consider the actual implementation of your AD design.

When you're planning the actual implementation of an upgrade or migration to Windows 2000, you'll often need to rely more on your business sense than your technical skills. The reality is that all of the planning you have done up to this point has been to put together an ideal AD structure. Your job now is to decide which steps will be taken to achieve this goal (or, as you'll see later in this chapter, a realistic version of your goal).

Critical Information

One of the most common mistakes made at this point in a design project is to lose sight of the goals of the process. Once the AD tree has been designed, the domain structure agreed upon, the OUs planned, and all of the rest of the details worked out, many design engineers become engrossed in the technical details and forget to look at the big picture.

Before beginning to plan the implementation of an AD environment, reevaluate the reasons for the migration or upgrade. Review the interviews that were made during the analysis of the business needs, and if possible, interview key individuals again. Your objective here is to establish the overall goals of the migration. Many technologists will build a list of technical issues here: move to Windows 2000 to reduce the network traffic, or move to Active Directory because of the advances in policy management. In reality, technology itself is rarely enough of a reason to justify the expense and effort involved in a major upgrade. Your list should be made up of a series of business needs and proposed solutions, as shown in Table 3.4.

TABLE 3.4: Business Goals for the Move to Windows 2000

Business Goal	Windows 2000–Based Solution
Reduce connectivity costs and/or increase performance of the WAN.	Define AD site boundaries and set replication schedules to minimize adverse effects on wide-area links.
Reduce desktop support costs.	Implement group policies to limit the amount of control users have over their desktop environment.
Decrease the overall IT administrative overhead.	Implement Active Directory to minimize the number of management arenas that exist.
Reduce network traffic overall.	Implement DDNS systemwide so that WINS can be removed from the system.
Reduce exposure to unwanted access to information.	Implement Windows 2000 security.
Control access to resources.	Implement Windows 2000 security.
Centralize management of application software.	Implement Group Policy to publish applications through Active Directory.
Improve security of confidential data.	Implement Windows 2000 encrypting file system.

Technology exists to meet business needs. If your list has needs that are not met or, worse, creates new business problems, then you will need to reevaluate the move to Windows 2000 or reevaluate the business needs of the company. In a successful design project, each business need will be met by some aspect of technology (or the redefinition of a business process).

Migration Considerations

Once you've determined that your proposed solution meets the business goals of the environment, you can begin to plan for the actual implementation. Here again, though, you will need to stop and evaluate another set of business needs—specifically, those needs that pertain to the process of migration. Your first list was really a set of goals to be achieved *by* the migration; this second list is a set of goals to be achieved *during* the migration process. You should build a table of these immediate goals and your proposed methods of achieving them, as shown in Table 3.5.

TABLE 3.5: Goals During Migration Process

Goal	Method
Minimize the effects of the migration on the business environment.	• Servers should stay online during business hours; all upgrades and new installations will be implemented and tested during nonbusiness hours. • A complete recovery plan will be in place and will be utilized in the event of lost productivity due to misconfiguration. • All key servers will be migrated to new hardware so that the old server will be available in the event of problems. • Group Policy changes will not be implemented until after the actual migration has been accomplished to avoid abrupt changes to the users' environment.

TABLE 3.5: Goals During Migration Process *(continued)*

Goal	Method
Security must be maintained throughout the process.	• All changes will be tested in a lab environment before being implemented on the production system. • Support personnel will monitor key access points (Internet connections, key files, etc.).
Minimize IT administrative overhead and intrusion into the workplace.	• User accounts will be migrated (not re-created). • Software distribution techniques will be used to minimize the number of visits to workstations.
Minimize immediate effects on users.	• User accounts will be migrated, including security information, account restrictions, and passwords.

As you can see, Table 3.5 lists the possible pitfalls of any migration and the specific steps you intend to take to avoid them. Although this list will change from project to project, many of the same potential problems will occur in *any* major change to an IT environment.

Reevaluating Your AD Design

Once you have your list of business needs and a general list of technologies that will meet them, it is time to take another look at your proposed AD design. At this time, you need to determine if your proposed design will facilitate uses of technology to solve your business needs. To put this another way, compare your design with the business needs to ensure that the business needs will be met. You would be surprised at the number of times the final suggestion does *not* fully meet the business needs of the environment! Taking the time to make this comparison at this point in the process helps to ensure that you do not implement a design that does not offer a complete business solution.

You'll want to look at each portion of your proposed AD design with an eye on the business and migration goals that you have identified. You'll want to examine the following:

Current and Planned Domain Structure   Windows NT 4 networks usually had more domains than are necessary in a Windows 2000 environment. You will need to plan for the consolidation of domains during your upgrade.

Plans for a Single or Multi-Tree Design   Upgrading to single-tree AD design is much easier than upgrading to a multiple-tree forest environment. If your proposed design includes multiple AD trees, you will want to consider the long-term ramifications—if you need to merge the trees later, the only way to accomplish it is to restructure your entire organization.

Proposed Site Boundaries   Compare your proposed site strategy to the business goals of the migration. For example, if high availability is a goal, you will want to have multiple domain controllers at each site. Also, reevaluate your replication schedule to ensure that AD replication does not conflict with periods of high network usage.

Administrative Management Model   At this point, it is a good idea to review your analysis of the IT management model—centralized or decentralized. Ensure that your proposed AD design is optimized for whichever model will be used.

Security Strategies   Ensure that your proposed AD solution facilitates all of the security features that will need to be implemented. Also, define a migration plan that maintains security during the actual implementation process.

Recovery Plans, Both in the Long and Short Term   Although a properly planned migration strategy should ensure that no problems are encountered, you should always have a plan for reversing the migration process if necessary. Your plan should include, at a minimum, complete documentation of existing services and applications. (Of course, if you have been following the steps we have outlined in this book, you already have this documentation.) Your minimum plan should also include a complete backup to tape of every server, and Microsoft suggests that you find a BDC in each domain (or install a new one if none is available) that can be left offline during any upgrades. This ensures that your NT 4 SAM database is preserved intact.

Mixed vs. Native Mode

In an effort to preserve backward compatibility and to allow a more relaxed upgrade process, Microsoft has included components that allow a network to support both Windows 2000 and Windows NT 4 domain controllers working together within the same domain. Specifically, the first domain controller upgraded to Windows 2000 within a domain assumes the role of PDC emulator. Basically, the PDC emulator replaces the functionality of the original NT 4 PDC within the domain, replicating changes to the account database on all NT 4 BDCs still active in the domain. This allows for an incremental migration to Windows 2000—you can upgrade the PDC of your old NT 4 domain and then take your time upgrading to Windows 2000 the other NT 4 domain controllers.

When a network is supporting domain controllers from multiple versions of Microsoft products (NT and Windows 2000), that network is said to be operating in *mixed mode*. Although this might sound like the perfect solution—especially for those companies with a limited upgrade budget, because it allows them to spread the costs of upgrading over a longer period of time—there are disadvantages to running in mixed mode. While in mixed mode operation, the domain cannot support universal or nested groups, and many of the advances made to group policies are not available.

Once all of the domain controllers within a domain have been upgraded to Windows 2000, Active Directory can be set to operate in *native mode*. An environment operating in native mode cannot have any Windows NT 4 domain controllers in operation. This allows the system to take full advantage of the features of Active Directory. The ultimate goal of any migration to Windows 2000 should be to move to native mode as soon as possible—either by upgrading all of the NT 4 domain controllers to Windows 2000 or by demoting them to member server status.

NOTE Technically, there is no easy way to demote a Windows NT 4 domain controller to member server status—Microsoft uses the word demote to soften the image. In reality, the only way to change an NT 4 domain controller into a member server is to reinstall NT 4.

Domain Upgrade Strategies

At this point, you have confirmed that your proposed Active Directory design is sound and that it will meet or exceed the business needs of the company. Now you need to consider each existing domain and the process that will be used to upgrade it to Windows 2000 and Active Directory.

Before we begin our discussion of upgrading domains, it is important that you understand the upgrade options available for your legacy NT servers. This information will affect your domain upgrade strategy and is the kind of information that Microsoft traditionally tests on in the MCSE exams. Table 3.6 lists the upgrade paths available for older operating systems.

NOTE Operating systems that do not have a direct upgrade path to Windows 2000 can still be upgraded. You will have to upgrade them to an intermediate operating system that *does* have a direct path to Windows 2000. For instance, you could upgrade an NT 3.51 server to NT 4 and then upgrade the computer to Windows 2000 Server.

TABLE 3.6: Upgrade Paths Available for Windows NT Servers

Legacy Operating System	Can Upgrade to Windows 2000 Server?	Can Upgrade to Windows 2000 Advanced Server?
Windows NT 3.51	No	No
Windows NT 3.51 Advanced Server	No	No
Windows NT 3.51 Workstation	Yes	No
Windows NT 3.51 Server	No	Yes
Windows 95/98	Yes	No
Windows NT 4 Workstation	No	No
Windows NT 4 Server	Yes	Yes
Windows NT 4 Server Enterprise Edition	No	Yes

TIP Exam Hint: Take a close look at Table 3.6. A few of the options are not what you would expect. For instance, NT 3.51 Server can upgrade to Windows 2000 Advanced Server but not Windows 2000 Server.

Designing an Upgrade Strategy

When upgrading an existing Windows NT environment, you will need to decide upon a strategy for upgrading your existing domain structure into your new Windows 2000 Active Directory domain structure. To create your plan, you will have to consider the following:

- The order in which domains will be upgraded

- The order in which servers will be upgraded

- When to move from a mixed-mode to a native-mode environment

- How many domain controllers will be required for each domain and at each site

You will also want to establish a checklist of actions to be taken after the upgrade to ensure that the process was successful.

Planning the Order of Domain Upgrades

Traditionally, the IT department was always the first area to be subjected to an upgrade. Given the fact that the user base in the IT department was usually the most technically savvy, they would work out any problems before the operating system was rolled out to end users. This philosophy of limiting the effect of changes to a select group was also applied to network operating systems. The first servers upgraded were often not mission critical. This reduced the effect of any problems on the productivity of the employees.

With Windows 2000, the rules change a bit. The first domain upgraded becomes the root domain for the forest. In other words, you must upgrade the most important domain *first* and then upgrade or restructure any additional domains. This does not mean that all servers within the domain must be upgraded immediately, but the PDC of what will be your root domain must be the first server in your new AD forest.

In general, you should upgrade your Windows NT account domains first because this provides the immediate benefit of management of user accounts through Active Directory. AD gives you much more latitude in the delegation of account administration, is much more scalable, and is able to support many more user accounts in a single domain than NT.

NOTE If you are not comfortable with the concept of account or resource domains, we suggest reading *MSCE Exam Notes: NT Server 4 in the Enterprise* (Sybex, 1999).

If you have multiple account domains, you will have to determine which should be upgraded first. Of course, the first one upgraded should be the domain that is going to act as your root domain. After that, though, there are a few guidelines to follow in choosing your order:

- Although you should have tested your upgrade process in a lab, it is still a smart idea to first upgrade those domains to which you have easy physical access. This ensures that you can easily implement your recovery plan without the delay of first traveling to the location of the domain controllers.

- Limit the effects of mistakes by upgrading the domain with the smallest number of accounts first. If you do have a problem, this will reduce the number of people affected.

- If you are going to merge or in some other way restructure domains, first upgrade those that will remain after the upgrade. Remember, if you intend to move users from one domain to another as part of your upgrade, the target domain needs to be in place *before* you move the accounts.

Once you have upgraded your account domains, the next step is to upgrade your resource domains. Because, by definition, resource domains do not contain user accounts, this should be a fairly straight-forward process with little chance to create adverse effects on the workplace (famous last words if we ever heard them!). Here again, there are a few guidelines to help you chose the order of upgrade:

- Upgrade those domains in which AD-dependent applications are running. If, for instance, you plan to upgrade to Microsoft Exchange 2000 (an application that uses the AD database to store information) running on a server in a domain, then that resource domain should be among the first upgraded.

- Unlike user domains, you should upgrade large resource domains first. This gives you the immediate benefit of the many desktop-management features of Windows 2000.

- Once again, if you intend to restructure your domains, upgrade early in the process the domains that will remain after the upgrade is complete. Remember, you can't move a workstation into a domain unless the domain exists!

When you upgrade the first PDC in the first domain, that computer takes the roles of schema master, domain naming master, relative ID master, and infrastructure master for the root domain. Because this is, by definition, the first domain in the AD tree, it also assumes those roles (schema and domain naming masters) that are forestwide. For our discussion here, though, the most important role that the new AD server assumes is that of PDC emulator. This role allows the server to act as the PDC for any NT BDCs that are on the network. This role is so important that, if you upgrade a BDC first, it will assume the role of PDC emulator and the old PDC will be demoted.

When the Active Directory Installation Wizard is run, it installs all of the necessary components on the domain controller, such as the AD database and any protocols used in authentication (Kerberos v5, for example). The existing SAM is copied to the AD database, thus pre-serving user, group, and computer accounts. When a child domain is upgraded into an existing tree, transitive trusts are automatically created to the parent domain.

There is really no order of preference in upgrading the BDCs of the domain. The only consideration you will have to take into account is to ensure that any applications running on your BDCs are compatible with Windows 2000. If you have incompatible applications in use on your network, the correct Microsoft answer it to upgrade them to AD-enabled applications to take advantage of Windows 2000 capabilities. If this is not an option (either because no such version exists or because of lack of funding), you can move the applications to a member server so that all of the domain controllers can be upgraded to AD.

TIP Exam Hint: Reread this section, "Planning the Order of Domain Upgrades." There are numerous rules to follow during an upgrade. Knowing these rules and suggestions will help when you are presented with a case study about upgrading an existing NT network!

Restructuring Domains

A domain upgrade maintains the existing domain structure, whereas a *domain restructure* is the process of redesigning your existing domains to match the business needs of your environment. Domain upgrades are the easiest and simplest form of migration, but domain restructuring allows for the creation of an environment that provides a robust solution to a business need. Given the complex domain designs that were forced upon many networks due to the limitations of Windows NT 4, it is safe to assume that many of the migrations to Windows 2000 will include domain restructuring during implementation.

By the time you are ready to study for the Designing a Microsoft Windows 2000 Directory Services Infrastructure MCSE exam, you should already be familiar with the tools and techniques used to accomplish a domain restructure. For the exam, though, you will need to reinforce the rules of the game—what needs to be done to prepare to restructure (and in what order), what can be accomplished, and what the results will be. You will also have to understand how domain security works in order to better plan a restructuring strategy.

Domain Security

The security systems of both Windows NT 4 and Windows 2000 rely upon *security identifiers* (SIDs) to determine which users or groups have permissions to resources. SIDs are domain-specific values that uniquely identify a security principal. Your user interface will display user-friendly names, such as Bking, but these names are mapped to the SID of the user for authentication purposes. During the logon process, users will identify themselves and provide whatever means of proof are necessary in the environment. (The most common means of proof being a password, but many other types of proof can be used in Windows 2000.) Once a user has proven his or her identity, the domain controller will return an *access token* to the user's workstation. This token contains the user's SID and the SIDs of any groups of which the user is a member.

NOTE For more information about other methods of identifying users, see *MCSE: Windows 2000 Network Security Design Study Guide* (Sybex, 2000).

When the user attempts to access a resource, the SIDs in the access token are compared with the SIDs in the resource's *access control list (ACL)* to determine if the user (or any groups of which the user is a member) has been granted permissions to the resource in question.

The process of using SIDs to authenticate to resources is fairly straightforward, but it does present a few problems when you are considering moving objects from one domain to another. Because the SID is domain specific (part of a user's SID is the domain SID for the domain in which the user exists), the SID generated for an object in one domain will not be valid for an object in another. In other words, if you were to move an object from one domain to another, the original SID would not be valid. In reality, the only way to move an object (such as a user) from one domain to another is to create a new object (thus generating a new SID) and then delete the old object. Unfortunately, this would result in a loss of permissions, because the ACL of resources would contain the old SID, not the new one. To eliminate this drawback to SID/ACL-based authentication, Active Directory security principal objects have an attribute not found in earlier Windows-based operating systems. Each security principal has the sIDHistory attribute. This attribute stores the former SIDs of restructured security principals. When a user attempts to authenticate to a resource, the sIDHistory information is also compared against the SIDs in the ACL. The sIDHistory information is automatically updated when an object is migrated from one domain to another. There is one caveat to the use of the sIDHistory attribute: it can be populated only in native-mode Windows domains. This means that the target domain (the domain to which the user is migrated) must be fully upgraded to Windows 2000 *before* any migration takes place.

Inter-Forest Restructuring

Inter-forest restructuring is the process of moving users, groups, and computer objects from either a Windows NT domain *or* a Windows 2000 domain in a separate AD forest to a new Windows 2000 domain. Figures 3.64 and 3.65 depict these two situations.

Inter-forest restructuring is a popular technique among consultants because it requires a new environment to act as the target for the moves. From an implementation perspective, this is the safest type of migration. In the event of problems, the old system is still up and available. You can easily reverse the migration process by unplugging the new servers and reattaching the old. You can then reevaluate your process and try again—all without affecting productivity.

FIGURE 3.64: **Moving accounts from NT to Active Directory**

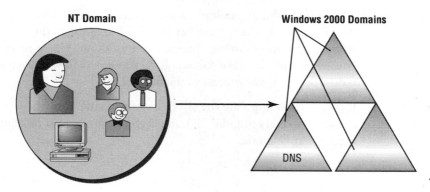

FIGURE 3.65: Moving accounts from one AD forest to another

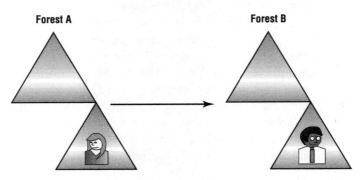

As with any other complex procedure, there are a few suggestions, requirements, and restrictions that must be considered before implementation.

Here is a list of suggestions:

- Even though the original system will still be available after the restructuring, make a complete backup of the source environment before copying any objects. This way, an accidental deletion won't prevent you from reversing the process.

- Make a complete backup of the target environment *before* copying in new objects. This allows you to easily revert to the beginning of the process without the hassle of re-creating any work configurations that you have already done.

- If you are combining multiple domains into a single Windows 2000 domain, back up the target after you finish copying in the objects from each source domain. Once again, this allows you to reverse your work back to a last-known-good status so you won't have to redo work that was successful the first time.

- If you wish to populate the sIDHistory attribute of the new accounts with its original SID, the target domain *must* be configured in native mode.

The requirements are as follows:

- The source domain controller's Registry must include the Registry entry HKEY_LOCAL_MACHINE\System\CurrentControlSet\ Control\LsaTcpipClientSupport: Reg_DWORD:0X1.

NOTE You must restart the domain controller after making this Registry edit.

- The user performing the restructuring operation must be a member of the Domain Admins group in the target domain and have administrative privileges in both the source and target domains.

- Account auditing *must* be enabled on both the source and target domains. (If the source is an NT 4 domain, you must enable both success and failure auditing of Group Management on the PDC.)

- Within the source domain, you must create a local group named <source_domain_name>$$$ (for example, Tampa$$$). This group should have no members.

And finally, there are some restrictions:

- The source domain controller must be either the PDC (in an NT 4 domain) or PDC emulator (in a Windows 2000 domain).

- All source objects must be security principals.

- The SID of the source object must be valid in the target domain. In other words, the SID must be unique. The SID must also not already be in use in the sIDHistory attribute of any existing object.

- Migration tools must be run on the target domain controller so physical access (or the ability to run the tools through a service such as Terminal Services) is possible.

The inter-forest migration strategy is the safest method of moving from a legacy NT environment or restructuring an existing Windows 2000 system. It is not only the preferred method used by consultants (because it reduces the risks involved in the process), but it is also Microsoft's preferred method. If, on your MCSE exam, you are presented with a question in which an inter-forest restructuring is possible—it will be the correct Microsoft solution.

Intra-Forest Restructuring

Intra-forest restructuring involves moving security principals between domains within the same Active Directory forest. This type of restructuring will commonly be used by companies that are performing a two-phase migration to Windows 2000. In a two-phase migration, all legacy NT domains are first upgraded to Windows 2000. After this is accomplished, resource objects are moved from domain to domain to match the target AD design. Any unnecessary domains can then be eliminated and their servers migrated into an existing domain. This approach to migration offers the advantage of moving the entire company to Windows 2000 quickly—allowing the administrators and users to take advantage of the new features and benefits as soon as possible. Restructuring can then take place at a more leisurely pace.

NOTE Intra-forest restructuring might also take place if there are changes to the business environment. If, for instance, users need to move from one domain to another, perhaps because the company has been reorganized, the process of moving the objects will constitute intra-forest restructuring.

When you're performing any type of intra-forest restructuring, the only migration option available is a *move*. When an object is moved, a new object is created in the destination domain and the original object is deleted. Because this leaves no option for returning to your original configuration (putting the object back where it started), this form of restructuring is considered more of a risk than inter-forest structuring. Don't let this warning scare you, though—moving user objects from domain to domain within an AD forest is a normal part of Windows 2000 administration. It should, however, stress the importance of a good system recovery plan!

As with intra-forest restructuring, there are a few suggestions, requirements, and restrictions that must be considered before implementation.

The suggestions are as follows:

- Back up! Back up! Back up! Remember, the original object will be deleted after the new one is created. (This is a move operation.) If you are moving just a couple of users to a new domain, this is probably not a big issue, but if you are restructuring 1,000 users, you will want to be able to recover in the event of a problem.

- If available, it is a good idea to preserve a BDC of any domain that will be absorbed into Windows 2000 until you have determined that the restructuring process has been successful.

Here are the requirements:

- The target domain *must* be operating in native mode.

- The source domain controller's Registry must contain the entry `HKEY_LOCAL_MACHINE\System\CurrentControlSet\Control\LsaTcpipClientSupport: REG_DWORD: 0X1`.

- The user performing the move must have administrative privileges in both the source and target domains.

- Auditing must be enabled in both domains.

And the following restrictions apply:

- The source object cannot be a built-in account, such as the Administrator account.

- The SID of the source object must not already exist in the target domain, including in the sIDHistory of any other security principal.

- You will use the Active Directory Migration Tool (ADMT) to perform the move. Administrative shares must be in existence on the computer upon which you run ADMT and on any computers upon which the ADMT must install an agent.

Restructuring Utilities

Although the Design exam does not test your ability to perform administrative tasks (that is tested in other MCSE examinations), it *does* test your ability to chose the right tool for the job. For that reason, we'll include a short description of the domain restructuring utilities that are available. You should be aware of the function of each of the following tools:

- Active Directory Migration Tool (ADTM)
- ClonePrincipal
- Netdom
- Ldp
- MoveTree

Active Directory Migration Tool

ADTM is an MMC snap-in that allows both inter-forest and intra-forest restructuring through a graphical interface. Microsoft licensed the software from Mission Critical Software to facilitate the migration to Windows 2000. It includes a series of reporting functions: what is migrated, accounts referenced in ACLs, and any name conflicts that might occur. It populates the sIDHistory attribute, and it allows many of the operations to be reversed if a problem develops. It is available for download at the Microsoft Web site.

ClonePrincipal

ClonePrincipal is a series of Microsoft Visual Basic scripts that copy users and groups from a Windows NT 4 or Windows 2000 domain into a Windows 2000 native-mode domain. As such, it is used to populate the target domain in inter-forest structuring. You are not responsible for knowing the individual components that make up the scripts, but you should know that they are located on the Windows 2000 Server compact disc.

Netdom

Netdom is a command-line utility that is used to facilitate both intra- and inter-forest restructuring. Its primary use is to query a domain for a list of existing trusts and create new trust relationships automatically (when used in conjunction with an automated migration script).

Ldp

Ldp is a graphical utility that allows users to perform LDAP operations against any LDAP-compatible directory (such as Active Directory).

MoveTree

MoveTree is a command-line tool used to move objects—such as OUs, users, and groups—between domains within an AD forest (intra-forest restructuring). The target domain must be running in native mode.

Restructuring Strategy

Now that we have discussed the fundamentals of domain restructuring, we can begin our discussion of planning a restructuring strategy. At this point in the design process, you have a proposed domain structure in hand. You must now find the best way to implement that proposal—and therein lies the bulk of the Microsoft exam objective. *Best* is a relative term—what is best for one company might not be best for another. At the beginning of this chapter, we discussed reevaluating the business goals for the company—both the long-term goals *and* the short-terms goals of the migration. You must now take those short-term migration goals and design a domain restructuring strategy that meets (or exceeds) them.

During your planning for the restructure process, you will need to perform the following:

- Determine what items need to be restructured.

- Determine the order in which domains should be restructured.

- Determine the order in which objects should be restructured.

- Choose a restructure method.

- Prepare the target domains.

- Test your results.

Determining What Items Need to Be Restructured

Because you have a model of what you would like your end result to look like, determining what changes have to occur should be a fairly straightforward process. Most of the time you will be reducing the number of domains during the migration process; legacy NT implementations often needed multiple domains to facilitate delegation of administration or to stay within the 40,000-object limit imposed upon NT account databases. With Windows 2000, and the large number of objects that the AD database can support (not to mention the ability to define AD sites to control replication traffic), most environments will require fewer domains than they did with earlier Microsoft networking products. Remember, the single-domain design will probably be the most common implementation. Do not create additional domains without justification.

Determining the Order in Which Domains Should Be Restructured

As we mentioned earlier, the first domain in an AD tree becomes the root domain. Because this domain defines the namespace of the tree, it is important that you consider your choice carefully. After that, many variables will come into play to determine the order in which domains should be upgraded or eliminated, including these:

- In most cases, account domains should be upgraded or eliminated before resource domains.

- If a particular group of users needs access to a feature of Windows 2000 (such as Group Policy objects), move them into a Windows 2000 domain early in the process.

- Many administrators prefer to experiment on a particular group of users (such as the IT department) before making changes to the rest of the user base.

- If you have an application that is not compatible with Windows 2000 running on an NT 4 domain controller, you might want to preserve that domain so that your Windows 2000 domains can run in native mode.

- Politics, as always, sometimes determines our course of action.

Determining the Order in Which Objects Should Be Restructured

Microsoft recommends the following order for migrating objects:

1. Restructure users and groups. This gives the administrator the fastest access to the improved management capabilities of Windows 2000.

2. Restructure computer accounts. This allows administrators to begin using the software installation and management features of Windows 2000 quickly.

3. Restructure member servers. Because member servers do not hold a copy of the NT 4 accounts database, they can easily be moved from domain to domain. Migrating them before attempting to deal with domain controllers gives you experience before tackling the more intricate project of migrating domain controllers.

4. Move the domain controllers into the Windows 2000 domain.

Choosing a Restructure Method

There are two philosophies from which to choose when deciding on the overall method of migration:

- Post upgrade

- Pristine install

POST UPGRADE

The *post upgrade method* involves upgrading your legacy NT domains first and then shuffling your environment to match your proposed design. This method offers the benefit of Windows 2000 administration immediately, but it does entail some risk, and it can take longer to finish the overall migration with this method than with other methods. This method of migration is best used in the following situations:

- If a business need mandates a fast move to Windows 2000 to take advantage of one or more of its new features.

- If no new hardware will be purchased during the migration process.

- If the company expects to implement drastic changes to its internal organization in the near future. These changes should be severe enough to force major changes to business relationships, wide area links, or internal processes.

The major risk to using the post upgrade method of migration involves the fact that the environment is changed on a production system—any challenges that might develop can have direct, adverse effects on the productivity of the business. Although a good recovery plan can alleviate many of these concerns, there is still a potential for unacceptable downtime.

PRISTINE INSTALL

The *pristine installation method* involves creating a completely separate Windows 2000 Active Directory. This new system is usually implemented in a lab environment so that it can be adequately tested before implementation. Security principals can be migrated from your existing domains, or you can create new ones. This method offers the safest path to Windows 2000 because the old environment is never changed. If there are problems, the company can easily switch back to the legacy system and the process can be corrected. The major drawback to this migration method is cost—you must have enough equipment to implement a redundant domain structure. Many large firms utilize this form of migration to minimize any potential negative effects of the migration on their business. The pristine installation method of migration is best used in the following situations:

- When downtime due to the migration is unacceptable

- When funding is available for the additional hardware required

- When an immediate move to Windows 2000 is not mandated by business needs

Once again, the major advantage of the pristine installation method of migration is safety. The major drawback is cost. Most consultants will tend to suggest using the pristine installation method to reduce their liability if there are problems—everyone wants an "out" in the event of catastrophe.

Preparing the Target Domains

Before you can actually implement your AD design, there are certain issues that must be dealt with. Attention to detail during this preparation process can reduce problems during implementation. There are certain things you must do to prepare the target domains:

- Ensure that adequate hardware is in place to support Windows 2000 and Active Directory.

- Ensure that any namespaces you define will be unique.

- Ensure that DNS has been properly configured to support your new namespace.

- In the target domain (Windows 2000), ensure that OUs exist that are appropriate for your proposed design.

- Create an administrative transition plan that outlines the roles and responsibilities of each member of the IT department.

- Test your recovery plan in a lab environment, ensuring that you can re-create the existing environment in the event that something goes wrong.

Checking Your Results

After any restructuring has taken place, you will want to confirm the success of the process before eliminating any excess resources. You should test to ensure that security principals are functional and that their permissions are set correctly. Check group memberships. Check any applications to ensure that they are working properly, and check your print environment.

When you have finished your test of the new environment, it is safe to decommission any domains that are no longer functional and reassign any remaining resources to your new environment.

One more time—Microsoft has recommended that you keep a domain controller from any decommissioned domain until you are satisfied that the migration process was successful!

Planning a Low-Impact Implementation

In every chapter of this book, we have stressed the importance of considering the business needs when making design decisions. In no other area is this as important as in the actual implementation of your design. A mistake made during implementation can bring an entire company to a halt. Bob has a sign hanging over his desk that reads, "Don't mess with the goose!" The sign reminds us of the importance of protecting our client's best interests—if they stop making money, we stop making money.

NOTE "Don't mess with the goose!" is a reference to the goose that lays the golden eggs—in this case, our "golden goose" is our client. Protecting the client's best interests is in *our* best interests!

We've all seen the math that goes into justifying the expense of a good backup strategy—take the average hourly salary times the number of employees and the result will equal the cost of an hour of downtime. We can take this a step further by calculating the lost revenue per hour of downtime and include that cost in our justification! This same cost analysis can be used to determine the cost of any downtime during your implementation of Windows 2000. Your goal during this process should be to minimize any negative effects of the migration upon the company's network, employees, and customers!

There are two distinct processes that can be involved in a migration to Windows 2000: upgrading domains and restructuring domains. Each of these processes can have an effect on the network. We'll look at methods to reduce these effects in the next couple of sections. From an exam perspective, you should be able to analyze a proposed solution to determine what its effect will be on the company's productivity. You should also be able to determine which migration strategy plans will have the least negative effects on productivity.

Controlling Impact During a Domain Upgrade

Any major change to an environment is bound to have some sort of effect. In the case of a domain upgrade, the adverse effects can range from mild inconvenience (such as users calling to explain that something new has appeared on their screen) to catastrophic (such as an upgrade going sour and taking the data on the computer with it). This brings us back to the premise that our first responsibility is to set expectations. Many of the support calls that are generated by users during an upgrade can be avoided by providing information *before* changes are made.

The first rule for upgrades (or any type of change) is to anticipate problems and proactively prevent them. That's really the point of this entire chapter—the more issues you anticipate (and alleviate), the fewer problems you'll have to face after the upgrade. There are four major goals in an upgrade from Windows NT 4 to Windows 2000:

- Maintaining uninterrupted network services
- Maintaining security
- Maintaining the availability of applications
- Maintaining acceptable network performance

Failing to accomplish any one of these four goals can result in an upgrade process that is perceived as a failure. This might not be a literal truth, but we must remember that perception is often reality and a perception of failure can affect your future employability. We'll discuss each of the four goals in the next few sections. Once again, though, our discussion will stay at a fairly high level because they pertain to an AD implementation—knowledge of the installation, configuration, and management is prerequisite information.

Maintaining Uninterrupted Network Services

Windows NT 4 Server includes the ability to provide numerous network services through the operating system and add-on components. Many of these services were critical to a healthy NT network—some will still be important after you have upgraded to Windows 2000. Your upgrade strategy must ensure that all critical network services continue to function throughout (and after, if appropriate) the upgrade process. The following list includes some of the more important network services:

- DNS
- NetBIOS name resolution
- DHCP
- LAN Manager replication
- Remote access
- System policies

Each of these services will present a unique set of challenges during your implementation.

DNS

Domain Name System (DNS) is a critical component of any Windows 2000 Active Directory environment. Windows 2000 uses DNS to locate network services, such as locating domain controllers during the logon process. In order for DNS to be used to find services, it must support SRV records, and unfortunately, the Windows NT 4 version of DNS dos not! This means that it is imperative that your DNS services be migrated to a Windows 2000 server as soon as possible in the upgrade process.

NOTE Upgrading to Windows 2000 DNS is one way of providing support for SRV records. Because the use of SRV records is defined in an RFC, there are other implementations of DNS that will also suffice. But we are concerned with Microsoft solutions, so we can avoid complicating this issue with a discussion of them. For more information on third-party DNS solutions, see *Mastering Windows 2000 Server* (Sybex, 2000).

There are two methods of upgrading DNS to Windows 2000. The first and simplest method is to upgrade to Windows 2000 the Windows NT 4 server that currently acts as the master DNS server. Once it's upgraded, you can configure the zone to allow dynamic updates and you are set to go. The second method involves installing a new Windows 2000 server and configuring it to be a secondary DNS server for the existing zone. Once a zone transfer has occurred, you can then switch roles so that the new Windows 2000 server is the primary DNS server and configure it for dynamic updates.

There is actually a third option available for providing DNS support for a Windows 2000 environment, but it is a method that is not favored by many administrators. You *can* stay with the Windows NT version of DNS and add the appropriate SRV records to the zone file manually. Although NT 4 DNS services do not technically support SRV records, you can create them and queries for them will function. The problem, of course, is that if you choose this method, you will be forced to manage SRV records manually—a task that most administrators find onerous.

As you upgrade your NT domains, be aware that Windows 2000 Active Directory–enabled zones cannot be replicated between domains. If you need a zone to be hosted on DNS servers in other domains, you will have to configure those DNS zones to be secondary DNS zones.

TIP Exam Hint: The bottom line is that DNS needs to be upgraded to Windows 2000 DNS services as soon as possible in the migration process.

NetBIOS Name Resolution

Windows NT 4 (and earlier) uses the Windows Internet Name Service (WINS) to resolve NetBIOS names into IP addresses. Although this service is not required in a Windows 2000 network, you need to ensure that no computers or applications are using it before you remove WINS from your environment. To determine if WINS is still required to support NetBIOS name resolution, you can track a few counters in Performance to see if it is still in use. The following counters are sufficient to check for uses of WINS:

Windows Internet Name Service Server: Total Number of Registrations/Sec   This is the total number of services that are registering with WINS each second. If this value is consistently zero, it is safe to assume that no WINS-dependent services still exist.

Windows Internet Name Service Server: Queries/Sec This is the rate at which the WINS server is resolving NetBIOS names for client requests. Once again, a value of zero indicates that WINS is no longer being used.

DHCP

Because Active Directory requires TCP/IP, and because manually configuring TCP/IP addresses is inconvenient at best, it is likely that Dynamic Host Configuration Protocol (DHCP) will be utilized in most environments. Maintaining reliable DHCP services during a domain upgrade is not difficult, but it does require a little planning. The solution is to provide a backup DHCP server to renew leases that expire during the upgrade process.

LAN Manager Replication

In Windows NT 4, the LAN Manager replication (LMR) service is used to replicate logon scripts, system policies, and other types of data. In Windows 2000, this service has been replaced with the File Replication Service (FRS). The major difference between the two systems is that LAN Manager replication is a single-master replication scheme and Windows 2000's FRS is multi-master. In LMR, changes are made on the export server and replicated to import servers. In FRS, changes can be made at any domain controller and those changes will be replicated to all other domain controllers in the domain.

If you must live with a mixed (NT and Windows 2000) environment for a time, there are a couple of guidelines that can help to reduce the number of replication problems you will have:

- If the NT export server is the PDC, move the export services to another server in the domain. This allows the replication to continue to BDCs until the upgrade has been completed.

- The Windows 2000 Resource Kit contains a script file that builds a bridge between the export directory and the NetLogon share point in Windows 2000. Basically, this allows files in the Windows 2000 NetLogon share point to be replicated to the NT export server—allowing you to manage those files from a central location.

Remote Access

Windows NT 4 Routing and Remote Access Service (RRAS) is commonly used to provide users with dial-in access to the company network. After you upgrade an RRAS server to Windows 2000, it will continue to function as before. If, however, you have multiple RRAS servers and a mix of Windows NT and Windows 2000 servers acting as RRAS servers, you might encounter a few difficulties due to the different ways in which these two environments authenticate users to use RRAS services.

In NT 4, the RRAS service uses the LocalSystem account to log on and does so with NULL credentials. This means that the service logs on to the server without providing a username or password. By default, Active Directory does not allow a NULL session to access the attributes of objects. In other words, if a user dials in to an NT 4 RRAS server but is authenticated through a Windows 2000 server, the attempt to use dial-in services will be denied (RRAS won't be able to read the user's object to determine if they have permission to dial in). The only way to work around this issue is to ensure that the user authenticates through an NT BDC. Because there is no way to control which domain controller will authenticate a given logon attempt, it's best to use one of the following solutions:

- Upgrade all RRAS servers to Windows 2000.
- Place the RRAS service on NT BDCs. Users will then log on through the local account database.

System Policies

This is one of the more difficult (and often important) network services to control during an upgrade. The problem lies in the fact that NT 4 system policies are not migrated automatically during the upgrade. This is because system policies exist *only* as a file (`Ntconfig.pol` for NT clients), whereas Windows 2000 group policies are managed through Active Directory. In a mixed environment of NT and Windows 2000, if clients authenticate through an NT BDC, they will receive only NT system policies, and if they authenticate through a Windows 2000 domain controller, only AD group policies will apply. Also be aware that AD group policies can be applied only to Windows 2000 clients. If a user logs on at a computer running a legacy operating system but authenticates through a Windows 2000 domain controller, by default no policies will be applied. You can configure your environment to process both system policies and group policies, but this can get confusing if a user has had both applied to them.

Maintaining Security

This is probably the most far reaching of the potential problem areas in an upgrade. Almost every aspect of your security strategy will be affected by the move to Windows 2000, so you will have to plan carefully.

First the good news: Because both Windows NT 4 and Windows 2000 use access control lists (ACLs) to control access to resources, the upgrade to Windows 2000 should not affect your permissions structure. The upgrade process maintains the user and group SIDs. SIDs will change only if the object is moved to another domain, and even then the original SID will be preserved in the sIDHistory attribute if the target domain is running in native mode. Group memberships are also maintained, as are share and file permissions, Registry permissions, and trust relationships. Remember that the default trust configuration for Windows 2000 domains is that parent and child domains establish a two-way trust between themselves and that trusts are transitive. The upgrade process will convert any one-way trusts into two-way trusts automatically. (If this is not what you desire, you will have to manually change them after the upgrade has completed.)

Because all of the one-way trusts from your NT environment are automatically converted to two-way trusts by the upgrade process, you will have to review a few of your security strategies. Many administrators are concerned with this change to their environment. In reality, the two-way trusts and their transitive nature will not have any real effect on your security. What it does change, though, is your ability to place users from one domain into the ACLs of objects in all other domains. (The purpose of one-way trusts in NT 4 is to limit which users can be assigned permissions in which domains.) This means that you will have to carefully review the membership lists of each of your security groups to ensure that an incorrect addition has not been made.

Maintaining the Availability of Applications

The likelihood of an application being completely incompatible with Windows 2000 is extremely low. (So far, the only applications we've seen that wouldn't run on Windows 2000 were custom written— we've had great results with off-the-shelf software.) You should, however, test each server-based application in your lab before performing your domain upgrade. If for some reason an application will not run correctly on a Windows 2000 server, you should take action to correct the problem.

Check to see if an upgrade or service pack is available to fix the issue. Most application vendors have already released Windows 2000– compatible versions of their product (or they will soon). If no upgrade or fix is available (or will not be released in an acceptable amount of time), you might be wise to consider replacing the application with something that *is* Windows 2000 compatible.

If your application does not run on a Windows 2000 server, test the application on an NT 4 member server. Moving incompatible applications to member servers will allow you to switch your domain to native mode. You can then upgrade or replace the application in a more leisurely manner.

Maintaining Acceptable Network Performance

The key to maintaining acceptable network performance during (and after) an upgrade is to control network traffic. This is accomplished through proper placement of servers and an effective site boundary strategy. Careful planning of these issues will not only give you the best control of network traffic, but it also might actually decrease the amount of traffic on key networks to amounts below that generated in your Windows NT 4 network.

The first step is to define your AD sites as soon in the process as possible. After you have upgraded the first domain controller in your forest, define the sites you agreed upon earlier in the design process. Then as new servers are added to the system, they will automatically be placed in the appropriate site. (Remember, sites are tied to TPC/IP subnets, so as soon as you configure TCP/IP on the server, AD can decide which site the server should belong to.) Implementing your site strategy early in the upgrade process will allow you to control when the domain data is initially replicated to new servers.

Another form of network traffic that needs to be controlled is traffic generated during client startup and authentication. Proper placement of Windows 2000 servers can help to keep this traffic off of your busy (and expensive) wide area links. The key to optimizing this traffic is to optimize the services that are involved. Optimal placement of the following services can have a dramatic, positive effect on network performance:

DHCP Server   As each client initializes, it needs to receive an IP address (among other configuration parameters). These IP addresses will determine the AD site in which the client computer is located.

DNS Server   As a client initializes, it obtains a list of available domain controllers by querying a DNS server for the appropriate SRV records. Those SRV records will direct a client to a domain controller within its own site if possible; if not, the process is completely random—with no control over which domain controller will be used for authentication.

Domain Controller   The domain controller is accessed during the logon process. The most efficient placement of domain controllers allows users to be authenticated by a local server. Site membership is used to find local domain controllers.

Global Catalog Server   If the domain is configured in native mode, the domain controller will contact a global catalog server at logon to determine universal group membership.

If any of these services are not available locally, the result will be a failed authentication attempt, authentication over a wide area link, or authentication using cached credentials.

Microsoft recommends the following procedures for controlling authentication and initialization traffic:

- Deploy your site strategy as soon as the first PDC is upgraded to Windows 2000.

- Place a domain controller in each site that contains Active Directory clients.

- Place a global catalog server at each remote site.

- Provide WINS for legacy clients (until all clients have been upgraded).

TIP Exam Hint: The list of suggestions for controlling authentication and initialization traffic will help solve many of the deployment questions found in the MCSE exam!

Exam Essentials

In many ways all of the other exam objectives lead to this one—planning for the actual implementation of Windows 2000 and Active Directory. As a test taker, though, you have to remember what this test is all about—it is not so much about implementation as it is about planning. For that reason, this is not a heavily tested exam objective. You will, however, need to be comfortable with the following:

Ensure that your design is appropriate to the environment. The last step before implementation is to compare your proposed solution with the business goals you defined early in the project.

Know the upgrade paths available for Microsoft products. Review Table 3.6 in the Critical Information section.

Upgrade domains in an order that limits your exposure to risk. Upgrade those domains that are easily recovered first, then smaller domains, then move on to your more complex migrations.

Know the Microsoft suggested procedures for inter-forest restructuring. See the Critical Information section for details.

Know the Microsoft suggested procedures for intra-forest restructuring. See the Critical Information section for details.

Know the use of each of the following utilities: ADTM, Clone-Principal, Netdom, Ldp, and MoveTree. See the Critical Information section for details.

Know the order in which Microsoft recommends that objects should be restructured. See the Critical Information section for details.

Key Terms and Concepts

Native Mode An Active Directory environment in which all domain controllers have been upgraded to Windows 2000. In such a system, the PDC emulation is no longer necessary.

Mixed Mode A Microsoft-based network in which both NT and Windows 2000 domain controllers exists. In this environment, one of the Windows 2000 domain controllers must act as the PDC emulator to perform SAM replication with the NT domain controllers.

Domain Restructure The process of redesigning the existing domain structure to meet the business needs of the environment.

Inter-Forest Restructuring The process of moving users, groups, and computer objects from either a Windows NT domain *or* a Windows 2000 domain in a separate AD forest to a new Windows 2000 domain.

Intra-Forest Restructuring The process of moving security principals between domains within the same Active Directory forest.

Sample Questions

1. Which of the following tools can be used for inter-forest domain restructuring only?

A. ATDM

B. ClonePrincipal

C. Netdom

D. MoveTree

Answer: B, D. ATDM and Netdom are used to facilitate both intra- and inter-forest domain restructuring. ClonePrincipal and MoveTree can be used only for restructuring between forests.

2. In most cases, which of the following objects should be moved to Windows 2000 first?

A. Users and groups

B. Computer accounts

C. Member servers

D. Domain controllers

Answer: A. In most cases, you will want to move your users and groups into Active Directory as soon as possible to give administrators access to the improved management capabilities of Windows 2000.

3. Which of the following would suggest a post upgrade method of restructuring?

A. The business needs indicate that a fast move to Windows 2000 is required.

B. All servers are being replaced with newer hardware.

C. A major restructuring of the company is expected soon.

D. The company has a high risk tolerance.

Answer: A, D. Performing a post upgrade method of migration moves users, groups, and computers to Windows 2000 as quickly as possible. After the upgrade has taken place, the objects are moved around within the forest to match the proposed AD design. This method has the highest risk factor because all changes are made on the production network.

4. Which of the following would suggest a pristine installation method of migration?

   A. The business needs indicate that a fast move to Windows 2000 is required.

   B. All servers are being replaced with newer hardware.

   C. A major restructuring of the company is expected soon.

   D. The company has a low risk tolerance.

   Answer: B, D.   A pristine installation migration involves creating a new AD structure on nonproduction equipment and moving to it after everything has been tested. Because the company is replacing hardware, this would be the best choice. Changes are made to a nonproduction network, so this is also the safest migration method.

Chapter

4

Designing Services Locations

MICROSOFT EXAM OBJECTIVES COVERED IN THIS CHAPTER:

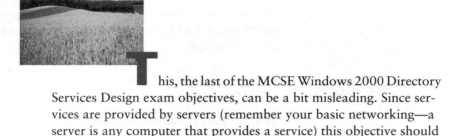

his, the last of the MCSE Windows 2000 Directory Services Design exam objectives, can be a bit misleading. Since services are provided by servers (remember your basic networking—a server is any computer that provides a service) this objective should really be titled "Server Placement."

In a real design project, determining the location of each server is a complex process that involves balancing network overhead, performance, cost, and access. In this chapter we'll discuss the design issues that must be considered when planning for the physical placement of servers within a network infrastructure. These considerations include performance, fault tolerance, functionality, and manageability.

Design the placement of operations masters.

We've discussed the difference between single-master and multiple-master environments. In short, a single-master environment uses a single instance of a database to accept and then replicate changes. A multiple-master environment allows changes to any replica of the database, and each replica is capable of updating all other replicas with changed data. Most of the changes made to the Active Directory database are handled in a multiple-master manner. The change will occur at any local AD server, and that server will synchronize those changes with the rest of the AD servers in the domain (and the global catalog server, if necessary).

There are, however, certain operations that, by the nature of what they do, need to be handled in a single-master manner. For these operations, one server is designated as the *operations master*. All updates or changes occur at the operations master, and this server is responsible for synchronizing the changes with all other servers.

Critical Information

Some of these single-master operations are forest-wide tasks. In other words, one server performs the task for your entire AD forest. Other operations are performed by one server in each domain. In either case, only one server performs the operation, so it is important that you take these tasks into account when planning server functionality and disaster recovery. By default, the first domain controller installed in your forest or in each domain, as appropriate, is assigned the role of operations master for each function.

For each class of server Microsoft recommends that you consider four main issues—performance, fault tolerance, functionality, and manageability. For each type of server, we'll end our discussion with a four-part list that covers these considerations.

Forest-wide Operations

There are two forest-wide operation master roles:

- Schema master
- Domain naming master

Schema Master

There is only one schema master server per forest. By default, it is the first server placed in the Active Directory environment. In most cases, this server should be in the root domain of the AD tree and must be available any time you need to make modifications to the AD schema. Although this server is not critical for normal operations of Active Directory, there will be times when it must be available, as, for example, during any schema modifications. The placement of this server is not a critical design factor, although keeping it close to the central IT staff might be a good idea because they will probably be in charge of all schema modifications. There is only one schema master server per enterprise.

Performance   Not an issue since the overhead of the task is only apparent during schema modifications.

Fault Tolerance   Not critical due to the nature of the process.

Functionality   Schema modifications are usually done during off-hours, so this role can be assigned to almost any server. Just ensure that the server is not heavily burdened during schema updates.

Manageability   The schema master is usually placed in close physcial proximity to the IT staff because they will usually be the people who perform schema updates.

Domain-Naming Master

Like the schema master, the domain master computer is used during a specific function—adding a new domain to the AD forest. By default, the domain master is the first AD server added to the environment. The domain master server ensures that no duplicate domain names are created within the forest. Although this job is critical, it is not necessary to the day-to-day functions of the network. There is only one domain master server per enterprise.

Performance   Performance is not an issue because the overhead of the task is apparent only during the addition of domains.

Fault Tolerance   Fault tolerance is not critical due to the nature of the process.

Functionality   Domains are usually added during off-hours, so this role can be assigned to almost any server.

Manageability   The domain master is usually placed in close physcial proximity to the IT staff because they will usually be the people who manage the domain structure.

Domain-wide operations

Certain AD server roles are domain specific. For each domain within the forest there will be one (and only one) of each of the following:

- Primary domain controller emulator
- Relative identifier master
- Infrastructure master

Primary Domain Controller Emulator

The PDC emulator replaces a Windows NT 4 primary domain controller to allow for mixed environments of Windows 2000 and Windows NT 4. When users change their passwords, the change is sent to the PDC emulator first. Whenever a user is denied access to the network due to an incorrect password, the authenticating servers will query the PDC emulator before denying the request. From a design perspective, this means that the PDC emulator must be a dependable computer that is centrally located to ensure access at all times (you never know when users will decide to change their passwords). There is one PDC emulator for each domain in the enterprise.

Performance   The overhead of this role is dependent upon the number of Windows NT 4 domain controllers that it must support.

Fault Tolerance   If it is at all possible, ensure that you have at least two Windows 2000 domain controllers for each domain—this will ensure that replication to the Windows NT servers is not interrupted in the event of a server failure.

Functionality   Once again, the overhead of this role will be dependent upon the number of Windows NT 4 domain controllers that must be supported. In general though, this server should be dedicated to network tasks (as opposed to offering other services such as e-mail or database access). The placement of this server should ensure that the NT domain controllers have ready access.

Manageability   There is not much to managing the PDC emulator—place servers for functionality rather than manageability.

Relative Identifier Master

Each object within the AD database is assigned a unique identifier known as its security identifier (SID). The SID is a combination of a unique domain identifier (created by the domain-naming master during the creation of the domain) and a relative ID (RID) that is unique within the domain. To ensure that the RIDs are unique, one AD server in each domain assumes the role of relative identifier. The relative ID master assigns to each domain controller within the domain a pool of values that are used as the RID for any objects created. If a domain controller uses all of the RIDs assigned to it, it will contact the relative identifier master for another pool. Once again, this roll is not critical to the day-to-day functions of the network. Once the original pools have been assigned, the relative identifier master can go offline with no real effect on the network. It must, however, be available when a domain controller exhausts its supply of RIDs or that domain controller will be unable to create new AD objects. There is one relative identifier master per domain.

Performance   Because of the nature of the process, performance is not an issue.

Fault Tolerance   Because of the nature of the process, fault tolerance is not critical.

Functionality   This role can be assigned to any Windows 2000 domain controller—the overhead of the task should not affect other processes. A centrally located server will be more likely to maintain communications with other domain controllers.

Manageability   There are no management tasks associated with this role. Place the server with regard for functionality rather than manageability.

Infrastructure Master

The infrastructure master for a domain is responsible for maintaining the cross-references between domains when an object is renamed. Put another way, if you rename an object within the AD database, the infrastructure master will ensure that the new name (and any changes to the SID) are replicated throughout the forest. Due to a quirk in AD, a global catalog server *should not* be assigned the role of infrastructure master. If this happens, the change will not be replicated across domain boundaries. Once again, there are no day-to-day functions that will be affected by the temporary loss of this server. At worst, if the infrastructure master is offline, updates will be delayed until it is brought online again. There is one infrastructure master for each domain within the forest.

Performance   The overhead of this role will be dependent upon the number of name changes made within the domain.

Fault Tolerance   A down server will only delay the replication of name changes, so fault tolerance is usually not an issue.

Functionality   The overhead of this role will depend upon the number of name changes made within the domain. In an environment with numerous name changes, do not give this role to an already busy server. Placing the server near infrastructure hubs can decrease the lag associated with name changes.

Manageability   There are no manageable features of the infrastructure master, so place the server for functionality.

Exam Essentials

This is not a heavily tested exam objective. Ensure that you are comfortable with the following concepts before attempting your exam:

Know the various server roles.   Be able to describe the function provided by the schema master, domain-naming master, primary domain controller emulator, relative indentifer master, and infrastructure master.

Know which roles are forest-wide and which are domain-wide. There are only two forest-wide server roles: schema master and domain-naming master.

Key Terms and Concepts

Forest-wide   A server role in which only one server is assigned the role for the entire Windows 2000 forest.

Domain-wide   A server role in which one server is assigned the role for each Windows 2000 domain within the forest.

Schema Master   A server that is responsible for the maintenance and modification of the AD schema for the entire forest.

Domain-Naming Master   A server that is responsible for ensuring that no duplicate domain names are used within an AD forest.

Primary Domain Controller Emulator   A server that is responsible for acting as the PDC for legacy (Windows NT 4) domain controllers in a mixed environment.

Relative Identifier Master A server that is responsible for generating pools of RIDs for all of the domain controllers within a domain. The RIDs are used as a part of the SID of each new object created, thus ensuring unique SIDs for every object within the AD domain.

Infrastructure Master A server that is responsible for ensuring that when an object is renamed, the new name and any changes to the SID are replicated throughout the AD forest.

Sample Questions

1. Which of the following best describes a multi-master environment?

A. Multiple changes are sent from the servers.

B. All servers can accept changes and replicate those changes to other servers.

C. It is a distributed management business model.

D. Two or more management consoles are run simultaneously at a server.

Answer: B. In a multi-master environment, all replicas are peers, can accept changes, and replicate those changes throughout the domain. This is the exact opposite of a Windows NT 4 domain structure, which is a single-master environment (one main copy of the accounts database, which is stored on the PDC, accepts all changes and replicates them to other domain controllers).

2. Which of the following server roles are forest-wide?

A. Schema master

B. PDC emulator

C. Domain-naming master

D. Infrastructure master

Answer: A, C. The only two server roles that are forest-wide are the schema master and domain-naming master roles.

Design the placement of global catalog servers.

The concepts of AD forests are fairly straightforward, but there are certain conditions that must be met during their creation. First, all domain controllers must share a common database structure, or *schema*. This means that any extensions made to the AD database in one tree must also be made to all other trees within the forest. Say, for instance, you add an application (such as Microsoft Exchange Server 2000) that extends the AD schema. You will have to add those extensions to all other trees within the forest structure. This is easy to do if your company controls all of the trees, but it does complicate matters in a situation where autonomous groups manage the trees.

The trees within the forest must also share a common global catalog (GC*)*. The global catalog for the forest will be that of the first domain created in the first tree (sometimes referred to as the forest root domain).

Critical Information

This is a very short section—there is not a lot to the decisions involved in placing global catalog servers within a network. We'll begin with an overview of the global catalog because understanding how it works will help make those placement decisions. Then we'll cover the four criteria: performance, fault tolerance, functionality, and manageability.

Global Catalog Servers

A *global catalog server* is an AD server that holds a partial replica of the entire forest. This replica holds a limited amount of information about every object within the forest, usually properties that are necessary for network functionality or properties that are frequently asked for.

The list of properties will be different for each class of object. User objects, for instance, will need to store certain information for network functions—a great example is their Universal Group Membership list.

During the logon process, the user's object is checked to retrieve this list. AD will then confirm the user's membership with each universal group using information stored in the global catalog. Once membership has been confirmed, the security IDs for each group can be added to the user's security token. The global catalog might also contain various properties that might be frequently searched for—telephone numbers, for example. On the other hand, the global catalog will probably store less information about printer objects because fewer of those properties will be needed regularly.

By default, the global catalog will be created on the first domain controller installed in the AD forest. The service itself has two major functions. First, it is critical to the logon process. When a user logs on to the network, a security token is created for the user. This token includes information about the groups of which the user is a member. If a global catalog server is not available during the logon process, users will not be able to log on to the network; instead, they will be limited to logging on to the local computer.

TIP   Test Hint: Members of the Domain Admins group can log on to the network without accessing the global catalog. If this were not the case, a malfunctioning global catalog server could conceivably prevent an administrator from logging on to fix the problem.

The second function of the global catalog is to facilitate searches of the Active Directory database. If you perform a search for, say, the phone number property of a user in another domain, your request could be answered by the global catalog server rather than a domain controller from the target domain. To put it more simply, searches can take place on servers that are more local to the user, thereby reducing network traffic and decreasing the time it takes to receive results.

The second function of global catalog servers brings us to an important design issue. By default, only one global catalog server is created, but the system can support an unlimited number of them. To reap the benefits of the global catalog, you must think about how many you would like and place them appropriately. It is best to have a global catalog server at each physical location; otherwise, your searches will cross your WAN links, thereby eliminating one of the major benefits of the AD service. This design also prevents the situation in which users are unable to log on to the network because a WAN line has gone down.

On the other hand, though, too many global catalog servers can increase network traffic. Remember that the catalog contains an incomplete copy of every object in your forest. Let's say that user Joe changes his phone number; this change would have to be replicated to every global catalog server in your environment.

NOTE The amount of network traffic that would be generated during replication explains why the global catalog does not contain every property of every object. The traffic generated to keep complete replicas up to date would probably exceed the bandwidth available on most networks.

Windows 2000 creates the first global catalog server for you and determines which properties of each object class it will store. In most cases, this default list of stored properties will be sufficient. There might be situations, though, where you want to add a property to the list that the global catalog stores. By using the Active Directory Sites and Services tools, you can control the attributes of each object class stored in the partial partition of the global catalog.

Placement Issues

This exam objective lists four criteria to be concerned with when planning for the placement of global catalog servers: performance, fault tolerance, functionality, and manageability.

Performance   Since global catalog servers are used during the logon process, you must ensure that the computer has as much (if not more) power than your domain controllers. If, for instance, you place three domain controllers in a location in an effort to limit the overhead of handling logon requests, you should also consider the fact that the global catalog servers would need to handle that overhead. Place global catalog servers near the users who will need to access them—limiting the number of network segments that queries will have to cross. This has two benefits: it controls network traffic and it increases the speed at which results can be received.

Fault Tolerance   In locations that support a large number of users (or that generate a large number of AD searches), you should have at least two global catalog severs. This eliminates the single point of failure, thus ensuring that logon traffic (or a search-AD request) does not have to cross WAN links.)

Functionality   In most cases it is best to dedicate a server to the task of acting as the global catalog server (if the hardware and budget allow.)

Manageability   Other than changing the object property list of the global catalog, there is not a lot of management involved in GC servers. Place the servers for performance rather than for management.

Exam Essentials

There is not a lot of essential exam information for this objective. Be aware of the following:

Remember that a global catalog must be available during the logon process.   This will effect your design considerations—always try to have a global catalog server near users.

Key Terms and Concepts

Global Catalog Server   An AD server that holds a partial replica of the entire forest.

Sample Questions

1. Global catalog servers hold which of the following?

   A. A complete replica of the AD database

   B. A limited replica of all objects within the AD database

   C. A catalog of all Web content within an IIS cluster

   D. A catalog of all registered software installed within a domain

   Answer: B.   The global catalog server contains a record for every object within the AD database, but only a limited number of the properties for each object.

2. Which of the following persons can log on to the AD network without a global catalog server?

   A. Members of the Domain Admins group.

   B. Members of the PowerUsers group.

   C. Members of the ServerManagers group.

   D. No one can log on if a global catalog server is not available.

   Answer: A.   Members of the Domain Admins group can log on to the AD network without access to a global catalog server.

Design the placement of domain controllers.

The bottom line in domain controller placement is usually performance from the users' perspective. Domain controllers must be placed so as to respond to user requests in a timely manner. This is, of course, a subjective matter. *Timely* will be defined differently in each environment. Your earlier analysis of the business will help in making these decisions.

Critical Information

In a homogenous network, made up of only Windows 2000 servers, planning for the placement of domain controllers is fairly straightforward. In a mixed environment, one that includes both Windows 2000 and Windows NT 4 domain controllers, planning becomes a bit more complex. The big difference between the two environments (all Windows 2000 versus a mixed network) is that the presence of NT 4 domain controllers will force you to consider the ramifications of a single-master replication process.

To review—a single-master replication environment is one in which all changes to the accounts database occur on a "master" copy (the SAM stored on the PDC.) In NT 4 networks, administrators often had to balance performance against network traffic. Placing domain controllers in each location would increase performance (logons would happen faster because the authentication process took place on a local server), but could increase the amount of traffic on the wide area links (because the remote domain controllers would have to be updated by the PDC).

As shown in Figure 4.1, placing all domain controllers in a central location would limit the amount of replication traffic on the wide area links, but it would also increase the amount of authentication traffic on those links and increase the time required for the logon process. This design also means that users would not be able to access local resources in the event of a wide area link failure, because they would be unable to authenticate themselves to the network.

In most cases, performance and fault tolerance outweigh the reduction of network traffic—so most administrators would place domain controllers throughout the network, as shown in Figure 4.2.

While this discussion does not seem to be relevant to our subject (the exam, after all, covers Windows 2000 and Active Directory), it does play a role in a mixed network. By mixed, we mean one in which there are still Windows NT 4 domain controllers. In such an environment,

FIGURE 4.1: **Centrally located domain controllers**

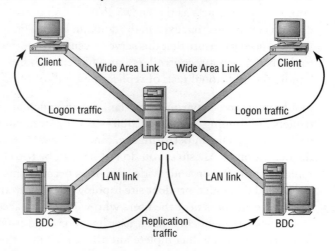

FIGURE 4.2: **Physically dispersed domain controllers**

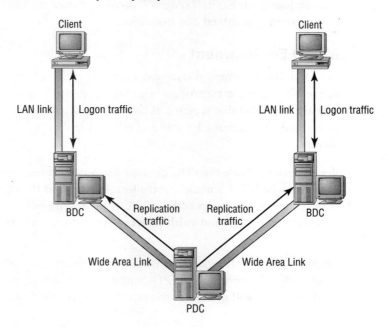

one domain controller in each domain takes on the role of PDC emulator. This server acts as the "new" PDC for all of the legacy NT 4 domain controllers that exist in the domain. From a design perspective, you will need to ensure that this server is centrally located (with respect to the NT 4 domain controllers), and has enough horsepower to handle the additional task of replicating to all of the NT 4 servers.

In a homogenous environment—i.e., one in which all domain controllers are running Windows 2000—server placement is determined with an emphasis on performance. Since Active Directory includes the definition of AD sites, you do not have to be too concerned with replication traffic on your wide area links because this traffic can be controlled through a prudent site topology design. In this case, place domain controllers near the users who will need to access them. The fewer network segments that a user has to cross during logon, the faster the process will complete and the less chance there is of a network problem affecting their ability to authenticate.

For our four testing criteria, we will break our answers into two types of environments: mixed and homogenous.

Mixed Environment

In a mixed environment you must concern yourself with the placement of the NT 4 domain controllers with respect to the Windows 2000 domain controller that is acting as the PDC emulator. Your major concern should be planning for fast and efficient replication to the legacy servers.

Performance   Place the PDC emulator in a central location with respect to the NT 4 domain controllers. Ensure that the connections between the NT 4 servers and the PDC emulator are reliable and have adequate available bandwidth to accept the additional replication traffic.

Fault Tolerance   If possible, ensure that there are multiple routes from each NT 4 server to the PDC emulator. This ensures that a network problem will not affect the replication process.

Functionality In an environment with numerous NT 4 domain controllers, your PDC emulator should be dedicated to network functionality (as opposed to offering multiple services such as print or file access).

Manageability Domain controllers do not require any special management—but place them, if possible, near the IT staff who might need management access. Remember, however, that performance is the key consideration.

Homogenous Environment

Planning the placement of domain controllers in a homogenous Windows 2000 environment is fairly straightforward. Because AD sites can be used to control replication traffic over wide area links, domain controllers should be placed so as to facilitate user access and management.

Performance Two factors are significant for domain controller performance: hardware and the perceptions of users. Purchase hardware that has enough power to handle the authentication overhead that it must support. Placing domain controllers physically near users will decrease the amount of time that the logon process takes, thereby giving the perception of increased performance.

Fault Tolerance Placing at least two domain controllers in each physical location will ensure that logon traffic will never have to cross wide area links.

Functionality Most experts recommend that domain controllers be dedicated to the task of supporting the network. In other words, in most cases, do not add services to a domain controller (such as print, file, or applications).

Manageability The domain controller service does not require much management. Place domain controllers to improve performance, rather than to facilitate management.

Exam Essentials

This is a short section but it contains two very important concepts for domain controller placement. Know the following two concepts and you should have no problems choosing the correct placement in the design scenarios on your examination.

In a mixed environment, place the PDC emulator in a central location with respect to the legacy NT domain controllers on the network. This ensures that replication to the NT 4 domain controllers will happen in a timely manner.

In a homogenous environment, place domain controllers near the users who will access them. Use AD sites to control replication traffic; place your domain controllers to increase end-user performance.

Key Terms and Concepts

PDC Emulator The Windows 2000 server that provides the functionality of a PDC to legacy NT 4 servers on the network.

Sample Questions

1. In an environment that includes Windows NT 4 domain controllers, which of the following should be placed in a central location?

A. All of the remaining NT 4 domain controllers

B. Any existing NT 4 member servers

C. All Windows 2000 domain controllers

D. The Windows 2000 domain controller that is acting as the PDC emulator

Answer: D. Placing the PDC emulator in a central location (with respect to any remaining NT 4 domain controllers) ensures the most timely replication process.

2. In a network made up of only Windows 2000 domain controllers, which of the following statements is most accurate?

A. The PDC emulator should be placed in a central location.

B. Place domain controllers near the users who will access them.

C. AD sites will not affect replication traffic.

D. Domain controllers should be placed to facilitate management.

Answer: B.   In a Windows 2000 environment, place domain controllers near the users who will access them to increase perceived network performance.

Design the placement of DNS servers.

Given the critical nature of DNS within an AD environment (DNS is used by the Netlogon service to locate domain controllers during the logon process), understanding the placement and integration of Windows 2000 DNS servers into a network is critical to designing an efficient network. DNS and all of its considerations are tested heavily in the Windows 2000 MCSE track.

Critical Information

The exam objective for this section asks you to consider performance, fault tolerance, functionality, and manageability when considering the placement of DNS servers. Most of these considerations will center on the WAN links in the environment.

TIP   Exam Hint: Remember that DNS is critical to the Netlogon service. It will always be better to have too many DNS servers than not enough.

Performance   During your analysis of DNS traffic on your network, you should have developed a good feel for the effects DNS will have on your infrastructure. Planning server placement will require subjective decisions based upon this "feel." Consider the effects of DNS query traffic and compare those effects with those of zone transfer traffic. For example, if you have two physical sites connected through a WAN link, you will have to determine whether you should place a DNS server on each side of the link or whether one central server will suffice. It is easy to trace the traffic generated by both processes and determine which will have a greater effect on performance (zone transfer or DNS client query). Unfortunately, we can't give you a hard-and-fast rule about which will have the greater effect; too many variables determine which function will generate more traffic.

Fault Tolerance   You must consider the effect of the WAN link going down. In such a situation, will your users still be able to log on to local resources? Remember that DNS is used by the Netlogon service to locate domain controllers. Without DNS, clients will not be able to log on to the network. The bottom line here is that a DNS server on both sides of most WAN links is the safest design.

Functionality   Here you will need to make a more subjective decision. Consider the distribution of computers across your various physical networks. As with most services, it is best to place DNS servers as close as possible to the users who will access them. If you plan on one DNS server and your office has a backbone-wiring scheme, place that server on the backbone. If you can limit the number of DNS queries that cross routers, do so. Analyze the traffic patterns and place DNS servers on subnets that will generate the most DNS traffic. Since DNS is used during every logon attempt, many larger environments will need to dedicate a server to act as a DNS server.

Manageability   Like functionality, this is a more subjective consideration. If your company uses a distributed management model (that is, you have site administrators), you should consider placing DNS services on local servers. If, however, you follow a centralized management model, keep the DNS servers on centrally controlled servers. Consider staffing—do you have a local person who is capable of managing the DNS service?

TIP   Exam Hint: For most of these types of questions (where should I place this or that?), Microsoft has a history of describing the management philosophy during the scenario setup. For the Design tests, this is critical information!

Plan for Interoperability with the Existing DNS

As might be expected, Microsoft recommends that you use the Windows 2000 implementation of DNS whenever possible. This Microsoft version of DNS services provides numerous advantages over traditional text-file-based DNS implementations. The advantages include the following:

SRV Resource Records *SRV resource records* are a new type of record (defined in RFC 2052) that identifies the location of a service rather than a device.

Dynamic Update Microsoft DNS is more properly called DDNS: *Dynamic* Domain Name System. It is capable of allowing hosts to dynamically register their names with the zone, thereby reducing administrative overhead.

Secure Dynamic Update Windows 2000 Server security is used to authenticate hosts that attempt to dynamically register themselves within the zone.

Incremental Zone Transfer With *incremental zone transfer*, only changed data is replicated to other AD servers.

Interoperability with DHCP A server running DHCP services can register host names on behalf of its clients. This allows non-DDNS clients to dynamically register with the zone.

Active Directory uses DNS to locate domains and domain controllers during the logon process. This is made possible by the inclusion of SRV-type records in the DNS database. Each Windows 2000 domain controller dynamically registers an SRV record in the zone. This record represents the domain Netlogon service on that server. When a client attempts to log on, it will query its DNS server for the address of a domain controller. The bottom line here is that even if you are not going to use DNS for anything else, you will have to install and configure it for the logon process to work properly. Let us stress this one more time—DNS is critical to an AD environment!

NOTE The process of installing and configuring DNS is covered in *MCSE: Windows 2000 Network Infrastructure Administration Study Guide* (Sybex, 2000).

If you are already running another version of DNS services, the correct "Microsoft" action would be to migrate to Windows 2000. If that is not feasible, then you must ensure that your existing DNS servers meet two criteria:

- They *must* support the Service Location resource record (.SRV record type.)

- They *should* support the DNS dynamic update protocol.

NOTE Notice that the second of these criteria is described as "should" rather than "must." Although dynamic update is not mandatory, it will make your network much easier to administer. Microsoft always includes it in any discussion of DNS criteria—so you can bet that the correct test answers will include it!

If your current DNS solution does not meet these criteria, you have three choices:

Upgrade the existing DNS server to a version that meets the criteria. You will need to consult the documentation of your DNS product to determine the minimum version necessary.

Migrate the zone to Windows 2000 DNS services. This is a Microsoft "non-answer." If you have control of DNS you should follow Microsoft's recommendation of moving to Windows 2000 DNS. If not, you will probably have a hard time convincing the current DNS administrators to give you control (otherwise this wouldn't be an issue in the first place). The Microsoft theory is that you should use Windows 2000 DNS servers as secondary servers for a while and that once you are satisfied with performance and reliability you can migrate to a Microsoft solution.

Delegate the DNS zone to a server that meets the requirements.
In this case, you would move the zone to a foreign DNS server that
meets the requirements (thus avoiding Microsoft DNS services.)

Exam Essentials

This is another small section of this manual, but a large topic for the
exam. As we said earlier, DNS is critical in an Active Directory environment! You must understand how DNS works, how to configure it,
and how to optimize its performance on your network. Luckily, the
two topics for this exam objective (placement of DNS servers and the
coexistence of Microsoft DNS with other vendor's solutions) have
one simple Microsoft "correct" answer—upgrade or migrate to Microsoft Windows 2000 DNS as soon as possible. Most of your exam
questions will have this as the correct solution!

Remember that DNS must be available during the logon process.
The Netlogon service uses DNS to find domain controllers during
the logon process, so your design must ensure that a DNS server will
always be available. This means planning for down network links and
providing a fault-tolerant solution.

Remember the two criteria for maintaining your existing DNS servers.
Your existing servers must support Service Location resource records
and should accept dynamic updates.

Key Terms and Concepts

SRV Resource Records   A type of DNS record (defined in RFC 2052)
that identifies the location of a service rather than a device.

Dynamic Update   A DNS system that is capable of allowing hosts to
dynamically register their names with the zone.

Incremental Zone Transfer   A DNS replication process in which
only changed data is replicated to other DNS servers.

Sample Questions

1. Within Microsoft's implementation of DNS, an incremental zone transfer is _____.

   A. An update of all DNS servers in which the entire zone is transmitted in 64K segments

   B. An update of a DNS server in which transmission is controlled using the GTSP (Global Timing Sequence Protocol)

   C. An update of a DNS server in which only the changed data is replicated

   D. The process of moving DNS services from one server to another

   Answer: C. One advantage of Microsoft DNS is that the entire zone file does not have to be replicated each time the content of the DNS database changes.

2. Which of the following is the primary reason that DNS is required in an AD environment?

   A. The Active Directory database is stored within the traditional DNS database.

   B. AD uses the DNS zone transfer protocol during replication.

   C. Netlogon uses DNS to find domain controllers.

   D. DNS is *not* required in an AD environment.

   Answer: C. The Windows 2000 Netlogon service uses DNS to find domain controllers during the logon process.

And so ends our fascinating journey through the exam objectives—we hope that you were able to stay awake through most of them! (One of the nice things about buying a book is that you can always reread those sections that put you to sleep.) Both of us sincerely hope that our work is of some value to you on your road to the Windows 2000 MCSE certification. Good luck—and drop us an e-mail to let us know how you did!

Index

Note to the Reader: Throughout this index **boldfaced** page numbers indicate primary discussions of a topic. *Italicized* page numbers indicate illustrations.